STROMBOLI · STROMBOLICCHIO

ALICUDI

VULCANO

D1395272

GULF OF MILAZZO

GULF OF PATTI

ROMETTA MAREA
MILAZZO
MESSINA
VILLA SAN GIOVANNI
REGGIO DI CALABRIA

GIOIOSA MAREA
CAPO D'ORLANDO
NASO
PATTI
Tindis
CASTROREALE TERME
BARCELLONA
POZZO DI GOTTO
SANTA LUCIA DEL MELA
MILI SAN PIETRO
ITALA
ALI
ALI TERME
ROCCALUMERA

ROMETTA

CEFALU
OFELICE
GIBILMANNA
CASTELBUONO
POLIZZI
PETRALIA

ACQUEDOLCI
SANT'AGATA DI MILITELLO
SAN FRATELLO
CARONIA
SANTO STEFANO DI CAMASTRA
MISTRETTA
NEBRODI MTS
CESARO
NOVARA
PELORITANI

MTS

RANDAZZO
CASTIGLIONE DI SICILIA
FRANCAVILLA DI SICILIA
FORZA D'AGRO
CASTEL MOLA
LETIOJANNI

NICOSIA
TROINA
BRONTE
LINGUAGLOSSA
TAORMINA
FIUMEFREDDO DI SICILIA

CALASCIBETTA
LEONFORTE
AGIRA
CENTURIPE
ADRANO
MT ETNA
Valle del Bove
GIARRE
RIPOSTO

ENNA
VALGUARNERA
AIDONE
Morganrina
PIAZZA ARMERINA
Villa Imperiale
PATERNO
NICOLOSI
Pietralunga
ACIREALE
ACITREZZA
CANNIZZARO

CALTANISETTA
CATALDO
BARRAFRANCA
SAN MICHELE DI GANZARIA
CALTAGIRONE
GRAMMICHELE
FRANCOFONTE
MILITELLO
CATANIA
PLAIN OF Symaethus
CATANIA

Naples

IONIAN SEA

GULF OF CATANIA

ICATTI
BUTERA
NISCEMI
VIZZINI
IBLEAN MTS
SORTINO
Pantalica
Megara Hyblaea
LENTINI
CARLENTINI
AGNONE BAGNI
BRUCOLI
AUGUSTA
MELILLI
PRIOLO
BELVEDERE

LICATA
GELA
ACATE
CHIARAMONTE GULFI
Akpai
PALAZZOLO ACREIDE
FLURIDIA
CASSIBILE
SYRACUSE

GULF OF GELA

VITTORIA
COMISO
RAGUSA
DONNAFUGATA
MODICA
ROSOLINI
ISPICA
NOTO
AVOLA

MARINA DI RAGUSA
SCICLI
DONNALUCATA
MARZAMEMI
PACHINO
PORTOPALO · CAPE PASSERO

GULF OF NOTO

80   90   100 kilometres
60   70 miles

Sicily

Travellers' Guide

Sicily

by Christopher Kininmonth

with 15 photographs by Herbert Spencer

Jonathan Cape London 1972

For R.B.F.

Μεθεισαν δεσπόται
με θεοῦ γύαλα τάδ᾽ ἐσιδεῖν   EURIPIDES

God would not have chosen Palestine for his own
if he could have seen my own Kingdom of Sicily.
                    FREDERICK II OF HOHENSTAUFEN

by the same author

The Children of Thetis
Rome Alive
The Brass Dolphins
The Travellers' Guide to Malta and Gozo
The Travellers' Guide to Morocco
Frontiers

First published 1965
Revised edition 1972
Reprinted 1974
Text and maps © Copyright Helga Greene 1965, 1972
Photographs © Copyright Herbert Spencer 1965
Maps by Janet Landau
General Editors: Judith Greene and Kenneth MacKinnon

ISBN 0 224 00612 6

Made and printed in Great Britain
by Richard Clay (The Chaucer Press) Ltd, Bungay, Suffolk,
for Jonathan Cape Ltd, 30 Bedford Square, London WC1

CONTENTS

CONTENTS

MAPS, CHARTS AND PLANS

Acknowledgments

From all possible aspects Sicily has been as intensively written about as any area of the world. As author of this guide-book I am grateful this should be so, for I must inevitably draw heavily on the published expertise of others, each in his specialized field. It is hard to imagine that you will choose to visit Sicily unless one aspect at least of its highly idiosyncratic character attracts you and, if we take this to be the case, I must assume you will want to know more about that than I have space to offer. Besides being of practical aid to a traveller, then, I would be happy if this book should help kindle your Sicilian enthusiasm, and therefore this guide should indicate also where this may best be fed. My own greatest debt is to other authors, and this I gladly acknowledge; but it would please me more if by stimulating your interest in their works I could repay some mite of my debt by increasing their sales. References are made to a number of books in my text and a Selected English Bibliography is given on pages 311–14.

I am extremely grateful to Dr Peter Davis of Edinburgh University for so generously supplying the section on flora, and to the late Sir Harry Luke, K.C.M.G., D.LITT., for the note on religion. Stewart Perowne, O.B.E., has very kindly consented to my including the results of his acute and informed observations made at the Imperial Villa at Casale on p. 298 (which I hope he will publish more adequately himself). I want, too, to offer my heart-felt thanks to Margaret Guido, Daphne Phelps, Gerald Guinness and Professor Woodhead for their generosity in making corrections to the first edition of this guide and for helpful criticisms and suggestions which I believe have contributed greatly to making this revised edition a better book.

I must gratefully acknowledge permission to quote passages from Professor Bernabò Brea's *Sicily Before the Greeks* (Thames and Hudson), Georgina Masson's *Frederick II of Hohenstaufen* (Secker and Warburg), Peter Quennell's *Spring in Sicily* (Weidenfeld and Nicolson), the Hon. Sir Steven Runciman's *The Sicilian Vespers* (Cambridge University Press), Bertrand Russell's *The History of Western Philosophy* (Allen and Unwin) and A. G. Woodhead's *The Greeks in the West* (Thames and Hudson). I have to thank Mary Renault also for her kindness in letting me quote from her novel

Fire From Heaven (Longmans). There is no subsection of the Bibliography in which I can list either this or the same author's *The Mask of Apollo* (Longmans), largely set in fourth-century B.C. Syracuse, and a vivid and well-researched evocation of life there at the period: a rousing novel to take as companion reading.

Monreale Cathedral: the cloister

Monreale Cathedral: apse

Monreale Cathedral: the cloister

Segesta: the temple

Agrigento: Temple of Herakles

Rural architecture: shrine

Rural architecture: chapel

Acitrezza: Isole dei Ciclopi

Mondello Lido

Syracuse: fishing

Piazza Armerina: mosaic floor

Noto: a balcony

Mount Etna: view towards Taormina

Syracuse: from Plemmyrion Point

(*following page*) Agrigento: the temple ridge

INTRODUCTION

This hand-book is designed for holiday-makers. We have supposed a reader who is visiting Sicily with a view to relaxation, yet ready to take an intelligent interest in that old, varied and historic island.

We have not attempted to produce a complete guide to every village, town, church, castle or archaeological site, but instead have tried to indicate where the visitor can best skim the cream off Sicily's many and scattered treasures. Some of these lie in rather isolated parts, but there is no road along which to drive is not to pass through beautiful landscape, and no excursion which will prove uninteresting to the inquiring traveller – and it should be possible to see the interior at the sacrifice of only one daily bathe.

The best roads and the best services by public transport follow the routes most trodden from earliest times, and on these we have based our division of the island. The route diagrams on pp. 76–77 and 288 show their direction; where two or three alternatives exist, we have described the most interesting.

It is annoying to read a guide-book from back to front, and we have tried to minimize this. We first deal with Messina – Sicily's chief link with the Italian mainland – and the road connecting it with Palermo, where there is the largest concentration of interesting sights; then with the western corner, working down the coast to Agrigento; thence to Syracuse and back to Messina; a final section covers the interior.

Palermo is the obvious base for seeing everything in the north; a night's excursion away would enable you to see something of Agrigento. On the east, Catánia is the best placed of the centres, though the least attractive to holiday-makers; better to base yourself on Syracuse or Taormina and excursion from there for one or two nights to see the other extremity of the island. The excursions chart facing this page will help you to plan your holiday to suit your own requirements. It lists the most important sights in each major town and indicates recommended day and overnight excursions from the main centres.

Somewhere in this revised edition I am bound to make certain reservations and criticisms about Sicily from the visiting reader's point of view, and that might as well be here.

The 'season' in Sicily now extends from February to November and there are scarcely enough beds to be had anywhere to lodge the great number of visitors who flock to the island. Gone are the days of casual touring, unless you don't mind the odd night in a station waiting-room. Most – not all, though most – of the new hotels and so-called 'tourist villages' now being built are designed to cater for not very well-off families, staying en pension, and interested primarily in sea-bathing. They do not much help the visitor with other interests besides and, it must be confessed, they tend to be so noisy as to be exhausting rather than relaxing places at which to stay. Plan your visit, therefore; book well ahead and deviate from your schedule at your peril.

To help those who have children whom they may want to abandon in safety while they themselves go excursioning, we mark those hotels (thus:†) which either have unobstructed access to the sea and/or private beaches. The conformation of the island made it inevitable that roads and railways should largely hug the coast; thus these hotels are fewer than anyone would now wish them to be.

At Taormina and neighbourhood – I have not yet encountered this vice elsewhere – by far the most of the hotels extort full-pension terms from visitors. They can get away with this because the demand for their rooms is so great and they do not give a god-damn how much or how eternally they turn you off the whole place by doing so. I don't know what come-back we have except, perhaps, not to plan to go there in the first place. Taormina, too, has need of more water and electricity than is available to it; the supplies of both are apt to be cut just when you most need them and, of course, your hotelier will pretend that each day's shortage is an exception instead of the rule. What was once a charming town has been rendered almost ugly – though nothing can diminish the splendour of its setting – through the raging greed of developers. It is dreadfully sad to have to say this, but a vulgar exploitation of all that once made this resort so delightful has now all but obliterated its foundation. One good thing, though – the network of overhead wires has gone and you get a liberated feeling by being without it.

Every town and village in the island has seen a very remarkable growth of new buildings – whole new quarters of them – and I must stress that, when I say (about Trápani, for instance) that 'it is a delightful and very Sicilian place', I mean the old parts of the town where one can forget the equally Sicilian though far from delightful new suburbs. It is an insoluble mystery how the occupants of these new buildings exist. Indirect pensionnaires of the Cassa del Mezzogiorno perhaps?

After some years' absence from Sicily, I am now struck more by the deceleration of cultural development there than, as when this guide was first written, its acceleration and achievement. This affects the visitor in various ways. I then put mention of the Mafia under Customs and wrote of it 'lingering now more in foreign imaginations than in dashing or sinister fact'. The Government tries its best no doubt to rid the island of this endemic sickness, yet it has proved more stubbornly resistant than was imagined. Inertia has, however, been broken and there is real hope that a cure can be effected, some time in the future. Meanwhile, it continues to do the island incalculable harm that is often irreparable.

Sicily gets its share of aid from central Government agencies (not all of which is rightly spent) but money is still short to rescue from long neglect so many things – leaving aside, without forgetting them, the people themselves – which deserve to be preserved. In particular the Soprintendenza ai Monumenti of Palermo seems to have become bogged down in lethargy. Restoration of the incomparable La Zisa and Aiutamicristo palaces has not advanced in seven years (though work slowly progresses to extend the National Gallery of Sicily in the Palazzo Abbatelli) and the National Museum of Antiquities remains cramped and unnecessarily gloomy. The key to San Giovanni dei Lebbrosi is, at the time of writing, lost. This important Norman church stands forlorn and bolted in the centre of a wasteland. Worse, indeed inconceivable, is the squalor surrounding the neighbouring and beautiful Ponte dell'Ammiráglio, which one had once supposed was temporary but must presumably now accept as the inevitable product of that same all too human ignorance and, probably, indifference that allows the surrounding slums to continue to exist. Something more sinister than indifference must surely account for the fact that the bombed old quarters of the town remain abominable slums with seven more years' squalidity added to them. The garden of La Favara is menaced by a new dual-carriageway road and will presumably soon disappear under speculative development, as have the surroundings of La Cúbula. The remains of the former palace of La

Favara are still a squatter-like slum. All right, the living are more worthy to be considered than the dead, but public parks in the midst of the cities are generally considered to be good for the living – except, presumably, those who can make millions by building over every square yard of the once fabled beauty of the Conca d'Oro.

An equally serious threat to Sicily's heritage is the situation of scheduled national monuments in private ownership, like La Favara. The Government does not aid these owners to maintain buildings which it will not allow to be destroyed, while the owners' miserly greed is often all too obvious. The Villa Palagonia was once reputed to have been bought for restoration by the authorities. This sale has never been effected and the state of that very exceptional building is now quite deplorable and dangerous. The owners, however, have sold or developed their large estate so that it has become the flourishing township of Bagheria – they cannot want for the price of minimal maintenance of the villa's fabric; they just think the Government should pay, not themselves. The awful earthquake of 1968 has rendered a number of other, less well-known protected houses semi-ruinous and a like stalemate now endangers these also.

The Church too rests on its ancient laurels. We have given up the idea that there will ever in fact be a Museo Diocesano and have dropped all mention of it from this guide except to say so here. In these not notably God-fearing days the safe-keeping of Caravaggio's last and masterly painting was apparently left to heavenly agency; so it was neatly cut from its frame over the altar in the Oratório della Compagnia di San Lorenzo one night during October 1969 and not seen again. I would have seen nothing to suggest there were not as many mad collector millionaires in Sicily as in California or Texas who might covet such a work of art, had it not been that the men who stole the bronze Ephebus from Castelvetrano could not locate one. This major work of art at least has happily been recovered. One must, however, tremble for the safety of many more.

Italy may be almost over-rich in its legacies from the past, but this wealth is not, once lost, recuperable. To put it no more damagingly, as guardians of their share of this treasure, Sicilians now *fanno brutta figura*.

The present, tragic condition of some buildings and neighbour-hoods in Sicily may so outrage you as to prompt you to want to do something towards their rescue. Most practical would be to join Itália Nostra's growing body of foreign supporters. (U.K. address: Brocklea, North Lyminge, Folkestone, Kent.)

It is good to be able in this reprint to make two corrections to the above. A key to San Giovanni dei Lebbrosi is again available, and the surroundings of the Ponte dell' Ammiráglio have been tidied up and saplings planted.

Needless to say, I shall be most obliged to anyone pointing out inaccuracies, or changes which may occur to outdate this edition – which I hope has corrected or brought up to date those mistakes which readers found in the earlier edition and were kind enough to tell me about.

Finally, it is always satisfying to pronounce place-names correctly. Usually in Italian the stress is on the penultimate syllable, but when the stress is on the last syllable the Italians use a grave accent. To help the tourist we have added an acute accent to show any ex-ceptions.

GETTING TO SICILY

The Italian State Tourist Offices (ENIT) are very helpful to intending visitors.

London office: 201 Regent Street, WI (tel. 01–734 4631).

New York office: 626 Fifth Avenue.

C.I.T., a partly state-owned travel agency, besides having branches in the principal island towns, has a London Office (10 Charles Street, SWI) and one in New York (11 West 42nd Street, New York 10036).

AIR

From all major cities via Milan, Rome, Naples, Réggio di Calábria, to Palermo or Catánia; also direct flights from London and Malta.

SEA

From England: sailings at irregular intervals (taking four to five days) to Naples (and occasionally continuing to Palermo). It is worth inquiring about the P. & O. Line's Amphibean (one-way) tickets, which take you and your car (the car is practically free if there are several of you) from London to Naples in two or three days.

From U.S.: no sailings to Sicily itself, but fairly frequent sailings to Naples (taking about a week).

From Naples there are regular steamer services to Messina and Palermo, also to Milazzo via Lípari (see p. 85). These Lípari ferries are not car ferries though one or two cars might perhaps be carried on deck.

RAIL

From London: to Messina, Taormina, Catánia, Syracuse or Palermo (taking roughly 48 hours; from Paris about 36 hours). The best way is to change at Milan or Rome, taking one of the fast trains to Messina (some of which have carriages which go direct through to Taormina, Catánia, Syracuse or Palermo). During the International Samples Fairs held at Palermo (in June) and Messina (in August) visitors to these cities are allowed a 25 per cent discount on fares from the Italian border.

ROAD

To take your own car to Sicily you need your normal driving licence and log-book. An International Driving Licence is needed for motorists driving Italian-registered cars. It is necessary to get a Carte Internationale d'Assurance (International Green Card) from your insurance company. A temporary membership of the Italian Automobile Club (A.C.I.), obtainable at the frontier, brings certain worth-while concessions, and there is a petrol concession available to all foreign motorists.

Driving is on the right hand of the road, of course.

Frequent car ferries operate to Messina from the mainland (see p. 79). It is normal to report about an hour before departure and the procedure is that you drive the car into the loading cradle yourself and out again on board ship; then you can lock the car.

PASSPORT AND CUSTOMS

Holders of U.K. and U.S. passports need no visa for a stay of up to three months, after which they must apply to the local *carabiniere* for a *permesso di soggiorno*. No visas are required either for subjects of most Commonwealth states and Ireland. Free entry through Customs is allowed for personal effects, including 200 cigarettes (or 50 cigars or 8¾ oz. tobacco), one bottle of spirit, one of wine, scent. A licence costing about 200 l. is needed for portable radios.

TRAVEL ON SICILY

AIR

Local services from Palermo to Catánia, Trápani, Pantelleria and Lampedusa.

SEA

For boats to the smaller islands, see under the appropriate entries.

RAIL

Good rail connections between the main centres, i.e. Messina, Palermo, Agrigento, Catánia and Syracuse. The fastest type of train is called a *rápido*, for which there is an extra charge.

BUSES, TOURIST COACHES AND GUIDED TOURS

Naturally there are local district buses, but as they stop very frequently, one can reckon that they average only about forty kilometres per hour. Sicily is not as well provided with a system of 'luxury' tourist Pullman coaches as northern Italy, but there is a service, which sweeps you round the chief sights of the island, called the Nastro d'Oro. This runs with varying frequency according to season, and is very well organized and conducted. It stops at the main sights round the island; luncheon is laid on at respectable places, where the tariff for 'group' meals is most reasonable; the night stops are in large towns where there is a good range of accommodation, which you pay for yourself at the usual rates, and where the coach will set you down in the evenings and collect you in the mornings. The only disadvantage of this is the brevity of some of the stops made, but, since you can leave your coach where you will and join another one a day or two later, this service does in fact make it extremely easy and comfortable for anyone to see all the main sights of the island without the harassment of coping with individual travel from place to place. Though the price (20,000 l. for the complete five-day circle) seems a bit steep, you will, I think, find that you save, when you consider that taxis to and from stations, hotels and bus terminals would otherwise have to be added to the basic fares you would lay out in getting from place to place. Europabus offers a similar service.

There are plenty of travel bureaux throughout Sicily which arrange for guides to conduct individuals or bus-loads of visitors to places of interest. C.I.T. offices (p. 32) offer the best tours, under the initials C.I.A.T., and, as they are semi-state-owned, their prices are regulated.

TAXIS AND CABS

Hire of taxis varies locally, but an average rate is 200 l. for the first 220 metres and 20 l. for each additional 220 metres. There is a surcharge of 150 l. after 10 p.m. Luggage costs 50 l. per piece. It is worth noting that Palermo International Airport lies far from the town (35 km.), making taxi-rides in and out an expensive business. Catánia and Trápani airports, on the other hand, are close enough to the towns for this not to be a serious matter.

Taxi-drivers should be tipped 100 l. or so, not 10 per cent of the fare. It is possible to make a price for a journey out of town, though you will have to battle for it.

Always make a price for a journey in a horse-cab; no tipping.

CAR HIRE AND DRIVING

Self-drive and chauffeur-driven cars can be had in Sicily although, being a law to itself in this as in all ways, these are more expensive than elsewhere. A Fiat 1600, really used for convenience and an exploration of the island, costs from £9 to £10 a day all in. With a driver, you will about double that cost.

Petrol (*benzina*) costs 152 l. (46p) per litre for Standard, 162 l. (49p) per litre for Super.

Familiarize yourself with the international code, signs, etc., and abide by them; but should you commit an *infrazione*, it is usually best to pay the fine on the spot and be rid of the matter.

Traffic is heavy in the towns and one-way streets take some getting used to. Outside the towns, traffic is still light and driving therefore unusually pleasant – with the very marked exception of the Messina–Catánia road, which is infernal. A motorway is in course of construction to relieve this road and is expected to be in operation in 1975. It may be longer before the Catánia–Palermo motorway is completed, though sections near Palermo are already open. In the 1980s this road will be linked with another connecting Palermo–Messina. Unfortunately these magnificent projects seem to absorb all the road fund and everywhere else the roads, whether major or secondary, have deteriorated.

Motorways – Autostrade – are toll roads in Italy. But while short sections only are open you may find no charge is made for their use.

MAPS

The Touring Club Italiano publishes excellent maps of all Italy, among which Nos. 25, 26 and 27 cover Sicily. These are kept reasonably well up to date but may lag a bit behind current motorway construction. Available from the R.A.C., Pall Mall, London sw1; Map House, St James's Street, London sw1; and Rizzoli International Bookstore, 712 Fifth Avenue, New York City.

HOTELS AND RESTAURANTS

HOTELS

The hotels listed in this guide-book and their classifications are taken from the latest *Alberghi di Sicilia*, a section of the *Annuario Alberghi*. Such is the rate of hotel building on the island that hotels may have been added and even categories changed by the time of publication. If you are touring the island, you are advised to arm yourself with the current issue of this useful and multilingual booklet which is given out free by the ENIT agency (ENIT, which stands for Ente Nazionale Italiano Turismo, is the Italian State Tourist Office – see p. 32) or travel agent.

Hotels are scheduled in this by categories and prices given, but we should say that a hotel wins its rating more for its plumbing and numerous bathrooms than for a general standard of service. Thus, you sometimes find the less grand places are the pleasanter all round. It should be said too that the prices of rooms do not always accurately reflect those of meals and other services because, the lower the category of a hotel, the lower the rate at which it is taxed, and some proprietors like the best of all worlds.

Book hotel accommodation ahead. A big change has come about since the Italians have started to take holidays – and a new interest in their own country – and only in the dead of winter could you rely on finding the accommodation you want wherever you should happen to drop in.

Hotel agencies are a useful help in making bookings. Some agency addresses:

C.I.T. (England) Ltd, 10 Charles II Street, London sw1 (01–930 6722);

Hotel and Resort Marketing, Chichester House, 278/282 High Holborn, London wc1 (01–242 9111);

Hotel Express, 66 Cannon Street, London EC4 (01-248 7011);
Hotels Abroad Ltd, 39 Jermyn Street, London SW1 (01-734 7511);
Italian Grand Hotels Company, 67 Jermyn Street, London SW1 (01-930 4147);
Utell International, 18 Berkeley Street, London W1 (01-499 2151);
Tophotels, 16 Berkeley Street, London W1 (01-493 9802);
R.M. Brooker Ltd, 11/12 Norfolk Street, London WC2 (01-836 1942).
(These tend to deal with the better-class hotels only.)

Jolly Hotels have, in Sicily now, lost their old monopoly of modern buildings and efficient service in the first-class category. With the exception of those at Érice and Taormina, they hardly expect you to use them as anything save overnight stopping-places and have adopted the abomination of illustrated menus as a symbol of the type of custom they expect from all nations.

The Italian State Tourist Office keeps up-to-date lists of tourist villages, which proliferate annually. They are usually formed of bungalows built around a service block. There is a Club Méditerranée at Cefalù (p. 97).

Categories and prices

Hotels are classified in five categories: de luxe, 1st, 2nd, 3rd and 4th; pensions into 1st, 2nd and 3rd. The charges are fixed in agreement with the local Provincial Tourist Board and vary somewhat according to season, position and services available. This makes it difficult to give a meaningful average price in any category but it is safe to say that all hotels in Sicily cost less than comparable ones in England, even the two luxury categories. Full-pension terms are normally available and offer a considerable saving (but see p. 28). Pensions approximate to 2nd, 3rd and 4th category hotels; you must usually stay not less than three days at them. Most hotel prices now include service and taxes.

We list hotels under the entry for the town in which they are situated.

Accommodation with bathing

The sign † beside a hotel's name indicates that it has unobstructed access to the sea-shore and/or a private beach. For those who attach particular importance to staying close to the sea we would suggest they consider the following places:

Agrigento Province: San Leone, Sciacca.

Caltanisetta Province: Gela.

Catánia Province: La Plaja, Acireale, Riviera dei Ciclopi near Acitrezza.

Messina Province: Lido di Mortelle, Maregrosso, Contesse, Milazzo.

Palermo Province: Mondello, Acquasanta, Sferracavallo, Romagnolo, Ísola delle Fémmine, Vetrana, Cefalù, Términi Imerese, Ústica Island, Terrasini, Cínisi (near Punta Ráisi airport).

Ragusa: Pozzallo.

Syracuse: Il Minareto; Il Villággio Turístico, by the sea 8 km. south of Syracuse, consists of bungalows with simple accommodation and a surprisingly good restaurant.

Syracuse Province: Pantanella, Sacramento, Penísola delle Maddalene.

Taormina Province: Mazzarò, Spisone, Giardini.

Trápani: Lido di San Giuliano.

VILLAS AND FLATS

Outside the Taormina neighbourhood there are few facilities for renting this type of accommodation, though the Azienda Autónoma di Soggiorno (see p. 41) for each district may prove helpful if applied to.

The Italian State Tourist Offices can suggest the names of firms dealing in the hiring of Continental holiday houses. Among others, the following will be found in the London telephone directory: Belvillas, Ltd; Continental Villas; Eurovillas; Holiday Villas; C.I.T. (England) Ltd; Villas Italia.

CAMPING

Organized camping sites abound in Sicily. Full details in the Touring Club Italiano's *Campeggi in Italia* – available from C.I.T. offices (see p. 32). For further information write to Centro Nazionale Campeggiatori Stranieri, Via Manueli 2, Florence. Camp sites with facilities charge 400 l. per day per person (children over six years of age generally less) and 150 l. for a car. Touring Club Italiano has its own sites with fixed tents, restaurants, etc.; for details write to T.C.I., Corso Italia 10, Milan.

YOUTH HOSTELS

Associazione Italiana Alberghi per la Gioventù (Via Guidobaldi del Monte 24, Rome) accepts Y.H.A. members. Charges are 500 l. a night with an additional 50 l. for heating when required; restaurant meals cost 550 l. and 150 l. for breakfast – or cook for yourself.

At Catánia and Messina there is a student hostel (Casa dello Studente). Apply on site or acquire the *Guide for Foreign Students* (500 l.) from the Ministry of Education, Viale Trastevere, Rome, which gives details of the many facilities offered students in Italy. There are youth hostels at Belvedere near Syracuse, on Lípari Island and Giarre.

If you wish to organize an educational party inquire of the Italian Cultural Institute in London or New York or the C.I.V.I.S. Via Caetani 32, Rome.

ALBERGHI DIURNI

These are a useful institution all over Italy, usually situated near the main railway station. In some there is a left-luggage office and a writing-room. They also provide baths, lavatories, washing facilities, barbers, shoeblacks, clothes-pressing, for either sex, for a moderate charge. In Sicily they are to be found in Palermo, Catánia, Messina and Syracuse.

RESTAURANTS

Prices vary of course – say, between 2,000 l. and 4,000 l. in the grander places, down to 600 l. or 1,000 l. in the more modest; which does not mean that you would starve on less in the kind of *trattorie* to be found around markets.

Sicilian cooking can be more pungent than is usual in the bland mainland style, but this good fare is disappearing from tourist-frequented places. Sicilians like their grub (if they get any at all) and you won't go far wrong if you eat anywhere they do themselves. Avoid the *tipico* joints where more attention is paid to the décor and the bill than the food.

We give the names of some restaurants under place entries but must insist that these are recommended on personal experience and perhaps reflect an idiosyncratic taste. Mention of a restaurant represents a tribute to a happy experience, not the outcome of an exhaustive investigation into all the available alternatives. We hope no crises or changes will have altered their standards, should you follow our advice and visit them, and we hope, too, that you will find others as good on your own.

PRACTICAL INFORMATION

CLIMATE AND CLOTHES

Average temperatures vary from about 52°F in the shade in January to about 84°F in the shade in July. It can be rather wet in November, December and January, but spring comes very early. Even in the height of the summer there is often a breeze in the evenings, and you may be glad of a pullover or cardigan. Women will naturally need something to cover their heads and their bare arms when visiting churches.

HEALTH AND DRINKING WATER

The water is drinkable everywhere, including the fountains. You may wonder why, in that case, Italians often drink bottled water. The main reason is that it is fashionable; also, it is effervescent and therefore slightly more refreshing, while most kinds claim to have some medicinal value as well. If you should suffer from an upset stomach, this is most likely due to the sun and the sudden change of diet. People who overdo things during their first few days in Sicily are asking for trouble; take a siesta after lunch, or at least go and sit in the shade. Sicilians go to sleep during the afternoon, and they are accustomed to the bright sun and the food cooked in oil. There is no reciprocal National Health Service arrangement, and, there-fore, no free medical treatment in Sicily, but a Tourist Insurance Policy is available from the M.A.E.C.I. Insurance Company, Via Panzeri 10, Milan, or Via Geantureo 11, Rome. The price of this policy, covering theft, accident, medical/surgical expenses, illness, disablement and death, is 800 l. for ten days, 1,150 l. for twenty days and 1,500 l. for thirty days. This may prove easier to collect on the spot than a home-based policy.

TOURIST INFORMATION

Information of every kind can be obtained from E.P.T. (Ente Provinciale per il Turismo) offices, which operate in all provincial capitals and in some cases there is also an information office called Assessorato Regionale per il Turismo, and/or a branch of the Azienda Autónoma di Cura Soggiorno Turismo. The address of the E.P.T. and Azienda Autónoma di Soggiorno offices are given under the appropriate town entries. See also information about ENIT and C.I.T. offices on p. 32.

MUSEUMS

Museums are open from about 09.30 or 10.00 to 16.00 or 17.00 on weekdays and during the mornings only on Sundays and holidays. They are closed one day a week. Maddeningly, this day varies in a whimsical way, though it is usually Monday. We give times and closing days – to the best of our knowledge – under individual entries. The local E.P.T. office will not be able to give you the exact opening times for each museum or for all other places of interest.

The charge at museums and art galleries, etc., is so nominal that it really adds very little to the cost of the holiday. Sicily is not a rich country and needs these contributions to keep up her museums, so we should not grudge these small sums. Students and teachers, however, can obtain free passes by applying well in advance to the Italian Cultural Institute, 39 Belgrave Square, London sw1, and 686 Park Avenue, N.Y.C., or get an International Student Identity Card (N.U.S. members only) from 3 Endsleigh Street, London wc1.

MONEY-CHANGING AND BANKS

The best exchange rates are to be had at banks. The cashiers there, particularly at the Banca Commerciale, Banca d'Itália or Banco di Sicília, are used to effecting the exchange and you will waste less time over the chore. Hotels give shocking rates. Banks are open from about 08.00 to 12.30 on Mondays to Fridays (closed on Saturdays and Sundays). Although they are sometimes open for an hour in the afternoons (usually 15.30 to 16.30) this hour varies, so you are advised to get your transactions over in the morning. You can also change money at C.I.T. offices. At present £1 = 1,482 l. and $ = 637 l., but you should check exchange rates with your bank as they are subject to considerable fluctuation.

SHOPPING

Most of the larger shops and some smaller ones have fixed prices which are marked on each article.

At about 12.30 or 13.00 they close and re-open generally at 16.00 and then close again around 19.00 on weekdays (including Saturdays). Some of the smaller shops where you are served by the owner remain open still later, and may be open on Sundays. Most hairdressers and barbers are open on Sunday mornings but are closed on Mondays.

The equivalent of Woolworths or Marks & Spencer are UPIM and STANDA, which can be found in the larger towns. Italian cigarettes are cheaper than English or American brands; but the latter are easily obtainable.

TIPPING

Tipping is a worry to most travellers: any suggestions we make are based on the present rate of exchange. Use your own discretion, naturally, if anyone has been particularly helpful. Packets of English or American cigarettes are appreciated. In restaurants an extra 5 per cent tip, over and above the service charge, is welcomed; but in small *trattorie* you would just leave 50 l. or so, and, if you are served by the proprietor, nothing. Give about 200 to 250 l. to a guide, and 100 l. per bag to porters, though you may find the official rate raised above that sum at any moment. There is no absolute rule about tipping barbers and hairdressers. While some Italians do not tip them, others do, and the tourist would probably be expected to tip in the region of 100 l. to the barber; for a shampoo and set, 200 l. to the girl who helps would be most acceptable, and 10 per cent of the bill to the man, unless it is quite clear that he is the proprietor. It is not necessary to tip in theatres, but it is usual to give a small tip to the girl who shows you to your seat in a cinema, between 50 and 100 l. depending on the price of your seat.

No one likes feeling cheated, but keep in mind that a suspicious attitude can completely wreck a whole holiday and that you would not be there at all if you could not afford to pay just a little more than the local population, especially when, as in Sicily, the smallest amount of money has a desperate importance. All the same, check your bills – this is common sense and not considered offensive – and Sicilians themselves will advise you not to leave your car unlocked, even for a few minutes.

OUTDOOR SPORTS

Swimming, underwater swimming and fishing, skin-diving, surf-riding and water ski-ing are all available in Sicily. There are water ski-ing clubs in Catánia and Palermo and the Aeolian Islands have special facilities for skin-diving. Underwater fishing can be found on the Aeolian, Egadi, Pelagic islands, also on Pantelleria, Lampe-dusa and Ústica islands. Underwater fishing requires no licence and is prohibited only in harbours. Sailing is possible to arrange, but it is not highly organized. For bathing possibilities, see p. 37. For freshwater fishing, tackle may be imported free on a temporary basis; a local permit must be obtained from the District *Prefettura* – 1,300 l. to 4,500 l., according to type.

For climbing, information can be obtained from offices of the Club Alpino Italiano, at the following addresses: Viale Regina Margherita 10, Catánia; Piazza Matrice, Linguaglossa; Via del Vespro 75, Isol. 269, Messina; Via R. Séttimo 78, Palermo; Pr.Ins. Geraci A, Via Roma, Petralia Sottana. Winter sports are carried on, particularly on Etna and the Madonie. Shooting can be had, mainly for hares, duck and geese, and all migratory birds. A permit, obtainable at all Italian consulates (£3·34 or $8), is obligatory. Further information of all kinds from the Federazione Italiana Caccia, Viale Tiziano 70, Rome.

Football is the popular sport on Sicily. Although you may not find tennis-courts very easily, they are available and, in fact, important tennis tournaments take place in Palermo (April–May) and Taormina. There is, as yet, no golf course on the island. Other sporting events include the International Air Tour of Sicily the Targa Florio) in July; Grand Prix races at Syracuse and

Pergusa; horse shows at Palermo (October), Catánia and Messina; and an 'International Review of Underwater Fishing', etc., at Ústica Island (August).

CONCERTS AND THEATRES

Opera and concert seasons are held in Palermo (January–May) and Catánia (February–April); and in summer there are open-air operas and concerts at Palermo, Taormina, Segesta, Tíndari, Enna, Trápani and Messina.

Performances of plays in the Greek Theatre at Syracuse are given every two years in May and June by the well-known Classic Theatre.

FEAST-DAYS AND HOLIDAYS

OFFICIAL HOLIDAYS
On the following holidays, shops, banks and museums are closed.

January 1st (New Year's Day).
January 6th (Epiphany).
February 11th (Concorda half-holiday).
March 19th (St Joseph's Day).
Easter Monday.
April 25th (Liberation Day).
May 1st (Labour Day).
Sixth Thursday after Easter Sunday (Ascension of Christ).
Ninth Thursday after Easter Sunday (Corpus Domini).
June 2nd (Proclamation of the Republic).
June 29th (SS. Peter and Paul's Day).
August 15th (Assumption of the Virgin Mary).
October 4th (St Francis's Day half-holiday).
November 1st (All Saints' Day).
November 4th (Victory Day).
December 8th (Conception of the Virgin Mary).
December 25th (Christmas Day).
December 26th (Boxing Day).

FEAST-DAYS
Each church or parish celebrates the feast-day of its patron saint as the climax to several days of jollity; these varying, according to the popularity of the cult and the amount of money spent on them,

from humble village festivities to great fairs in which a whole city takes part. They are invariably pleasant occasions, however poor, with bands, processions, decorated streets and fireworks. A calendar of the more interesting *feste* follows:

December 31st	*Vigília di Capodanno: New Year's Eve* – services in all larger churches, often fireworks; traditionally, one gambles to test the next year's luck.
January 1st	*Capodanno: New Year's Day* – public holiday; celebrations at home.
January 6th	*Epifania: Epiphany* – present-giving day.
February 3rd–10th	*Almond Blossom Festival* at **Agrigento**.
February 3rd–5th	*Sant' Ágata*, patroness of Catánia. Carnival at **Acireale**.
Easter	*Giovedì Santo: Maundy Thursday* – services in cathedrals recall Spanish custom with foot-washing and other symbolic ceremonies. Sometimes heavy crosses are carried in procession – at **Caltanisetta** with national costumes.
	Venerdì Santo: Good Friday – a big day for the Sicilian death cult. Processions of the Stations of the Cross, with penitents, of which that at **Trápani** is most famous and where a passion play is also given, as at **Isnello** and **Sezze** also. **Enna** and **Acireale**, for national costumes.
	Pasqua: Easter Sunday – celebrations in all churches and a dinner of lamb in all houses that can afford it. Celebrations according to Byzantine rites at **Piana degli Albanesi**.
Whitsun	*Pentecoste* – religious celebrations on Sunday.
Corpus Christi	*Corpus Domini* – floral processions, notably that at **Petralia Sottana**.
April	Rally of Sicilian costumes and carts, **Taormina**.
May 1st–4th	Folk-lore festival, **Agrigento**.
May 2nd	*San Sebastiano* at **Melilli**.
May 5th–12th	**Monreale** week.
First Sunday in May	Festival of the *Patrocínio di Santa Lucia* at **Syracuse**.

May 8th	*Sant' Alfio* at **Trecastagni**, with national costumes, painted carts, etc.
June 2nd	Public holiday to celebrate foundation of the Republic of Italy.
June 3rd	*Madonna della Lettera* at **Messina**.
June 29th	*SS. Peter and Paul* – a major fiesta everywhere, lasting several days.
July 11th–15th	*Santa Rosalia* – religious and folk-lore festival at **Palermo**; procession up **Monte Pellegrino**.
August 15th	*Ferragosto: Assumption of the Virgin* – a nation-wide fiesta; see it especially at **Petralia Soprano** for odd usages, at **Messina** for the procession of the giants.
September 4th	*Santa Rosalia* pilgrimage up **Monte Pellegrino** at **Palermo**.
September 8th	*Birth of the Virgin* – notably at **Tíndari** and **Gibilmanna**; **Piana degli Albanesi** for costumes.
September 27th	*SS. Cósimo e Damiano* – fishermen's festival at **Palermo**.
October 4th	*San Francesco* – the veneration in which St Francis of Assisi is held makes this a great festival everywhere.
November 1st	*Ognissanti: All Saints* – children are given presents 'from the dead' during the night; these are bought at special fairs set up everywhere.
November 2nd	*Il Giorno dei Morti* – the high holiday of the death cult: cemeteries are visited, graves decorated and illuminated, masses sung continually.
December 13th	*Festa della Santuzza* at **Syracuse**.
December 24th	*Vigilia di Natale: Christmas Eve* – midnight masses. Only chance to see interiors of dark churches.
Christmas Day	*Natale* – the cribs erected in every church are visited; that at **Acireale** is famous. Christmas is very much a family festival throughout Italy.

POSTAL INFORMATION

Postal services in the Italian provinces are erratic. If you must get hold of someone quickly, telegraph or telephone. Telephones are now fully automatic. A local telephone call – made from a public telephone – is paid for by means of a *gettone* (a counter) which can be bought wherever there is a public telephone. Stamps are sold (also salt) at all tobacconists.

WEIGHTS AND MEASURES

Italian weights and measures are, as usual on the Continent, according to the metric system:

1 kilo (1,000 grammes) = approx. 2·2 lb.
Half-kilo (500 grammes) = approx. 1·1 lb.
Quarter-kilo (250 grammes) = approx. $\frac{1}{2}$ lb.

The term 'quarter-kilo' is never used. Ask for *due etti e mezzo*. The *etto* is a local weight which equals about $\frac{1}{4}$ lb. (English).

1 litre = approx. 1$\frac{3}{4}$ pints.
1 metre = 39·37 inches.
1 kilometre = 0·62 miles (roughly, $\frac{5}{8}$ of a mile).

TEMPERATURE

The Centigrade scale is used. To convert Fahrenheit to Centigrade, subtract 32 and multiply by $\frac{5}{9}$. To convert Centigrade to Fahrenheit, multiply by $\frac{9}{5}$ and add 32.

ELECTRICITY

Most electric plugs in Sicily are two-pin Continental size, but supposing you have an electric razor or non-battery torch which needs recharging, the most practical thing is to take an adapter to fit a *screw-in* bulb socket. Voltage is 125–220 AC 50 cycles per second.

TIME

The normal time in Sicily is one hour in advance of Greenwich Mean Time, i.e. the same as British Summer Time. Italian Summer Time, operating between late May and late September, is an hour ahead of British Summer Time, i.e. two hours ahead of G.M.T.

GEOGRAPHY, FLORA AND FAUNA

The island of Sicily, which is a detached part of the Italian Apennine range of mountains, was also at one time (the Diluvial Period) nearly connected with North Africa by a table-land. The division from the Italian mainland came later, in the Tertiary Period, when a number of fissures radiating from the Tyrrhenian depression led to the region splitting up into islands. The Sicilian mountains resemble those in Calábria, on which bare peaks surmount heavily afforested slopes; but the highest peak in Sicily, Mount Etna (10,742 feet) was raised by volcanic action, to which are owed also Strómboli, the other Aeolian Islands and Pantelleria. A number of thermal springs and small mud-volcanoes exist. The oldest geological characteristics – Triassic limestone, gneiss and granite – are found on the north coast.

Nearly 90 per cent of Sicily is under cultivation, and such areas are of two strikingly different types: (1) A mainly coastal fringe of fruit trees and olive groves. This rich green belt extends along the terraced hillsides of the north coast and girdles the foot of Etna and most of the towns. (2) A more extensive area of cereal cultivation (mostly wheat) which covers most of the interior and the south coast. Although green in spring, by midsummer the cornfields have become parched and desert-like. Almond trees – one of the glories of Sicily in the spring – and olives grow along the windy southern coast.

Surviving natural woodland now covers only $\frac{3}{4}$ per cent of the island. It survives mostly on the north slopes of the northern range, particularly in the Madonie and Nebrodi above the limit of cultivation, and on Etna. On the north coast there are still quite extensive forests of sweet chestnut, often mixed with holly, ash and maple. Higher up the mountains, beech is the dominant tree. Holly-oak and cork-oak grow mainly on very rocky hillsides. The endemic silver fir, *Abies nebrodensis*, survives as one wild population of about twenty trees, but is being replanted at Polizzi and Castellammare. Many herbaceous plants characteristic of central European woodlands are found in the mixed forests in north Sicily. On the mountain slopes of Etna, a woodland belt of sweet chestnut, deciduous oaks, beech, birch (*Betula aetnensis*) and black pine extends from 4,000 to 6,600 feet. Above this altitude is a community of low shrubs, including species of *Genista*, the dwarf spiny *Berberis aetnensis* and *Astragalus siculus* (both confined to Sicily) and a low prickly race of juniper. Alpine plants extend nearly to the top of the cinder cone and include such attractive species as *Viola aetnensis*, *Saponaria depressa* (with long, sticky, red calyces), *Aubrietia* and *Cerastium montanum*. The Oxford ragwort, *Senecio squalidus*, is native on Etna, where life on cinder slopes has no doubt pre-adapted it to the railway cuttings and bomb sites which it has so rapidly colonized in England.

In many lowland areas and on stony hillsides, previous woodland is now replaced by those *macchie* and dwarf scrub communities, fragrant with myrtle, cistus and lavender, so characteristic of the Mediterranean region. Here many beautiful bulbous and tuberous plants, including bee orchids and anemones, flower in early spring.

Two interesting African plants grow in Sicily: papyrus (*Cyperus papyrus*) on the banks of the rivers near Syracuse, and a dwarf palm, *Chamaerops humilis*, abundant in many parts of the island.

Many of the rarest and most beautiful plants in Sicily grow on inaccessible limestone rocks. Near the theatre at Taormina one may see a magnificent shrubby scabious with silver leaves and pink flowers, *Scabiosa cretica*, and a handsome knapweed with big yellow heads, *Centaurea tauromenitana*, confined to this area; here, too, grows a bushy, pink-flowered catchfly, *Silene fruticosa*. The limestone cliffs towards Trápani are richer still. Here may be found – if you are lucky – a large flowered heath, *Pentapera sicula*, a shrubby white candytuft, *Iberis semperflorens*, and two rare cliff shrubs which also grow on Capri: *Lithospermum rosmarinifolium* (with gentian-blue flowers) and the pink and silver *Convolvulus cneorum*. *Scabiosa limonifolia* adorns the cliffs of Maréttimo. Many of these remarkable plants have no doubt survived on the limestone cliffs of Sicily since pre-Glacial times and represent one of the most interesting elements in the island's flora. If you come across them, please do not make them any rarer than they are!*

Sicily is suprisingly lacking in interesting wildlife. Foxes, wild-cats and martens are occasionally seen and, even more rarely, a wolf. Rabbits are few, hares more frequent. There is a large variety of wild-fowl and migratory birds.

* An account of the vegetation of Sicily – with reference to botanical literature – will be found in Rikli's *Das Pflanzenkleid der Mittelmeerländer* (Berne, 1943–8, 3 vols.).

HISTORY

PREHISTORY

The island was not colonized by man until the middle of the Würm glaciation, the last stage of the long Ice Age. The people whose culture was characteristic of that human phase which we call Upper Paleolithic then crossed the Straits of Messina.

The inhabited sites already found belonging to this period are very numerous. Upper Paleolithic man seems to have kept fairly close to the coast – as indeed all subsequent cultures have done – perhaps because his diet depended largely upon sea-food; and he may not have found it necessary to penetrate inland in search of the game then teeming in the forests.

These people have left vivid and sometimes exquisitely beautiful records of themselves on the walls of the Grotta della Cava dei Genovesi, on Lévanzo Island, and in the Grotta dell'Addaura, on the north side of Monte Pellegrino, where the incised drawings and paintings are apparently of differing dates, certainly of uneven skill, but always alive and illustrative.

The comparatively near presence of the ice-fields – which never reached Sicily – naturally affected its climate. The immense rainfall cut the deep, dry ravines so noticeable in south-east Sicily. When the retreat of the ice allowed the climate to become stabilized to its present type, a new culture arose in the Mediterranean coastal lands, the Mesolithic. As so often, Sicily proved a rare bird even then. A true Mesolithic culture was imported, but the Upper Paleolithic cultures of the island seem to have developed along Mesolithic lines rather than to have been supplanted; and the subsequent Neolithic period mingled with the Mesolithic.

The techniques of Neolithic culture were distributed over the Mediterranean from north-east Syria by peoples on the move, though the provenance of the particular people whose culture is dubbed 'Stentinello' (after the site where Professor Orsi first identified it) and who were the first to employ them in Sicily is not yet known. They were farmers, seamen and traders, lived in villages rather than in caves and made weapons from obsidian, basalt and greenstone as well as flint. They made rough, moulded pottery, coarsely decorated by impressions or incisions made in the soft clay before baking, the patterns often being made with the edges of shells.

This was previous to the year 4000 B.C. These basic Neolithic techniques were soon followed by a much advanced culture of which painted ware is the hallmark and which also had knowledge of copper smelting.

From then on the pace of civilization was ever accelerating. New techniques, enabling men more easily to support life, were resulting in an ever-growing population, while primitive scratch-farming was exhausting the lands settled by cultivators. Until techniques of crop rotation and fertilizers were worked out, there was an unending pressure of land-hungry peoples outwards from the 'nursery lands' of the Near East; and this was given a new impetus as the science of metallurgy advanced from copper to bronze, bronze to iron.*

The Straits of Messina, perhaps, mitigated the force of the impact of these successive waves of new peoples; though, by the time that the Greeks began their colonization, the island seems to have been shared by peoples who recognized only one division between them and whom we can call the Sikels and the Sicans, the first in the east and the second in the west of the island.

Confusion is rife over these names. The Sikels of the east, pacific by nature, appear to have been related to the mainland Latin peoples while the western Sicans, more belligerent, belonged to an older, pre-Aryan stratum and were probably descendants of immigrants from Africa, driven thence like the Ligurians by the progressive desiccation of the Sahara region.

The Greek colonists found a third people settled in the west, the Elymians. These claimed Trojan refugee descent and their origin remains obscure; some place-names of the region, however, suggest a Ligurian connection rather than, as has been suggested, an Iberian one, any similarities there being explained by concurrent exodi from North Africa.

At least as early as the fourteenth century B.C., the peoples of Sicily and southern Italy were in frequent contact with Mycenaean adventurers and traders. The *Odyssey* and other epic poems, though written down much later, contain many references to these early contacts.

* Recommended further reading: Luigi Bernabò Brea, *Sicily Before the Greeks*, trans. C. M. Preston and L. Guido (Thames and Hudson, London, 1957).

During the 'Dark Age' of Greek civilization following the over-throw of the Mycenaean kingdoms this contact did not entirely cease. A true Iron Age culture was meanwhile introduced into Sicily by the Apennini peoples, who resembled the Villanovans of Tuscany and made pots of immense elegance and distinction.

GREEK PERIOD (eighth century B.C. to 241 B.C.)

Beginning in the eighth century B.C., the Aegean Greeks began to seek agricultural *Lebensraum* outside Greece. The first colonists in the Tyrrhenian area may have been the Etruscans, who seized the iron-ore country of Tuscany. Greeks from the Euboean cities of Chalcis and Eretria followed about a generation later, colonizing Ischia, and then Cumae on the Bay of Naples about the year 756 B.C. Owing to considerations of winds and currents, they usually sailed south and west of Sicily to reach the west Italian coast, but returned to the Aegean through the Straits of Messina. To protect their lines of communication, therefore, the Cumaeans founded Naxos, north of the modern Catánia – the first Greek colony in Sicily (735 B.C.).

Other colonies followed along the south and east coasts of Sicily and the west and southern coasts of mainland Italy. On these rich and comparatively virgin lands, into which the colonists introduced the olive and the vine, the colonial cities prospered beyond all Greek imagining. This success caused disquiet to the Phoenicians (who were more traders than colonists) and from their one import-ant colonial base at Carthage (the modern Tunis) they occupied points on the western tip of Sicily, at Marsala and Palermo. Trápani already belonged to their allies, the Elymians. Thus the Phoenicians threatened the Greek sea route.

The rivalry of these three powers – Greek, Phoenician and Etrus-can – together with their often mutual commercial interests, explains their history of veering alliances and sudden antagonisms. This pattern was further complicated as the Greek cities, especially of Sicily, grew richer and more powerful than those of Greece itself. Taken together, the Italian colonies came appropriately to be called 'Magna Graecia' or 'Greater Greece'; and, like the cities of Greece, they developed violent rivalries among themselves, the crucial division being between those of Chalcidian and Corinthian origin, Syracuse leading the latter faction.

While the Cumaeans and their allies held an Etruscan advance southwards in Italy, the Sicilian Greeks succeeded for a time in confining the, by now, much alarmed Phoenicians to western Sicily by winning a great battle at Himera (near Términi Imerese) in 480 B.C. The following century saw the heyday of Greek Sicily, when Syracuse, the greatest city of the day in all the world, defeated the huge expedition which Athens made against her.

This power and splendour had been achieved first under the archaic and oligarchic rule of aristocratic colonial families and, later, by city tyrants who, usually beginning as champions of the masses – too many of whom had fallen into virtual serfdom through debt to the nobles or belonged to the growing caste of traders – soon came to realize the benefits of absolute rule both to themselves and to their states. Some even founded reasonably stable dynasties. But the Greeks, to their ruin, invented democracy, which, in their case, meant parochialism. This new, proud weakness gave the mountain peoples of Italy and the Carthaginians of Sicily their chance to whittle Magna Graecia away.

From Sicily's point of view, ruination had already set in. The great fleets which Greeks, Carthaginians and Romans built called for vast amounts of wood, the cutting of which went a long way to deforest the island, leaving the upland soil to be washed away, changing the climate to a more extreme one and, eventually, silting up many a once prosperous port.

The history of this important period for Sicily is given in fuller detail under that of Syracuse (p. 212), the most successful of the Greek colonies, whose fluctuating fortunes influenced those of all the rest.*

ROMAN PERIOD (241 B.C. to A.D. 318)

In Italy, the Latins of Rome proved the dominating people and gradually came to control all southern Italy. Their victories inevitably brought them into conflict with Carthage and the Phoenicians.

---

* Recommended further reading: A. G. Woodhead, *The Greeks in the West* (Thames and Hudson, London, 1962); M. I. Finley, *Ancient Sicily: To the Arab Conquest* (Chatto and Windus, London, 1968). Those interested in this period, with the Roman also, should supplement this guide with Margaret Guido, *Sicily: an archaeological guide* (Faber and Faber, London, 1967).

The first of the two Punic Wars, seventeen-year-long and devastating (it lasted until 241 B.C.) was inconclusive, though it left most of Sicily in Roman hands, only Syracuse remaining independent (until 211 B.C.). Hieron II of Syracuse had allowed Messina to fall into Carthaginian hands; it was this threat to the Straits which directly involved Sicily in the Romans' war.

Hannibal carried the second Punic War into Italy, and, after his great victory at Cannae, most of Rome's southern possessions deserted to him; but, with Rome's eventual triumph in 201 B.C., the defaulters' day of reckoning came. The citizens of Agrigento and Taranto were sold as slaves; those of Capua butchered; while the Neapolitans, who had been staunch, proved to have founded their city's fortunes. Eventually even Syracuse was reduced by the Romans after a two-year siege. However, since both the Roman consuls and Hannibal had resorted to scorched-earth tactics, the depredations of the war were such that neither the South nor Sicily has ever fully recovered from them.

Sicily was now, for the first time, a provincial place, a melancholy state made worse by the savage revolt of the slaves which further impoverished the island.

Under the governorship of a praetor and two quaestors (stationed at Syracuse and Marsala), the Sicilian cities enjoyed a measure of home rule and stood in various relationships to Rome – their significance largely having to do with their tax assessments. The raising of wheat was officially fostered and rich Romans invested in estates on the island. These absentee landlords in effect founded the disastrous tradition of the *latifúndie* which has bled the country-side ever since. C. Verres, the notorious governor who plundered the island between 73 and 71 B.C. did not affect its potential wealth, only the current prosperity of its people and their temple treasuries. Far more burdensome and damaging was Sextus Pompeius's seizure of the island (44–36 B.C.). His war with Octavius Caesar (Augustus) interrupted the flow of wheat to Rome, leading to its later decline. His shipbuilding further denuded the vanishing forests. Victorious, Augustus founded a half-dozen colonies of veterans, pioneering further settlement by mainlanders. The specifically Greek character of the old cities persisted, however, into Byzantine times and even later.

Under the Empire, the emperors themselves increasingly became the biggest landowners and the *latifúndie* generally increased enormously. Yet the ports on the Mediterranean sea routes prospered. The Romans built Palermo into a place of importance, but Syracuse was still the chief city. The vast extent of its catacombs may indicate that it was as important a seat of early Christianity as Rome itself.

BARBARIAN PERIOD (A.D. 318 to 535)

With the break-up of the Roman Empire of the West, Sicily fell to the Vandals of North Africa; from them the Ostrogoths took it, thus reuniting it to Italy. The barbarians sorely neglected their magnificent conquests. Things were everywhere left to fall into ruin, even aqueducts. It was the golden age of heresy – evidently an absorbing distraction in hard times. Because Italy was dependent on Sicily for its bread, the Sicilians were well treated by the Ostrogoths; but this did not mollify the Sicilians, who so enthusiastically welcomed the Byzantine invasion under Belisarius (A.D. 535) that the Ostrogoths withdrew without resistance.

BYZANTINE PERIOD (A.D. 535 to 827)

During the quiet period that followed, the anopheles mosquito made its appearance in Sicily and, as a result of malaria, the population began to dwindle in low-lying parts. All the same, Sicily enjoyed a period of almost unbroken peace lasting about a century. Elsewhere were interminable wars and dissensions and, if the Byzantines' preoccupation with these led to their making little of Sicily's potential wealth, at least the islanders were not harassed. From the mid seventh century A.D. onwards, however, Sicily became gradually more involved with the world again. The southern coasts, particularly, were troubled by Arab raids – early Muslim expeditions coming direct from Syria and Egypt. But its history would have been a sadder one over this time had not the powers surrounding it then been so debilitated themselves.

None the less, the Emperor Constans, despairing of holding Constantinople against the Muslims and perhaps dreaming of reconstituting the western Empire of Rome, moved his court west and settled at Syracuse. His officials rightly disapproved of his abandonment of Constantinople, and in A.D. 668 a courtier brained him with a soap dish while he was taking a bath – after which, the Government very properly returned to the Bosphorus for a further 750 years.

By early in the eighth century A.D., the Arabs had ousted the Byzantines all along the African coast facing Sicily. Thus their pressure on the island was much increased.

ARAB PERIOD (A.D. 827 to 1061)

In 827 Euphemius, the Byzantine admiral, dismissed from his post because of his liaison with a nun, revolted and invited Arab help. It was an opportunity not to be missed; a large force, landing at Mazara, seized Palermo in 831. Euphemius met a violent, mysterious end and slowly the whole island was occupied, the significant fall of Syracuse occurring in 878. Resistance was stubborn: Taormina held out until 902, Rometta, on the northern slopes of the Monti Peloritani, until 965.

Since the Arabs had conquered the eastern, southern and western littorals of the Mediterranean, Sicily was brought back into the centre of that sea's life. And the Arabs of the expansion were an active lot. They were at pains to resettle rural areas and their inheritance laws helped break down overlarge latifundian estates. Their reverence for water and scientific bent combined with intelligent self-interest to restore and to extend ancient irrigation works. They introduced citrus trees, sugar-cane, flax, the date-palm, cotton, mulberries and the silkworm, papyrus, pistachio nuts, melons and the sumac for tanning and dyeing. Probably they improved on the ancient tunny-fishing techniques, innovating the *mattanza* of today. They mined and produced silver, lead, mercury, sulphur, naphtha, vitriol, antimony, alum and rock-salt. Sicily really prospered again.

But, politically, Arab Sicily was bedevilled by internal rivalries – those between Ommayed Spanish and eastern Arabs, between true Arab and Berber, even between southern, Yemeni Arabs and those from northern Arabia. At the outset the island was a dependency of the Sunni, orthodox, Aghlabid rulers of Tunisia, but when in 909 the heretical, Shiite Ubaydallah el-Mahdi established the Fatimid dynasty in mid North Africa, a still further cause for dissension was added: that between Shiite rulers and orthodox subjects.

Under Gawhar (seemingly a Sicilian Christian by origin), the

Fatimids conquered Egypt and in 969 removed their capital to Cairo. After this they lost interest in their western possessions, which lapsed into anarchy. By this time, however, a governor appointed by the Fatimids in 948, al-Hassan al-Kalbi, had established his own virtually independent dynasty in Sicily, maintaining it as an island of stability. Visiting it in the middle of the century, ibn-Hawqual found Palermo to be a splendid city. His figures seem exaggerated (300 mosques, for instance), but even a conservative estimate shows it to have been a larger city than any Christian one of the era except only Constantinople, or Cairo in the Arab world. Between 989 and 998, under the emir Abu el-Futuh Yussef ibn-Abdullah, truly Arab Sicily saw a fine flowering too soon to decline amid the family quarrels and civil wars of the Kalbite dynasty's rule. This weakness also encouraged increased Byzantine attacks from the Basilicata of southern Italy.

Of these, that made in 1038 under the great general George Maniakes was the most important. Messina was stormed and much of the east of the island taken; Syracuse too in 1040, just before Maniakes was recalled in political disgrace, whereafter the invasion speedily collapsed.

A large contingent of Normans had, most significantly, accompanied the Byzantine army. The eldest of the astonishing de Hauteville brothers, William 'Bras de Fer' was among them, earning his iron-armed nickname by felling the emir of Syracuse with one blow. He and his fellows liked what they saw of Sicily and, though they quarrelled with Maniakes, they withdrew determined to come back on their own account.

NORMANS : HOUSE OF DE HAUTEVILLE (A.D. 1061 to 1194)

Chaos across the sea in near-by Africa considerably isolated Sicily from the Muslim world while internal dissension minimized what government survived on it. In 1060 open war raged between two emirs; getting the worst of it, ibn at-Timnah aped Euphemius, personally crossing to Calabria to invite Roger – the youngest de Hauteville brother – to possess himself of the island. Roger complied, though not without an initial set-back and a protracted struggle thereafter. Summer by summer, Roger pressed the Arabs back from Messina (captured in 1061) to Palermo (1072) then, more slowly and destructively, over the south and far west until, by 1091, he held it all.

In his thirty years a-conquering, Roger had acquired great administrative skill and consolidated his gains by evolving a method of ruling his multiracial subjects of diverse religions and cultures with a liberal firmness and equity (not lightly to be ignored today) that laid a sure foundation for Sicily's second epoch of significant prosperity and importance.

Roger the Great, Count of Sicily, died in 1101 to be succeeded by his eight-year-old son Simon, who himself died two years later. Roger's widow, Adelaide, continued as regent for her younger son, also called Roger.

Born in 1095, Roger II was Count at ten, inherited the dukedom of Apulia at thirty-three and was crowned first King of Sicily on Christmas Day, 1130. The splendid and turbulent Norman kingdom of the South became fully established under this best and best-remembered of its rulers. He reigned until 1154 and made his kingdom the third power in Europe. Yet it was barely a European place – or rather its Sicilian base was barely so; the mainland duchy was differently administered, differently peopled; a more conventionally European feudal estate. Under Roger II and his son, Sicily produced some of the finest contributions to Islamic culture and, at a time when Arabs were world leaders in the intellectual field, Sicilian Muslims were more instrumental even than the Spanish in passing the fruits of that leadership into European culture. The Arabs had restricted, though never persecuted, their Byzantine Greek Sicilian subjects – representatives, then, of all that was finest and most civilized, most generally admired, in Christian culture. These were preserved to add lustre to Roger's state as were their fellows in Norman Italy. The Normans of the south were therefore the Europeans the most exposed to both the best civilizations then extant in the West and if the kingdom drew upon Norman blood for its vigour, its creative talent arose from a marvellous cross between Greek and Arab which permeated all its manners, thought, art and interests. Roger himself epitomized his kingdom and actively created it from the materials his wise father had bequeathed him.

Alas, there is not space here to extol Norman Sicily enough, nor to detail its entrancing though saddening history. (But see the note on p. 60.)

Roger II was succeeded by his son, William 'the Bad' – not at all as bad as all that, but probably a manic depressive, very oriental by habit, misunderstood by and not popular with his uppity barons. His reign marks the beginning of a decline – of racial tensions, arrogance by the Latin baronage and increasing pressure from the papacy (from which the early Normans had been able to maintain an unusual and valuable independence; on this independence were laid the foundations of the awful, subsequent struggle between Guelph and Ghibelline factions which was to ruin Sicily). William was succeeded by his young son, William II 'the Good', a great builder and far from insignificant ruler of a still most prosperous though organically failing state. Roger II had extended his rule to Tripoli and Mahdia, in Tunisia, which provided an important commercial foothold and, for his Muslim subjects, a sustaining social link with Islam. The loss of these possessions under William II was most serious in that it isolated Sicilian Arabs, the bulk of the productive rural population, and left them a prey to increasing Latin bigotry. Other destructive factors have contributed, but it was the sheer stupidity of making life impossible for the Muslim farmer which did most to make a wasteland of Sicily's once bountiful lands. The Muslim was the least assimilable section of the community but, instead of latitude, this was met with increasing restriction, leading to an antagonism which bred only a counter-antagonism: a fatal chain of cause and effect. A baronage, too, which took pride in its illiteracy – in place of de Hautevilles and their agents who were expected to speak and write Latin, Greek and Arabic as naturally as they breathed – were just the kind to re-establish the *latifúndie*.

However, it was William's early death in 1189 that precipitated disaster. Roger II had married his sister Constance to Henry of Hohenstaufen, heir to the Holy Roman Emperor Frederick Barbarossa, and Constance was the only legitimate heir to the throne. Henry had lately inherited the Empire and at once claimed Sicily in his wife's name. The barons opposed him, electing Tancred, a bastard of Roger's, king. Although Tancred was able and active, that invidious smell of failure and dissolution hung about the state. His French ally – Roger's second wife was French – failed him and his English, King Richard, whose sister was William's widow, instead of helping him, sacked Messina. Henry won his new kingdom in 1194, after Tancred's death, with little difficulty, his campaign partly financed by the ransom England had paid him for

Richard. Tancred's infant son, William III, disappeared with his mother as Henry, having accepted the keys of the treasury, crowned himself king on the sixty-fourth anniversary of Roger's crowning.*

HOUSE OF HOHENSTAUFEN (A.D. 1194 to 1268)

Henry wanted a docile southern kingdom with all its wealth for a private subsidy. He may have been firm rather than sadistic, at least until the Sicilian revolt of 1196, which he was in course of repressing with exemplary ruthlessness – and even vindictiveness – when he died in 1197 from dysentery.

His widow, Constance, became regent for her infant son, Frederick, who was crowned King in May 1198, when he was three and a half years old. Constance had been forty when he was born, and she died six months after his coronation.

Constance had appointed Pope Innocent III her son's guardian but, as was inevitable during a minority, there was much quarrelling and dissension. Frederick I of Sicily, also Holy Roman Emperor Frederick II of Hohenstaufen (or Swabia), found when he took over, at the age of fourteen, a kingdom saddled with debt and largely dispersed among great lords. He was a most able ruler, reforming laws, stabilizing the currency and promoting education and industry; but he was never a popular ruler with the Sicilians, who resented his quarrelling with the Pope and his imperial pre-occupations, the endless wars that took him so often outside the island. Indeed, Sicily was the part of his dominions perhaps the least to benefit by the genius of Frederick 'Stupor Mundi', that most fascinating first modern man.†

HOUSE OF ANJOU (A.D. 1268 to 1282)

Frederick's heirs held the throne of Sicily until 1268 when the Pope invested Charles, Count of Anjou and Provence, brother of the saintly King Louis IX of France and champion of the Guelph cause,

* Recommended further reading: J. J. Norwich, *The Normans in the South* (Longmans, London, 1967) and *The Kingdom in the Sun* (Longmans, London, 1970) strictly for the Norman period; Denis Mack Smith, *Medieval Sicily (800–1713)* (Chatto and Windus, London, 1968) for these and later times.

† Recommended further reading: Georgina Masson, *Frederick II of Hohenstaufen* (Secker and Warburg, London, 1957).

as King of Sicily, leaving it to him to conquer the realm. This he did with diabolic ruthlessness. Charles was an ambitious ruler; he taxed his kingdom heavily and to impose his rule he resorted to the harshest methods which, in 1282, provoked the Sicilians to a general massacre of the French in the island – the well-known 'Sicilian Vespers'. The vehemence of this popular uprising carried the day – or, rather, the month – and a 'parliament' of Sicilian nobles invited King Peter of Aragon to accept the Sicilian crown on his wife's behalf. This he did. Charles failed in an attempt to retake Messina and the ensuing War of the Vespers lasted, with many interruptions, for twenty-one years – though mainly waged in Spain and at sea.*

HOUSE OF ARAGON AND THE VICEROYS
(A.D. 1282 to 1734)

Peter and his successor Alfonso having died, James of Aragon, succeeding, started negotiations to return Sicily to the Pope's wardship, but the Sicilians proclaimed James's younger brother Frederick as their king. The Peace of Caltabellotta (1302) confirmed Sicilian independence under Frederick – King of Trinácria, as he was styled. (The continued existence until 1815 – in title at least – of the Sicilian parliament which had elected the king, was more than a mere symbol of the Sicilians' spiritual independence of Italy, as of all other places. That this nationalistic sentiment is now anachronistic does not make it a whit less real, and one is very sensible of it throughout the island today.)

For seventy-five years the kings of Trinácria were resident on the island, their main concern its government. This was a golden age of comparative peace and prosperity, evidence of which remains in the many beautiful Catalan-inspired Gothic buildings. But the death of Frederick III in 1377 brought Sicily squarely into that anarchy – aided by the Black Death – in which the old feudal world of Europe collapsed. One Aragonese prince after another claimed the Trinacrian throne which, after 1442, under Alfonso V of Spain, included rule over Naples, then called 'Sicily this side of the Straits' (*Sicília di qua del Faro*).

* Recommended further reading: Steven Runciman, *The Sicilian Vespers* (University Press, Cambridge, 1958; also Penguin, Harmondsworth, 1960) describes the Norman and Hohenstaufen background to Charles's conquest, that campaign, his rule, the revolt and subsequent war.

During this disturbed period something of great consequence to Sicily was happening in the East – the Seljuk Turks were over-running the Levant. Except for its westerly connection with Spain, Sicily was now abandoned to the position of most southerly outpost of Europe – and it does not thrive as an extremity.

Alfonso was the first to appoint a viceroy to rule Sicily, a method which the kings of Aragon and, later, of Spain continued until 1713. The trouble with viceroys is that their hearts are at home and their courts are subsidiary to those of their kings elsewhere; appeal is possible over their heads – which is as well when the viceroy's rule happens to be too outrageously corrupt – and the unifying force of snobbery (immense in an aristocratic society) is, in time, directed away from the community of which it should be a pillar. Sicilian aristocrats – and no one else counted until the late eighteenth century – have, however, been content to be Sicilians and to stay insularly at home or, rather, in Palermo. A visit to the Spanish court – as to the Papal court – was doubtless a polishing experience for a Sicilian noble, but the point of the polish was that it would shine on the Cássaro Vécchio.

The Inquisition was introduced into Sicily and clerical tyranny so successfully defended the island from the pernicious influence of the Renaissance that one might think, to judge by the architecture, that nothing happened there between 1400 and 1550.

Everything, in fact, conspired to retard Sicily's growth, even to constant raids upon its coasts made by Turkish pirates, a menace finally put down by the combined efforts of the Knights of Malta and the Austrians at the naval victory of Lépanto in 1571. Austria had come upon the southern scene after the death of the Emperor Charles V and the division of his inheritance, but the Napoletano and Sicily did not escape from Spain until the conclusion of the War of the Spanish Succession landed them in Austrian hands – out of the frying pan and into the fire, the Sicilians thought. The Treaty of Utrecht (1713) awarded Naples and Sardinia to Austria, and Sicily to Savoy. By the Treaty of the Hague (1720), however, the islands were exchanged and Sicily went to Austria.*

* Recommended further reading: Denis Mack Smith, *Medieval Sicily* (*800–1713*), is particularly useful for the Spanish period, and the same author's *Modern Sicily: After 1713* for all subsequent periods.

HOUSE OF BOURBON (A.D. 1734 to 1860)

The Austrians were thoroughly unpopular and when, in 1734, the young Infanta of Spain, Charles of Bourbon, marched to claim the Kingdom of Naples on his own behalf, the people met him with a welcome compounded of relief at having a king of their own and distaste for the Austrians.

The Bourbons of Naples adored *il Regno* – their kingdom – but this fondness did not really extend to Sicily. Although it was not forgotten, it was not brought into the jolly circle of the Neapolitan court, and Ferdinand IV, with his basically stupid Austrian wife, Maria Carolina, though twice forced to resort to Palermo during the war with Bonaparte, were not made at all welcome there and enjoyed neither stay.

That most delightful of travellers, Patrick Brydone, visiting both Naples and Palermo in 1770, notes in his book *A Tour through Sicily and Malta* the marked difference between the mores and the tempo of the two societies. Palermo, he found, was the less licentious, but very much the freer. Where continental girls were kept in convents until marriage, the Palermitans were educated at home and entered society, as it were, at birth. Their mothers, who were usually married by fifteen, were in the habit of receiving company in their bedrooms on the evening after their confinements, and, thereafter, nightly until their convalescence was over. Family life struck Brydone as close and happy; he was surprised at the number of virtuous and loving couples to be met with and delighted by the amicable, if formal, arrangements made for those not so well matched. There was a general *conversazione* – a sort of club for the nobility, like the provincial Russian ones, with its own assembly rooms – which opened at sunset. Here everyone repaired to *talk* – Brydone particularly stresses the moderation with which they played cards or gambled and the exuberance of the talk – until midnight, when the nightly concert began at the Marino. The Marino is now called the Foro Itálico and lies outside the sea-wall of the town. It is still a shady walk where there are cafés in eighteenth-century pavilions interrupting the austere face of the wall. Parties enlivened with fireworks, given at the villas on the Piano dei Colli and at Bagheria, varied this summer routine, and every day there were dinner parties – afternoon occasions these. Daily life was moderate and even frugal, though entertainment lavish, and the one great extravagance was an abundance of carriages. To walk was an unthinkable social suicide. To speak English was fashionable with the young and Brydone was surprised how many learned people there were in society.

However, Brydone was a humanist and a liberal:

> The poor people of the village have found us out and with looks full of misery have surrounded our door. Accursed tyranny – what despicable objects we become in thy hands! Is it not inconceivable, how any government should be able to render poor and wretched, a country which produces almost spontaneously, everything that even luxury can desire? They [the Spanish] make it their boast that the sun never sets on their dominions, but forget that since they became such, they have left him nothing to see in his course but deserted fields, barren wilderness, oppressed peasants, and lazy, lying, lecherous monks. This village is surrounded by the finest country in the world, yet there was neither bread nor wine to be found in it, and the poor inhabitants appear more than half starved.

That village lay between Agrigento and Palermo – it could have been Casteltérmini, or Bivona – and if one were today forced, as Brydone was, to lodge there the night, one would write home in the same vein, one's strictures but slightly modified in tone.

Brydone's liberalism was aristocratic and land-owning; he enjoyed the aristocratic society of the several thousand landowning Sicilians and ascribed to 'the Spanish' his friends' own misrule of their feudal lands, their apathy, wilful ignorance and manic conservatism which, combined, at the time (and more or less ever since) rendered themselves and all the islanders both poor and ungovernable. Savoy, Austria and even the Bourbons sent them quite able and sensible viceroys, but the Sicilian nobles, abetted by other interested parties and incompetent officials, took care to sabotage all their reforms.

The French Revolution sealed the fate of this world in which amiability was so oddly mixed with abominability. Circumstances forced Naples into the first coalition against France (1793) and, Napoleon having been defeated on the Nile (1798), Ferdinand IV was persuaded by his wife, Maria Carolina (who was a sister of Marie Antoinette), to go to war with France. This brought the French down on Naples, which they entered in January 1799.

Maria Carolina and Ferdinand, with the British Ambassador, Sir William Hamilton, and his wife, the beautiful goose Emma, fled for Palermo on Nelson's flagship *Vanguard*. They weathered a tremendous storm in appalling conditions – the Queen's youngest son died of convulsions in Emma's seaworthy arms – and the whole company arrived twelve days later either prostrated or hysterical. Ferdinand hunted the – to him – fresh pastures of Sicily while Maria Carolina, who thought Sicily unbearably African, built La Favorita. The Bourbon court did not return to Naples until 1802, and then it was only to be chased thence once more, in 1805, by Napoleon's brother, Joseph, who assumed the throne.

Back in Palermo, the royal couple found themselves in an altered place; where the upheavals of the time had made frightened reactionaries of them, their subjects had been precipitated into the nineteenth century. Now representing the English power which maintained their throne, was the efficient and progressive Lord William Bentinck. The Sicilian parliament (a purely aristocratic preserve, of course) was at perpetual loggerheads with the King who, cornered by Bentinck, was finally forced to grant Sicily a British-type constitution in 1812.

In May 1815 Ferdinand dissolved parliament, however, and signed with Austria a treaty to regain Naples. He was restored in June, and now styled himself Ferdinand I of the Two Sicilies, proclaiming the kingdoms of Naples and Sicily one realm and abolishing the Sicilian constitution, army and flag. His tyranny, however, led to the successful Carbonarist mutiny in 1820 and he was forced to grant a constitution in Naples. A popular rebellion had also broken out in Sicily, demanding the reintroduction of Bentinck's constitution, and Ferdinand had recourse to Austrian aid to restore his autocracy.

He was succeeded by his son, Francis I, a weak king under whose rule corruption became rife. Ferdinand II, inheriting the kingdoms in 1830, was believed to have liberal inclinations; but the mid nineteenth century was a difficult time for European monarchies, and corruption in the turbulent Two Sicilies had reached a point where the throne, government and officialdom had sold their authority to anyone with money. Ferdinand had to attempt to rule firmly, and his twenty-nine years as king earned him a vile name for his political prisons, his galleys to which political offenders were condemned for life, and his multitudinous police spies.

The populace of the Mezzogiorno is both fickle and conservative – and full of grumbles. A Sicilian rising in 1837 was easily put down. Another in 1848 – the year of revolutions – which began in Palermo, where the local parliament declared the island's independence and an end to Ferdinand's rule over it, was put down with so much violence and cannonading that it earned Ferdinand the nickname of Re Bomba – King Bomb. Now, over a century since his death, and with the centenary of Garibaldi's triumphant entries into Palermo and Naples passed ten years ago, one often hears King Bomba mentioned in the same affectionate tone as all the family *Borbone* is referred to. If Bomba knew himself to be a Neapolitan, all his erstwhile subjects knew it too, and at heart they would rather be citizens of their own *Regno*, with their own master, than the least-considered Italian electorate. His son, Francis II, succeeded him.

Things, however, were coming to a crisis by 1860. There was an abortive rising in April, at Palermo, which awakened and stirred all the island. Francesco Crispi and Bixio appealed to Garibaldi to help them in Sicily. Garibaldi sailed in May from Genoa with his famous 'Thousand' and landed at Marsala. He was surprised to be greeted with astonishment on the shore and with lack of enthusiasm in the interior of the island, for the Sicilians as a whole had not bargained for a Sardinian invasion in the name of unification. On the 15th, he defeated 3,000 Bourbonist troops at Calatafimi and was joined by dissident Sicilian bands; still more to the point, he found he had captured the Sicilians' imagination. By skilful manoeuvring, Garibaldi outflanked the commander of Palermo and entered the city from Misilmeri and over the Ponte dell'Ammiráglio, where, despite the citizens' enthusiasm for the invaders, there began three days of street fighting. Garibaldi, who had almost run out of ammunition, granted General Lanza's request for a day's truce, and bluffed so well that this was extended to an unconditional armistice granted by the Bourbon commanders. On June 7th, 15,000 Neapolitan troops embarked for the mainland. In July, Cavour, minister of Victor Emmanuel, the King of Savoy, arrived with reinforcements and ammunition. Cavour wanted the annexation of Sicily to Sardinia, but Garibaldi was able to prevent this and maintain the island as, so to speak, a central base for a unifying expedition against the mainland. He met the Bourbonists in a desperate battle at Milazzo, which Garibaldi won. This made Francis decide on the evacuation of all Sicily except the fortress of Messina (which only surrendered in the following year) and, on August 19th, Garibaldi crossed the Straits and stormed Réggio. He entered Naples in triumph and, by winning the battle of the Volturno on October 1st and 2nd, made Italian unity inevitable under the House of Savoy.

HOUSE OF SAVOY (A.D. 1861 to 1946)

As part of the Kingdom of Savoy, Sicily became an integral part of a unified Kingdom of Italy, over which Victor Emmanuel ruled as constitutional monarch, in September 1870.* As such (earthquakes and eruptions apart), she ceased to have an individual history until Operation Husky, the invasion of Sicily by the Allies during the Second World War, began on the night of July 9th–10th, 1943, with an assault-landing by the U.S. 7th Army under Patton, on the great beaches on either side of Gela, and another by the British 8th Army under Montgomery on the beaches between Pozzallo and Pachino in the extreme south-east. Three hundred ships and 160,000 men took part – an army unequalled in size in all Sicily's long history of warfare. The Germans made Etna their fortress, and the Americans, having easily occupied the west of the island, were able to mount a flanking attack to support the British advance on Etna from the south. Messina – ever the last fortress to succumb – fell on August 18th and the last Germans withdrew the next day, thirty-eight days after the campaign had begun.

Sicily was granted regional autonomy, not unlike that of Northern Ireland, in 1946, the same year that the all-Italian electorate declared for a republican form of government and dismissed the House of Savoy.

* Recommended further reading: Denis Mack Smith, *Modern Sicily: After 1713* (Chatto and Windus, London, 1968) covers the whole period; Harold Acton, *The Bourbons of Naples* (Methuen, London, 1957) and *The Last Bourbons of Naples* (Methuen, London, 1961) covers that dynasty's association with Sicily, and G.M. Trevelyan's three-volume life of Garibaldi (see Bibliography) the history of the Risorgimento.

GOVERNMENT ADMINISTRATION

Sicilians feel themselves to be a different race from Italians of the mainland and, since 1860, have borne the north of the country a grudge for neglecting Sicilian needs. Aggravated by the aftermath of war, this discontent produced a Sicilian separatist movement which won a royal decree on May 15th, 1946 (converted to a constitutional statute on February 20th, 1948), setting up a regional government with considerable autonomous powers.

The Sicilian assembly (or regional parliament), whose headquarters are in Palermo, elects a president from among its ninety members. The president not only promulgates regional laws but acts also as chief minister of the *giunta*, the executive committee of the assembly. He represents Sicily in the national council of ministers – though without a vote – and also represents the national government in the island.

The significant areas in which Sicily enjoys autonomy are agriculture, industry, commerce, education and taxation. Order is maintained by the assembly through the agency of national forces seconded to local control.

RELIGION

While the great majority of Sicilians are Roman Catholics, the 'Greeks' (or 'Italo-Albanians', as Mussolini decreed they should be called), for instance, of Palermo and Piana degli Albanesi are in general Uniates of the Byzantine rite, a break-away sect from the Greek Orthodox Church in communion with Rome. Each group has its Uniate bishop, though these are under the jurisdiction of the Latin archbishop in whose see the community resides, that is, Palermo and Monreale. The church of La Martorana at Palermo shares co-cathedral status with the *duomo* of Piana degli Albanesi.

The celebration of Easter in the Byzantine rite is rather splendid and interesting.

LANGUAGE

With the history they have been submitted to, it is not surprising that Sicilians speak a hybrid language of their own. In response to historical pressures this has been increasingly, first Latinized, then Italianized, and although the foreign Italian speaker can more or less read modern Sicilian he would have to learn to speak it. In ordinary conversation nowadays, however, he will find that Sicilians generally use Italian with a heavy accent and a broad dialect of their own, and always when speaking to a foreigner they use Italian of sorts, but the educated, naturally, speak it perfectly.

Albanian is spoken in the colonies at Contessa Entellina and Palazzo Adriano, Greek of a dialectal kind at Piana degli Albanesi (the name was altered from Piana dei Greci for political reasons by Mussolini) where, as in one or two other remote places, there is a residual Greek colony.

SICILY IN MYTH

THE CHTHONIC DIVINITIES

Sicily was the scene of Hades' rape of Persephone, the Great Goddess. This took place by Lake Pergusa which, since it has no visible outlet, was thought to be an entrance to the Underworld – Hades' realm of death. To say that, however, is to state the myth in the late form in which it has come down to us.

Before there were gods, there was only the Goddess. She was, essentially, motherhood: the source of life most apparent to primitive people since – as it seemed – woman bore children of herself, parthenogenetically. These she nourished with her milk, though, presently, she weaned them and drove them away to fend for themselves, forsaking them to a perilous independence during which a part of their natures, rather cravenly, longed for the lost security of her womb. We all feel this, though people with underdeveloped minds feel it far more strongly. Thus, to them, it was natural to envisage death as a return to that perfect haven. In this way, then, the Goddess was life- and death-giving. And she was the promise of rebirth, the Resurrection.

The history of mankind is essentially the story of his struggles to adapt himself to, and to fend for himself during the period of, his independence from motherly protection. During it he must exercise his wits. The more primitive a people the more noticeably it is the men who do this. They have a psychological need to assert their independence of the mother before they can feel themselves to be men – while the women are comparatively more content to be mothers as their own mothers were. This male independence can really be achieved only through attainment of an intellectual liberty. The greatest impetus towards this assertion came with the realization of man's role in procreation. The social revolution which this caused was reflected in the religion authorizing the usages of society. A male deity had to be created to mate with the Goddess, so she bore herself a son to be her lover. Slowly, as masculine 'superiority' was asserted here below, so in heaven it became necessary for a God to usurp the Goddess's throne: Hades abducted Persephone and raised her to his side – a blasphemy which rendered the religion meaningless.

Meanwhile the concept of the Goddess herself was also changing. This probably began long before the creation of gods as it sprang from the phases of a woman's life: pre-pubertal childhood, the fertile years and sterile age – three aspects of one entity. The Goddess went by different names in different localities – yet all of them were descriptive, allusive, as if her real name could not be spoken because it was the identity of her power; thus we find the Goddess's three aspects called by such names as Parthenia, maiden; Demeter, barley mother; Persephone, bringer of destruction.

One aspect of some local deities gradually gained a greater significance than the others: Pallas Athene, the Goddess's virginal name in Athens, came so far to predominate that we can now only conjecture what were the names of her other aspects in early times. Ancient polytheism was accidental, the result of society's tendency always to form itself into larger and larger units; but the unity of what seems to us a chaotic proliferation of deities was not forgotten until Hellenistic and Roman times, when Christianity reunified the religion in the inverted concept of God the *father*, God the *son*, the *lesser* divinity the Virgin mother, plus that crucial new, ostensibly unifying inspiration, the Holy Ghost.

We must remember that the religion of the Greek colonists was much further evolved along this path than that of the Sicilians of the eighth century B.C. Thus, in Sicily, the settlers found a purer, more archaic form of their own religion. It seems to have impressed them deeply; their ardour for the worship of the 'Chthonic' divinities – Demeter, the mother, Persephone, the destroyer who was also the maiden (there are various 'playmates' connected with the rape myth among whose names may have been the original virgin one), and Hades, the child-lover and later master – had a reformatory zeal. Indeed, the cult of death in Sicily is still now rivalled only by the cult of motherhood, and the Holy Virgin is by far the greater deity than her Son.

APHRODITE OF ERYX

Aphrodite had an important shrine on the summit of Mount Érice – Eryx to the Greeks. When Butes the Athenian, sailing past the sirens' island with the other Argonauts, hearkened to the bird-women's song rather than to Orpheus who was singing against them, and threw himself into the sea – that is, choosing death – Aphrodite snatched him up to her temple of Eryx and there made him her lover. There, too, Daedalus offered the goddess a honey-comb made of gold.

Aphrodite represents the Goddess in her child-bearing aspect. Her cult was primarily an Eastern one; its emphasis having been originally upon fertility, it gradually came to stress the ecstasy of love. The goddess of Eryx was symbolized as a queen bee (Eryx meant 'heather'). Her rites had probably evolved upon lines resembling those of the Near Eastern Aphrodite–Astarte goddess with whom – as early as the Bronze Age – the Greeks and the Phoenicians identified her. By doing so, they enriched and enlarged their own conception of Aphrodite – that single aspect of the Goddess which had crystallized into a deity on its own. When this happened to an aspect, when one absorbed its peers in the trilogy and became identified with similar goddesses from other places, it assumed 'surnames' to recall the two eclipsed aspects and the places of its origin or 'birth'; thus there is Paphian Aphrodite as well as Aphrodite of Eryx; and 'golden' Aphrodite was surnamed such things as 'the grave-digger'. Like Persephone, her popular image retained her own maidenhood; by bathing and by assuming her girdle, she constantly regained her virginity.

Butes (his name means 'herdsman') was a bee-keeper. Mountain-top goddesses tended naturally to have herdsmen lovers, and the association with bees and honey is also an obvious one. The bee-goddess of heathery Eryx links up with a whole complex of myth and symbolism from elsewhere, from the Troad to Athens, which is expressed in references to heather-colour, honey-cakes, winds off the heather and so on. This last suggests its connection with a belief of great antiquity, holding that the wind impregnated women. A sombre light is thrown on Aphrodite of Eryx by the bee analogy, for the queen bee destroys her drone lover when she frees herself from his embrace by tearing out his genitalia. In distant times, when the priestess of the Goddess took consorts for a limited term in the Goddess's name, Butes and his fellows suffered this cruel fate.

DAEDALUS AND HERAKLES

Daedalus, semi-divine master-craftsman and engineer, came of the royal and divine Erechtheid family of Athens, although he is best remembered for his works in Crete. His is an obscure legend, masking a yet more obscure myth which links him with the mysterious smith-god Hephaestus, Hera's parthenogenetic son, Athene's lover and Aphrodite's 'husband'. The tenuous connections this suggests are hardly now to be unravelled except intuitively; Hephaestus was probably a deity older than metallurgy, a Promethean figure who became a metal-worker, and therefore, like all craftsmen who applied their intellect to practical uses, eventually a servant of Athene. Daedalus' divinity must have been Hephaestan; his name may have denoted a guild or tribe of metal-workers and builders; his journeyings most probably incorporate in one man's story a number of events and travels having to do with this guild. When he escaped from Crete, flying with the wings he made for himself and his ill-fated son Icarus, he landed first at Cumae where he built Apollo a temple, then came to Sicily where he built works for Cocalos of Camicos. Minos of Crete, his former master, made an expedition to recapture him, but the daughters of Cocalos, with Daedalus' help, murdered Minos in his bath. This tale is probably a recollection of a Mycenaean expedition to Sicily that had more to do with command of the sea than with Daedalus – although the death of Minos, like that of Agamemnon, has about it a strongly ritualistic flavour.

Various stories of Herakles' exploits in Sicily are thought to have been concocted in the Greek period to illustrate the spread of his cult among the colonists. But even Herakles, whose name means 'glory of Hera', brings us back to the ubiquitous presence in Sicily of the Goddess.

CUSTOMS

The folk arts and customs once so beloved of foreign visitors are, now, not much in evidence in Sicily.

Painted carts of traditional design drawn by feather-tufted horses, harnessed with splendid accoutrements, can still be seen, though the paint is more often faded than not, the brass tarnished and the feathery cockades kept for festival times. These splendours are costly and farmers now save their price to buy a three-wheeler Vespa or Lambretta – those superb, if less romantic, replacements for carts. Cart painters at work can still be found, holding to their traditional manner and subject matter of heroic epic, but they grow increasingly rare.

Boats have still almost invariably an eye painted on either side of the prow. This most ancient symbol wards against the evil eye, as do cerulean blue beads, a twisted horn, and the index and little finger extended outwards from an otherwise closed fist, and even an agnostic and anti-clerical seaman will employ it. The eye symbol (it is Osiris' eye) has always entreated good fortune; you will see it – an implied toast – on Greek drinking-cups.

Marionette theatres persist in Palermo, Catánia and Messina. They are most unpretentious and incline to be intermittent; their programmes arc long and often (though by no means always – some classic dramas given in Italian were the only occasions when the poor heard that language) delivered in uncompromising dialect. The plays are traditional and recount such epic themes as the stories of el Cid or Roland and Oliver – as the carts illustrate – since the chief influence upon them has been Spanish. As the Sicilian marionette is of an antique design mechanically, the long-drawn-out performances are not enhanced by any particularly lifelike movements or appearance; a little of this sport seems to me to be enough, although it is, for a time, quite entertaining. To visit the theatres it is best to consult your hall porter; he will be able to find out where and when they are showing. In Palermo and Cefalù there are permanent theatres.

Marionette performances are also given during major provincial festivals which, in Sicily, are usually the occasion for a fair lasting several days. A list of festivals with their dates is included (pp. 44–46). Some nice pottery, copper pots, basket-work and suchlike can be bought at them.

Another Sicilian custom is the Mafia – something of which nobody is proud or finds attractive. I have mentioned this on p. 29 and would add only that there is a very good essay on the subject of the Sicilian Mafia in E. J. Hobsbawm, *Primitive Rebels* (Manchester University Press, Manchester, 1959), while noting that the tourist is unlikely to encounter this despicable skeleton in the island's domestic cupboard.

FOOD

When communications within the island were poor – i.e. a century ago; travel was always by sea, while very narrow bridges made the interior impracticable for vehicles – there were marked differences between the gastronomic specialities, at least, of one region and another. A town might be famous for its dried figs or cheeses, or a dish dependent on ingredients produced locally, though not elsewhere. If it sometimes seems that Sicily remains obstinately behind the times, since recent years it has caught up with the age as deplorably as elsewhere in the matter of food. When I asked a maid from a very poor family to make *tagliatelli*, she laughed in my face: 'It's not *made*; it comes from the shop in a packet!' (Her mother now does make it, at a considerable saving, from Elizabeth David's recipe, and the family thinks it tastes better than the bought kind.) It is really only in houses and the poorer *trattorie* that you are likely to find really unexpected food. When you do, it will almost certainly be strongly flavoured – and that is something which can also be said in general about those restaurants that do care about the fare they provide.

The sea food is *fresh*. Eating it, you are astonished to rediscover the genuine taste of fish. *Spada* – swordfish – cutlets are a summer stand-by everywhere, but try to find fresh sardines and anchovies. Also tunny in season. In autumn, there should be *dendice*, which is a particularly good large fish of, presumably, the mackerel family.

SICILIAN WINES

Apart from the obvious Marsalas, the following places have special wines which you may still be able to find.

Carini: a strong white wine called *Zucco*; usually medium sweet.
Linguaglossa: 'wines of the half mountain', *vini di mezza montagna*; dry for Italy. Red or white.
Noto: *moscato di Siracusa*; a sweet white wine.
Pantelleria Island: *Zibibbo*; as it sounds, an Arabic name and an odd anise-flavoured wine; for the adventurous rather than the perfectionist. White.
Also *moscato*; sweet and excellent of its sort. White.
Vittória: *cerasuoli*; rosé wines. Also a peach wine.
Lípari Island: *malvasia*; sweet, white.
Catánia/Taormina: *vini dell'Etna*; red and white, dry.

Routes round the Island

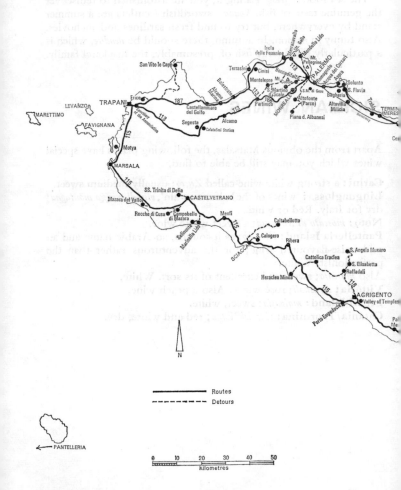

USTICA

San Vito lo Capo

Terrasini
Isola delle Femmine
Cinisi
Boccadifalco
Mt. Gallo
Mondello Lido
Mt. Pellegrino
Sferracavallo
PALERMO
113

Montelepre
Mt. Cuccio
113
S. Martino
d. Scale
Partinico
MONREALE
S.M. di Gesù
Altofonte (Parco)
Acquasanta
Acqua dei Corsari
Bagheria
Aspra
Soluto
S. Flavia
Altavilla Milicia
Piana d. Albanesi

Balestrate
Alcamo Marina
Castellammare del Golfo
187
113

San Vito lo Capo

Erice
TRAPANI
Sanctuary of the Annunciation
113
Castellammare del Golfo
Segesta
Calatafimi Station
Alcamo

LEVANZO
MARETTIMO
FAVIGNANA

Motya

MARSALA
115

Mazara del Vallo
SS. Trinità di Delia
CASTELVETRANO
115
Rocche di Cusa
Campobello di Mazara
Selinunte
Marinella di Selinunte
Menfi
115

S. Calogero
Caltabellotto
Ribera
SCIACCA
118
Cattolica Eraclea
Heraclea Minoa
Raffadali
S. Angelo Muxaro
S. Elisabetta
AGRIGENTO
Valley of Temples
Porto Empedocle
115
Pal
Me

TERMINI IMERESE
Cefa

N

—————— Routes
- - - - - - Detours

0 10 20 30 40 50
kilometres

PANTELLERIA

ALICUDI

FILICUDI

SALINA

PANAREA

LIPARI

VULCANO

Punta del Faro

Lido di Mortelle

Ganzirri

Castanea d. Furie

113

MESSINA

Spadafora

MILAZZO

Terme Vigliatore

Castroreale Terme

Olivarella

S. Filippo d. Mela

Antennamare

Barcellona Pozzo di Gotto

S. Lucia d. Mela

Mili S. Pietro

Mili Marina

Tremestieri

Capo d'Orlando

Gioiosa Marea

Tindari

Patti

Falcone

Castroreale

Gliaca di Piraino

Torrenova

Naso

Frazzano

Sant'Agata di Militello

S. Marco d'Alunzio

Ali

Ali Marina

Atala Marina

114

Ali Terme

Roccalumera

San Francesco di Paola

Forza d'Agro

Letoianni

Mazzaro

Giardini

Cape Schiso

Naxos

Fiumefreddo di Sicilia

Mascali

Giarre

S. Venerina la Badia

Acireale

Aci Trezza

Acicastello

Cannizzaro

CATANIA

115

Ponte Primosole

Agnone Bagni

Brucoli

AUGUSTA

Megara Hyblaea

Priolo

Penisola Magnisi

Thapsos Castle

Belvedere

Scala Greca

SYRACUSE

Olympieion & Fonte Ciane

Cassibile

Noto Antica

287

Noto

115

Marzamemi

Pachino

Portopalo

CEFALU

113

Cerda

Gibilmanna

Castelbuono

Tusa

113

Castel di Tusa

Pollina

Campofelice

Milianni

San Stefano di Camastra

Acquedolci

Acquedotto di S. Fratello

Castel di Tusa

Caronia Marina

San Fratello

Sant'Agata di Militello

289

Mistretta

Cesaro

Nicosia

Bronte

MT. ETNA

Observatory

Milo

Zafferana Etnea

Casa Cantoniera

Fleri

Viagrande

Trecastagni

Pedara

Nicolosi

Massannunziata

Mascalucia

Gravina

S. Agata li Battiati

S. Giovanni la Punta

Randazzo

120

Linguaglossa

Castiglione di Sicilia

Francavilla di Sicilia

Castel Mola

TAORMINA

114

284

Adrano

PIAZZA ARMERINA

'Villa Imperiale'

117b

115

Gela

GELA

115

Vittoria

Comiso

RAGUSA

Donnafugata

Modica

Camarina

Marina di Ragusa

Scicli

Donnalucata

Ispica

Rosolini

Pozzallo

Symaethus

LENTINI

Archaeological Zone

Carlentini

Sortino

Necropolis of Pantalica

Ferla

193

Floridia

Cassibile

Licata

Licodia

S. Caterina

Belpasso

INTRODUCTION TO ROUTES

Routes on Sicily are divided into two main sections. The first of these is concerned with travel round the island in an anti-clockwise direction, following what are largely coastal roads. The routes are described between the main towns on this tour of the island. These centres themselves are described, with their environs, as the route reaches them; starting with Messina, then (260 km. onwards) Palermo; Trápani (103 km.); Agrigento (187 km.); Syracuse (223 km.); Catánia (60 km.); Taormina (52 km.); and back to Messina (48 km.). The whole round by the shortest alternative routes (and excluding even the shorter diversions which it is difficult to believe you would visit the island without wanting to make for the sake of what lies at the end of them) totals 933 km. See diagram of Routes round the Island (pp. 76–77).

The second section deals with travel in the centre of the island, Enna being the radial point. See diagram of Routes in Centre of Island (p. 288). For links between routes round the island and in the centre, see the endpaper maps.

In both sections, distances are given in kilometres and are one-way, detours being described but not included in the reckoning of route distances. At the beginning of each route description, information is offered on alternative means of travel from one centre to the other and on accommodation *en route*. Further details about accommodation are given under the relevant entries for towns along the route.

To help the traveller to plan combinations of routes, a Chart of Excursions is provided (facing p. 27). Distances on the chart are one-way. Times offered beneath the names of centres are minimum times for seeing those centres, and do not take excursions into account.

ROUND THE ISLAND

MESSINA

Population*
250,000.

Air and sea
Ferry-boat from the mainland: from Villa San Giovanni (8 km. – 35 minutes) or Réggio di Calábria (15 km. – 50 minutes) to Stazione Maríttima. Transport for cars available.

Aliscafo (hydrofoil) from Réggio di Calábria (20 minutes) or Taormina (docks opposite Jolly Hotel at Messina). Passengers only; light baggage.

Steamer (twice weekly; winter, once) from Naples via Aeolian Islands (p. 85) (24 hours, book cabins in advance).

Air: from Réggio di Calábria, then cross over as above, or via Catánia.

Rail
Stazione Maríttima (*Map* **5**) is connected by rail with the Stazione Centrale (*Map* **7**), the station for Catánia, Palermo, Syracuse. If you have come by train from Italy, crossing by the ferry in that train, you may as well get off at the Stazione Maríttima.

Bus
Frequent bus and coach services to Catánia, Taormina and Palermo.

Information
E.P.T. office (*Map* **6**), Via S. Maria Alemanna 3.
Azienda Autónoma, Viale San Martino 227.
Tourist Information Office, Stazione Centrale (*Map* **7**).

Consulates
United Kingdom, Corso Garibaldi 267A.

Bathing
Bathing can be had in the immediate Messina area at Lido di Mortelle (p. 85) Maregrosso; Contesse.

Hotels
1st Class	*Jolly Hotel dello Stretto,* Corso Garibaldi 126;
	†*Riviera Grand Hotel,* Viale della Libertà.
2nd Class	*Belvedere,* Viale San Martino 146;
	Excelsior, Via Maddalena 32;
	Venézia, Piazza Cairoli 4.
3rd Class	*Commércio,* Via 1 Settembre 73;
	La Lucciola, Colle San Rizzo on S.S.113;
	Milano, Via dei Verdi 65;
	Moderno Terminus Via 1 Settembre 15.
4th Class	*Centrale,* Via T. Cannizzaro 127;
	Dante, Via S. Maria Alemanna 40;
	Marconi, Via Risorgimento 25;

* Population figures represent a rough estimate based on the 1961 census and an increase thought to be about 4·3 per cent. Nobody knows at present the current rate of emigration from Sicily to elsewhere in Italy and the Common Market countries.

Mediterraneo, Via Peculio Frumentario 6 ;
Monza, Viale San Martino 63 ;
Nuovo Peloro, Via N. Fabrizi 37 ;
Piemonte, Via T. Cannizzaro 1 ;
Roma, Piazza Duomo 3 ;
Romeo, Via Santa Barbara 6 ;
Savóia, Largo Seggiola 168 ;
Touring, Via T. Cannizzaro 17.

Pensions
3rd Class   *Bel Sit*, Via Cavalieri della Stella 21.
Hotels in environs of Messina
(At Ganzirri)   4th Class   *Fata Morgana*.
(At Giampilieri Marina) 4th Class   *Al Carlton*.
(At Lido di Mortelle)   1st Class   †*Lido*.
                         3rd Class   *Faro*.

Guardian of the Straits and principal link between Sicily and the mainland of Italy, Messina is a provincial capital.

Messina has had the most calamitous history of any Sicilian town. This is not only on account of the excellence and strategic importance of its harbour for naval control of the Mediterranean but also on account of its lying upon the earthquake belt running from Vesuvius to Strómboli and Etna. All the same, it is, these days, a prosperous place of a quarter of a million intrepid inhabitants living in a wholly modern town.

I will begin with the explanation for this odd fact. At twenty past five in the morning of December 28th, 1908 – a month when few Sicilian townsmen are abroad so early – a violent earthquake shock wrecked the entire town and tremors continued almost daily for two months. The initial shock caused a subsidence of the Messina shore of two feet. In the chaos of the ruined and waterless city, where scores of thousands of dead lay under the ruins of their homes, rats from the broken sewers scavenged, bringing to the survivors a raging epidemic of cholera. Eighty-four thousand people died in Messina, 16,000 more in the neighbourhood.

Dr Axel Munthe's book *The Story of San Michele* (John Murray, London, 1959), contains a graphic account of this aftermath, as does Giuseppe di Lampedusa's 'Places of My Infancy' – see *Two Stories and a Memory*, trans. Archibald Colquhoun (Collins and Harvill Press, London, 1962).

The whole world helped to rebuild the city, but this was far from completed when the American bombardment of 1943 reduced a great part of the work to rubble, killing 5,000 more unhappy citizens.

Under these circumstances one cannot look to see picturesque antiquity in Messina; but it turns out to be a very pleasant town, largely due to its situation on the shore and foothills of the delightful Monti Peloritani.

HISTORY

Messina was first founded, as Zancle, by settlers from Cumae, in the eighth century B.C., and from Naxos, and later resettled from Euboea. The name derives from a native word for a sickle and refers to the shape of the harbour. Its value was almost wholly strategic and its fate bound up with that of Rhegium (Réggio di Calábria), which it helped to found. In order to subsist, the colony required land on the north coast of the island and the citizens founded Mylae (Milazzo) as their frontier post. Himera was also a Zanclean colony, though territorially detached. The city was captured by Anaxilas, tyrant of Rhegium and renamed Messana by him in 493 B.C. For its subsequent history, see that of Syracuse (p. 212) and the general history of the island (p. 50).

The great size of the cathedral reflects the importance of eleventh- and twelfth-century Messina to the kings of Sicily, and its importance also to medieval Europe as the linking port between France – even England – and Italy with the eastern Mediterranean where lay the Crusaders' Outremer – the Kingdom of Jerusalem, Frankish Constantinople and Greece. Messina then was almost as rich as Palermo, though perhaps less regally Sicilian for being so international. The citadel was also one of the most splendid palaces of that luxurious age, and in 1190–91 Richard Cœur de Lion, wintering here *en route* for Outremer, sacked the place as a warning to King Tancred to surrender Richard's widowed sister, Queen Joan, and her dowry. The city, having withstood Charles of Anjou's furious attempt to take it in 1282, continued a noble and a prosperous place until the last few centuries; then in 1743 plague gripped it, and earthquake in 1783, naval bombardment in 1848; cholera in 1854 and yet another earthquake in 1894 prepared it for the later onslaughts of fate.

A note about the artist Antonello da Messina, less known elsewhere in Europe than his contemporary peers, Giovanni Bellini and Piero della Francesca, seems most appropriate here in his own town. His work can be seen at Messina, Syracuse, Cefalù and Palermo.

He was born about 1430 and died here in 1479. He is not known of until 1457, when he was here, and after 1465 he is untraceable for eight years, as he is between 1457 and 1461. In August of 1475 he was in Venice, where his success was phenomenal and he undoubtedly both learned from the Venetians and profoundly influenced them. He went to Milan the next year, but, by the autumn, was home, where he stayed until his death.

He seems to have been the first Italian to use the Flemish technique of painting in oil (as opposed to tempera), and this, since it was the perfection of his art that gained him the acclaim he met there two years later, he must have used before Vivarini introduced it to Venice in 1473. Where did he learn it? It seems most possible that he journeyed to the Low Countries and learned it from pupils of the Van Eycks. But what this very great artist made of his skill was something both southern and wholly personal. Every painting shows him passive towards the subject he works upon, but enormously perceptive and deeply reflective about the meaning of its stimulus upon him. He creates his visionary pictures out of his own genius – on this aspect of his art the subject has little bearing except an initial suggestion which is transmitted by its passage through his own imagination. And all that fantastic ability of his to control paint – to make it sing and shine and slumber as light does, but paint too rarely – he used only to serve his ends.

His cousin, Antonello de Saliba, was the best of his pupils, all of whom painted evocative pictures.

PRINCIPAL SIGHTS

Cathedral
Between Piazza del Duomo and the Corso Garibaldi; Map **3**.

This is a post-war reconstruction of the post-earthquake reconstruction of the Norman original. A contemporary act of faith, it is also one of the finest and most splendid Norman monuments on the island. The original cathedral was begun by Roger II and consecrated in the presence of the Emperor Henry VI in 1197.

The *façade* upon Piazza del Duomo – which was laid out in the eighteenth century and holds the restored *Orion fountain* by Montórsoli – retains quite a lot of the original sculptured fabric. That in the central portion was by Pietro de Bontate and belonged to

Messina

1 Museo Nazionale
2 Post Office
3 Cathedral
4 Church of SS. Annunziata
  dei Catalani
5 Stazione Maríttima
6 E.P.T. Office
7 Stazione Centrale
  (Central Station) and
  Tourist Information Office

Urban Buses – Piazza
Roma, Curvone Gazzi

A Route to SS. Pietro e
  Páolo (p. 284), Punta del
  Faro, Lido di Mortelle
  Circonvallazione ai Monti
B Route to Circonvallazione
  ai Monti, Antennamare,
  Palermo
C Route to Taormina,
  Catánia

PORT

0   500   1KM
metres

1468. The *side-doors* are by Polidoro da Caravággio. The *campanile* was designed to hold its *clock*, an astronomical one and the largest in the world, built in Strasbourg in 1933. It performs its elaborate tricks at noon, heralded by a cannon-shot. The bulk of the rest of the exterior is of the grandest Norman design.

The earthquake shattered the twenty-six monolithic columns of granite that had probably come from a temple to Poseidon upon the Punta del Faro. The northern corner of the west front, with some interior monuments such as royal tombs and frescoes and mosaics, survived, as also the contents of the Treasury. Now, the original contents are reduced to a restored *Baptist* by Antonello Gagini (1525) – well worth the restoration –, the *tomb* of Archbishop De Tabiatis by Goro de Gregório (1333), and the *sculptured slab* from the tomb of Archbishop Palmer of Messina, a notable Englishman of the age who arranged William II's marriage to Joan of England in 1177, and who died in 1195. Reconstructed items include the *font*, Montórsoli's distinguished *altars* in the aisles, the *baldachin*, the *stalls* designed in 1540 by Giorgio Veneziano, and the *mosaics* that survived the earthquake.

To say all this, however, is to do nothing to suggest the spacious majesty of the interior – this would be a wonderful church whenever it had been built. For many visitors it will be their first taste of the Sicilian Normans' splendour and it is remarkable to see it as new-cut and pristine as it was – though lacking its former, incredibly rich decoration – when Palmer was its bishop.

Church of SS. Annunziata dei Catalani
Corso Garibaldi and Via Césare Battisti; Map 4.

A fine twelfth-century Norman (though rebuilt) church whose beautiful *apse* only has so far withstood all disasters.

Museo Nazionale
Viale della Libertà, to the north of the town; Map 1.

Open 09.30–16.30. Sundays and holidays 09.30–13.30. Closed on Mondays.

Notable are a *Virgin and Child* by the exquisite Francesco Laurana; a Caravággio *Nativity* – less extraordinary than that at Palermo (now lost; temporarily, one hopes) but the master in his own idiom, vigorous and tender, and ever alive to the drama of life and paint; and, finally, the earthquake-shattered remains of a *polyptych* by the incomparable Antonello da Messina, dated 1473, in the central panel of which a ravishing Madonna offers cherries to the Child – a real baby, not grown to godhead – who holds an apple, while two angels hold a crown of roses over her head; of the flanking *panels* (in better condition than the central), the two above show the Annunciation and the lower two St Gregory and St Benedict, marvellous figures which must have been portraits.

ENVIRONS

A particularly pleasing walk or drive is by the Circonvallazione ai Monti, a road along the hills behind the town which passes the *Cemetery* – the Napoleonic British Cemetery was transferred here from the port area – in a beautiful garden with enchanting views, and the *Botanical Gardens*.

For those who like walking, the *Monti Peloritani* range is worth exploring. One can take a car as far as **Antennamare** (22 km.). Leave town by the Palermo road (S.S. 113; Route Exit B). At the cross-roads, where the right turning goes off in the direction of Castanea degli Fúrie, fork left.

14 km. to the north of the town on the tip of the cape *Punta del Faro* (Bus 8) is a good viewpoint. To reach it, take the coast road from town (Route Exit A). **Ganzirri** village on the way has a good restaurant, the *Fata Morgana*, bathing and some interesting mussel-beds. The pylon, carrying electric cable from Calabrian power-houses, is more than 750 feet high. There was once a temple to Poseidon here on the cape. About 3 km. to the west of Punta del Faro is **Lido di Mortelle** where there is good bathing and the *Hotel Lido* (1st Class) and *Hotel Faro* (3rd Class).

Excursion to Aeolian Islands

Sea

From Messina: Twice-weekly steamer (winter, once-weekly) to Naples via the Islands (dep. morning; arr. Lípari midday; arr. Naples following morning). Book cabins in advance. Also *Aliscafo* (hydrofoil) on summer Sundays only (dep. Messina morning; ret. afternoon), also a service from Cefalù and Palermo during the summer season.

From Milazzo (p. 91): daily steamers to Lípari (dep. early morning; ret. late afternoon).

Local boats connect the islands.

Hotels

Lípari

2nd Class	†*Carasco*, Porto delle Genti;
	†*Rocce Azzurre*, Porto delle Genti.
3rd Class	*Augustus*, in town;
	Gattopardo Park Hotel, in town;

4th Class	*Giardino sul Mare*, in town.
	Europeo, in town;
	Oriente Plccolo Hotel, in town;
	Regione, in town.

Pensions
2nd Class	*Villa Diana*, Diana-Tufo.
3rd Class	*Neri*, in town.

Vulcano
2nd Class	†*Arcipelago*;
	†*Garden Vulcano*, Porto Ponente;
	Les Sables Noirs, Porto Ponente.
3rd Class	*Eros*, Porto Levante;
	Faraglione, Porto Levante;
	Mari del Sud, Porto Ponente.
4th Class	*Casa Fiorita*, Porto Ponente.
	Casa Sipione Porto Ponente.
	Conti, Porto Ponente.

Pensions
3rd Class	*Agostino*;
	Orsa Maggiore.

Salina
3rd Class	*L'Ariana*, Leni.
4th Class	*Bellavista*, Santa Marina;
	Didyme, Santa Marina;
	Le Palme, Santa Marina.

Pension
3rd Class	*La Marinara*, Língua.

Panarea
3rd Class	*La Piazza*;
	Raya;
	Residence.
4th Class	*Lisca Bianca*;
	Villággio Turístico Cincotta.

Strómboli
2nd Class	*La Sciara Residence*.
3rd Class	†*La Sirenetta*.
4th Class	*Miramare*;
	Villággio Strómboli.

Alicudi and **Filicudi** both have very simple, unlisted accommodation to offer, as can also be found on the other islands

This archipelago of seven volcanic islands (excluding the un-inhabited Basiluzzo) is a strange and beautiful, and, sometimes, awesome, world of its own. The chief island is Lípari (after which the group is sometimes called); it has everything to recommend it as a base for visiting the others, although one can stay on Vulcano, and also elsewhere if one does not mind plain living and accommodation of a very simple sort.

The name 'Aeolian' derives from Aeolus, a legendary god-king of the islands who, it was said, had the winds bottled up in a bag which he kept in a cave here. Odysseus visited him and was given a favourable wind in a bag, which he let out carelessly and so got blown beyond his objective.

The weather here can still be wild and unpredictable, and the sight of storms and sunshine, black clouds, raging seas and water-spouts among the craggy islands is extremely dramatic.

HISTORY

The Greek colonization of the Aeolian Islands makes a strange story. Around the year 580 B.C., a contingent of Rhodians and Cnidians attempted to colonize Lilybaeum (now Marsala) and helped Selinunte in a war against Segesta. The Carthaginians aided Segesta against this alliance and, though Selinunte that time survived, the Greeks of Marsala did not. Pentathlus, their leader, was killed and the remnants of his followers sailed away to find another home. This they did in Lípari. Diodorus says they were refugees from their homelands, then under Oriental domination, but that their defeat at Marsala had so discouraged them that they were returning to the Aegean when the welcome given them by the 500 remaining 'descendants of Aeolus' at Lípari persuaded them to stay.

From Lípari, the colonists waged war upon the Etruscan pirates while themselves preying upon merchantmen. They divided their labours between those assigned to work the land – and these would sail over to cultivate the nearer islands also – and those assigned to the fleet. The land was held in common and the loot from the sailors' successes was divided among them all. Later on, the land was parcelled out among every man, equally, every twenty years, while the number of the tithes which the Liparians offered to Apollo of Delphi out of the spoil from victories over Etruscan pirates became famous.

LÍPARI ISLAND

Lípari is the largest of the group, the most populated (about 12,000 inhabitants) and the most highly cultivated, also the liveliest and best furnished with the amenities of life. In fact, the town of the same name, with its twin ports, romantic citadel and very attractive main street, is one of the very nice little places in the Mediterranean, its people unaffected and friendly. A bus crosses to **San**

Calógero – where there are hot springs – on the west coast; a drive which gives one a good idea of the island. One of the attractions of the place, however, is the walks over the hilly country-side. Lípari has its own modestly baroque style of domestic architecture and the country farms are enviably pretty. I like, too, the restrained, though lively baroque of the Liparian churches.

The *citadel* of **Lípari town** is notable because a continuous and uninterrupted record of its inhabitants, from Neolithic villagers to the present day, was disclosed by digging there – a stratification most important in dating central Mediterranean prehistory.*

Museum. The former bishop's palace in the citadel now houses an important and lucidly arranged collection of Aeolian and Sicilian prehistoric finds.

Across the cobbled path in front of the museum, archaeological digs are preserved to reveal the bases and lower walls of prehistoric stone huts. One, larger than the rest, is believed to be the chief or headman's house, and another, of a more elaborate plan, a shrine.

The crater of an extinct volcano, unusually stratified, *Monte Sant' Ángelo*, 1,950 feet high, makes a good steep walk recompensed by marvellous views, the strangeness of the pumice quarries which you pass and two remarkable veins of volcanic glass, or obsidian. It was this obsidian that lent the island its importance in Neolithic times, since the demand for it, because it made finer tools than flint, turned Lípari into a trading centre. The Neolithic peoples of Malta are known to have used Liparian obsidian, which may well have travelled even farther afield. Obsidian makes the dark sand of the beaches sparkle – though here the best bathing is rocky.

On the sail from Lípari to Vulcano you pass some surprising columns – or stacks – of basalt which include the *Pietralunga*, an impressive natural obelisk 236 feet high.

* Recommended further reading: Margaret Guido, *Sicily: an archaeological guide*. This is a good place again to draw attention to this essential companion to the present guide for those really interested in the prehistorical and ancient sites on Sicily and the lesser islands. Mrs Guido's résumé of the stratification here is particularly helpful.

VULCANO ISLAND

Vulcano Island is little more than the dramatic crater of an extinct volcano, last active in 1890. The small settlement on the sandy bay houses about 400 people. There are prehistoric sites here, but the chief interest is in the extraordinary formations and volcanic manifestations to be seen: *Vulcanello*, a volcanic cone which rose from the sea in 183 B.C.; the hot springs of *Acqua Bollente* and *Acqua del Bagno*; the *Faraglione della Fábbrica*, a high rock on which alum is quarried – all lying on the north of the island; and, to the south, *Monte Aria*, and the lower *Gran Cratere*, on which lies the *Piano delle Grandi Fumarole*, from which shoot jets of sulphur vapour – the whole island, indeed, reeks of sulphur.

SALINA ISLAND

Salina has 3,500 inhabitants largely supported by viniculture. It produces a good *malvásia*. It is the highest island, rising to 3,156 feet, but somehow bleak, remote and inhospitable-seeming – though this turns out not to be the case in any of its three villages. Between **Santa Marina** and *Capo Faro* there is a village of the pre-historic 'Milazzese' period.

PANAREA ISLAND

Panarea, an attractive island to look at, has a dwindling population – about 500 remain. There are several archaeological sites; on *Milazzese* headland, a Bronze Age village was found, dating from the fourteenth century B.C., which yielded Mycenaean pottery and local ware showing a Minoan influence. These finds, together with that of a village on Salina and a necropolis near Milazzo, go a long way to confirm those hints of early contact between the Aegean and Tyrrhenian peoples with which legend and myth abound.

STRÓMBOLI ISLAND

Strómboli is a tragic island from the human point of view, shocking from the physical. It is entirely composed of the cone of an active volcano which is in constant, mild eruption. The crater lies towards the east, on which side, down the *Sciara del Fuoco* (a tremendous scree of ash) it suppurates from its 3,038-feet-high tip to the sea. Interior explosions occur with a horrid regularity every hour or so, and, by day, send tall puffs of smoke into the air; by night, these appear as plumes of fire, awful and splendid. On days of greater activity, volcanic matter streams down the *Sciara del Fuoco*, glowing red, smoking and raising steam from the sea's edge. Around the islet of **Strombolicchio** to the north-east, a tall basalt block from which there is a marvellous view of the archipelago, strong mysterious currents wax and wane.

Along the western side of the island, having a gentler slope and being free from lava streams, the village of **Strómboli** (really two parishes: San Bartolomeo and San Vincenzo) is strung out – mostly simple houses composed of blocks of rectangular shape, whitewashed or, sometimes, a dusky pink or ochre yellow; they have great charm and a certain austere architectural merit, but are largely ruined, locked up or abandoned. Up the slope of the mountain behind it, and on the narrow littoral plain, there is a riotous growth of bright green vegetation alternating with dark carobs and the silvery drifts of olive-yards – but almost all this recently well-cared-for terracing has been abandoned to bamboo and broom, the owners having emigrated to America. Twenty-five years ago a fleet of thirty fishing-boats would put out each night; now there are three. This very beautiful and strange place is now not merely lonely but melancholy.

All the cultivated islands produce good wine, but Strómboli's was once the best of all.

BASILUZZO ISLAND

Basiluzzo – a name recalling the Byzantines – is uninhabited, but there are visible traces of Roman occupation.

FILICUDI AND ALICUDI ISLANDS

Filicudi and Alicudi, the westerly islands, are less interesting, although there is a Bronze Age site on Filicudi, type-site of the Capo Graziano culture.

MESSINA TO PALERMO

Route S.S.113 (Route Exit B). A good and delightful drive through rich country close to the sea. This was the ancient Roman Via Valéria, now officially called the Settentrionale Sicula. 260 km. You can join the Catánia–Palermo motorway just before Buonfornello, 55 km. short of Palermo.
Rail A *rápido* makes the journey in 3 hours 45 minutes.
Bus Connections taking 7 hours 15 minutes.
Accommodation en route At Spadafora; Santa Lucia del Mela; Milazzo; Barcellona Pozzo di Gotto; Castroreale Terme; Terme Vigliatore; Falcone; Tíndari; Patti; Gioiosa Marea; Gliaca di Piráino; Capo d'Orlando (Naso); Torrenova di San Marco d'Alúnzio; Sant' Ágata di Militello (Alcara li Fusi); Acquedolci di San Fratello; Caronia Canneto (Mistretta); Castel di Tusa (Tusa); Milianni (Castel-buono); Cefalù /Calduca (Gibilmanna); Cerda; Términi Imerese; Trabia Vetrana; Santa Flávia/Sólunto/Olivella; Bagheria.

[28 km.] Spadafora.

Hotel
3rd Class   *Centrale.*

[40 km.] Olivarella. At cross-roads in village, left-hand turn to **San Filippo del Mela** and **Santa Lucia del Mela.**

Hotel (at Santa Lucia del Mela)
4th Class   *Itália.*

At the same cross-roads, a right-hand turn to Milazzo (6 km.).

Milazzo

Hotels
2nd Class   †*Diana;*
             Flora;
             †*Silvanetta.*
3rd Class   *Rosa.*
4th Class   *Capitol;*
             Stella d'Itália.
Restaurant *Salamone* (2 km. up the peninsula), and those on the port can be quite good.

A port of embarkation for the Aeolian Islands and a nice, if not a very lively town of over 20,000 inhabitants where the interest is centred on the quayside, fishing, etc. Boats leave daily for the islands (see p. 85).

The town, called Mylae, was founded by the Greek colony of Zancle in 716 B.C. The Carthaginians were defeated off Milazzo by Duilius in 260 B.C., and it was here that Garibaldi drove Francis II of Naples to evacuate all Sicily except the citadel of Messina.

The *castle*, on the site of what was, presumably, Mylae's acropolis, was enlarged by the Emperor Charles V and restored in the seventeenth century. It still has a fine *keep*, and a *Gothic door* and *great hall*. A prison these days, it may be visited if you apply to the commander.

A new *cathedral* was begun in 1937 and is not yet completed.

In the *Church of San Giacomo* there is an *Annunciation* by Antonio Giuffrè and two parts of a *polyptych* by Antonello de Saliba.

[46 km.] Barcellona Pozzo di Gotto.

Hotels

2nd Class	*George;*
	Tirreno.
4th Class	*Aliquo.*

From here a pretty road leads inland, left, to **Castroreale**, favourite residence of Frederick II of Aragon, from whose royal *castle* it takes its name. Built in 1324, this is now a ruin. The churches of the town are interesting and contain some good things.

[51 km.] Castroreale Terme.

This straggling place and Terme Vigliatore mark the rough boundaries of an area of thermal springs boasting several hotels, some of them by the sea, for which you turn right by any of the roads.

Hotels

1st Class	†*Grand Hotel Terme.*
3rd Class	†*La Giara;*
	†*Liola.*

Pension

3rd Class	*Lido Marchesana.*

[55 km.] The No. 185 road branches left to Francavilla di Sicília (p. 275).

[57 km.] Terme Vigliatore (see above).

[61 km.] Falcone.

Hotel

4th Class	*Moderno.*

[68 km.] A turning right to **Tíndari** (1 km.), the site of the ancient *Tyndaris*, on its headland. The excavated areas lie around the *Sanctuary* of the miraculous Madonna of Tíndari – a black-faced icon of Byzantine date and revered all over Sicily and the neighbouring mainland (pilgrimage on September 8th and preceding days).

The branch road from the S.S.113 twists to climb the hill and also to avoid the better-preserved sections of the ancient city-wall, whose line it crosses in making the third S-bend, the walls thereafter lying on the left hand, below. A curve circles the inside of the remains of the interesting old *main gate* (a dipylon with barbican and narrowed, pincer-shaped inner gate) before arriving at the Sanctuary church – an appalling building in process of construction – behind which lies the *chapel* where the icon is kept. This part dates from a rebuilding of 1549 made after the older structure had been destroyed by the pirate Barbarossa.

You can drive beyond the car park to the entrance of the Archaeological Zone.

Tyndaris

Tyndaris was founded by Dionysius I of Syracuse in 396 B.C. to guard the Syracusan borders, peopling it with Greeks who had left home after the Peloponnesian War and naming it for their specially revered twin gods, the Dioscuri or Tyndaridae. The small colony prospered and Hieron II remade and strengthened its defences during his war against the Mamertines of Messina (mid third century B.C.), when the main gate was built. The inhabitants favoured the Romans and were favoured by them, and the town seems to have been occupied until destroyed by the Arabs.

An *Antiquarium* lies just inside the entrance to the excavations. The reconstruction of the original scene-building of the theatre, a model, is the most obviously interesting exhibit.

Beyond the museum lies the *decumanus* that has been cleared, running from the small *theatre*, to the left, to the '*basilica*' and the *agora* area to the right. There are some *Roman houses* to the north of the agora. Most imposing remains are those of the so-called basilica, probably of Augustan date (latter-first-century B.C.), which is in fact a monumental, arched propylaeum leading into the agora. At present it is closed off, but can be well enough seen all the same. This is a very beautifully placed site; less silted up then than now, one can see how this somewhat isolated hill guarded a useful river-mouth port, and how it could hold the passage along which the coast road must run, and while these strategic advantages must have over-ridden other considerations, one may be sure the Greeks were delighted that they were allied to this beautiful outlook upon mountains and islands and their beloved, feared sea.

Hotel
3rd Class   *Tyndaris.*

[76 km.] **Patti.** In the nineteenth-century *cathedral* at the top of the town, the *sarcophagus* of Roger II's first wife, Queen Adelasia, is preserved. (She died in 1118, to the great distress of her husband.) Also an Antonello de Saliba *Madonna.*

Hotels
4th Class   *Canape';*
             Modernissimo.

[89 km.] **Gioiosa Marea.**

Hotels
2nd Class   †*Capo Skino Park Hotel.*
4th Class   *Púglia.*

[94 km.] **Gliaca di Piráino.**

Hotel
3rd Class   †*Calabrese.*

[104 km.] Cross-roads: left for **Naso** (12 km.) on the 116 road to Randazzo (p. 310).

Hotel
4th Class   *Miravalle.*

At the same cross-roads, right (2 km.) to *Capo d'Orlando* headland, *sanctuary* of SS. Maria di Capo d'Orlando, and tiny seaside resort.

Hotels
2nd Class   †*Al Capriccio;*
             †*Bristol.*
3rd Class   *Flora;*
             Piave.

[112 km.] A turning left (11 km.) to **Frazzanò**, 2 km. beyond which, on the right, stand the remains of a Basilian *monastery* built by Count Roger in the late eleventh century. Its church of *San Filippo di Fragalà* is well worth the detour to see – ask the people on the site to let you in. It is of the early T-plan inside, with three apses and an octagonal domed cupola over the crossing. Rather shadowy Byzantine frescoes survive on the walls. The *bell-tower*'s top was rebuilt in the eighteenth century.

[116 km.] **Torrenova.** From here a road leads left (8 km.) **to San Marco d'Alúnzio,** known to the Romans as Aluntium and probably a pre-Hellenic settlement by origin. As you enter the hilltop town you see a free-standing building of obviously ancient masonry: a small *temple* to Herakles later transformed into the church of San Marco but now a shell. The Badia Grande del SS. Salvatore was founded in 1176 by William I's wife Margaret; of the original fabric little remains to be seen amongst that of a seventeenth-century rebuilding.

Hotels (at San Marco d'Alúnzio)
4th Class   *Piro*;
            Roma.

[122 km.] **Sant' Ágata di Militello.**

Hotels
2nd Class   *Roma Palace Hotel.*
3rd Class   *Parimar.*
4th Class   *Gloria.*

[125 km.] The No. 289 road turns left to Cesarò. Along it (14 km.) lies **San Fratello,** splendidly situated. It is worth visiting to see the small Norman church of *Sant' Alfio* at the crown of the hill. This noble building has an interestingly individual dome raised on a tall drum. This hilltop was once the site of the Sikel town, much Hellenized, of Apollonia. It has been prone to landslides and disaster, yet the local dialect preserves Gallic traces from the Lombards with whom Roger II's queen settled it. Also some of the women still – not only on festival days – wear long, black, pleated mantles of purely local design. The most outstanding local custom, however, is the *Festa dei Giudei* held as part of the mysteries of Holy Week (Thursday and Friday) when 'penitents' go wild. Prevented from flogging themselves with the long chains they once wore, the masked figures now tend to inflict on themselves a bacchic penance; but the desperateness of all orgiastic, self-obliterating rites is still there.

Hotel
4th Class   *Monte Soro.*

[127 km.] Acquedolci di San Fratello.

Hotel
4th Class   *Belvedere.*

[142 km.] Caronia Marina.

Hotel
4th Class   †*Za' Maria.*

[152 km.] Santo Stefano di Camastra.

[154 km.] The No. 117 road leads left to **Mistretta** and **Nicosia** (p. 308) – an exceptionally beautiful road even among so many lovely ones crossing the Monti Nebrodi.

Hotel (at Mistretta)
4th Class   *Sicilia.*

[161 km.] Branch road left (10 km.) to **Tusa.**

Hotel
3rd Class   *Dei Nebrodi.*

[162 km.] Castel di Tusa.

Hotels
3rd Class   *Rocca Marina.*
4th Class   *Alesa.*

[167 km.] Milianni.

Hotel
4th Class   †*Relax.*

[170 km.] Póllina station. A huge hotel complex will open hereabouts by 1973.

[177 km.] A turning left (14 km.) to **Castelbuono,** a seat of the once too powerful princes of Ventimiglia. (A Tourist Village opens by the sea at this turning in 1972.) The massive, semi-ruinous *castle* at Castelbuono contains a *chapel* decorated with stuccos by Giuseppe Serpotta (brother of the wonderful Giacomo) of 1683. The *Matrice Vécchia* church was consecrated in 1494, though mostly built rather earlier, and is a fine Catalan-Gothic building containing much decoration and church furniture, altar paintings, etc., of the period.

Hotels
3rd Class   *Villággio dei Faun .*
4th Class   *Ariston ;*
            Delle Rose.

[186 km.] You arrive at Cefalù.

Cefalù

Population
Over 12,000.
Sea
Hydrofoil service calls between Palermo and Lípari Island during summer season.
Information
Azienda Autónoma, Corso Ruggero 116.
Marionette theatre
Via Roma 72.
Post office
Via G. Matteotti.
Hotels
2nd Class   *A.R.T.U.*;
                †*Baia del Capitano*;
                †*Kalura*, Caldura district – east of headland;
                †*Le Calette*, Caldura district – east of headland;
                Santa Dominga;
                Tourist.
3rd Class   *Astro*;
                †*La Siesta d'Oro*, Caldura district – east of headland;
                †*Riva del Sole*;
                Terminus.
4th Class   †*Riva del Sole*.
Pensions
2nd Class   *La Giara*;
3rd Class   *Germania*;
                Santa Dominga;
                Villa Belvedere, SS. Salvatore district.

There is a Club Méditerranée.

This pleasant, little-spoiled little town nestles against a notable crag, but Roger II's glorious cathedral rides triumphantly out from it.

As Cephaloedium (the name refers to the cephalic-shaped crag), the town was a frontier fortress of the Himerians. It is extraordinary that the cathedral could have survived the comings and goings of warring armies along this vital highway.

Cathedral

Though begun by Roger II in 1131 to honour a vow, made when he was in great peril on the sea, that he would found and build a cathedral where he came safely ashore, it was a century a-building, beginning from the east end where, from the exterior, the three tall apses, the south transept and the embattled-looking southern wall are of magnificent Norman work, rich yet firm and strong. Very characteristic is the arched interlacing decoration in black lava upon the limestone walls, each arch supported by its very slender column. The west front, too, with its stout and simple flanking towers has great strength, though of a different genre. In the early Norman style a barbaric strength controls the Oriental richness of Byzantine and arabesque sophistication. It seems an immensely cultivated and not quite formalized thing, as though the emphasis might easily shift to reveal a changing splendour, like the lights in diamonds; but, by 1240, when Giovanni Panettera built this front with its double row of false loggias – a similar motif to the earlier – strength had become a less conciliatory matter; it is still frank, but less luxurious. The *narthex*, which stands as a porch before the doors, was rebuilt – tactfully, since it is plain yet graceful, and entirely of its time – by Ambrósio da Como in the fifteenth century; its plain beauty is perhaps explained by the architect's birthplace, Como. The quaint armorial bearing of a cat rampant on a shield upheld by angels is that of Mgr Chat, the bishop who consecrated the building.

The *interior* is currently being stripped of its overlay of baroque decoration – to its very great advantage already. It is one of those that open a door to the spirit: wide, long, culminating in the golden-walled shrine. The sixteen marble columns of the *nave* are Roman, taken from some temple site, and topped by Roman and Byzantine capitals; they carry an open-timbered roof which still shows traces of thirteenth-century painting. Their march culminates in a great *arch* at the crossing, borne aloft by two enormous columns– a first climax introducing another: the airy crossing itself, with, in either transept, triforium galleries; and the supreme climax, the *altar* beneath the central apse. Five steps rise to the *choir* where, on the right hand, stands the *episcopal throne*, on the left, the *royal seat*, both of marble with mosaic inlay, and a carpet of mosaic between them. Then the *presbytery*, where the mosaic decoration (a poor term for a major work of art perpetuated in stone, glass and gold) begins and curls, coves and rises within the apse. It is the earliest of its kind in Sicily: 1148.

From the conch, commanding the whole church, an immense *portrait of Christ* looms – in majesty and divine isolation. This extraordinary figure carries a Bible in the left hand while blessing us with the right; it surely constitutes the most perfect representation of the Redeemer in all Christian art. His Bible is opened to read, both in Latin and Greek, 'Ego sum Lux Mundi'. The best viewpoint from which to look at this is in line with the two thrones, by the altar. From here you see that the curve of the dome has been used to lend a three-dimensional, embracing effect to the arms which, from farther away, can seem weak – that effect of fore-shortening which is invariably recorded in photographs.

Below this inspired, yet profoundly human vision of God, the hierarchy of heaven soars, the Virgin in the centre, over the window, parting the apostles six by six. For grace and subtlety, this portrayal of the Virgin is unequalled in any mosaic, but its quietude in prayer is often overlooked.

On the presbytery walls stand patriarchs with prophets and saints in their rows, while on the vault are cherubim and seraphim, and pairs of angels. In the chapel north of the choir is a *Madonna* of 1533 by Antonello Gagini.

The *font* with its lions, in the south aisle, is twelfth-century.

From the north aisle a door leads into the *cloister*, between the bulk of the cathedral and the towering rock, a good example of the rather cosy effect of southern Norman Gothic.

Museo Mandralisca

Opposite the cathedral the Via Mandralisca leads to the Museo Mandralisca. Do not miss this; it contains Antonello da Messina's superb portrait (1470) of an *Unknown Man*. There is also a splendid *krater* of fourth-century B.C. Sicilian workmanship; Arab *vases*, and *ceramics* from the Liparian excavations; coins and other good paintings.

On the corner of the Corso Ruggero and the Via G. Amendola is a fragment of the so-called *Osterio Magno*, Roger II's palace here. There is rich, arched fenestration, a memory of architecture with a high sense of occasion.

The Rock

The rock behind the Cathedral takes some climbing, but rewards with its views and the romantic ruin of a *feudal castle*, among which are the remains, in great trapezoidal blocks, of a *prehistoric building*. Its doorways are later modifications, being fifth-century B.C. in form; and the whole is traditionally called the temple of Diana.

Inland from Cefalù (14 km.) the hill-resort of **Gibilmanna** straggles below the Pizzo Sant'Ángelo. There is a *sanctuary* of the Madonna (*festa*, September 1st and 8th).

Hotel
3rd Class *Bel Soggiorno.*
Pension
3rd Class *La Quércia.* The restaurant at the pensioni s simple and good.

You can circle back to the S.S.113 from Gibilmanna, 6 km., to **Gratteri**, where the *Church of San Giorgio* is still Norman enough to be worth looking at, and another 14 km. to *Bívio Láscari*, 10 km. west of Cefalù.

[205 km.] About 5 km. after **Campofelice** the *Fiume Grande* is crossed. On its left bank towards the sea, north of **Buonfornello** railway station and in the curve of the motorway, lie the ruins of a Doric *temple*, almost all that is left of *Himera*, a colony founded by Zancle in 648 B.C. and razed in 409 B.C. by Hannibal (Hamilcar's nephew) off which, in 480 B.C., the Greeks won their great victory over the Carthaginians.

The hexastyle temple was built in the fifth century B.C., in part a thanksgiving for the victory. It measures 55·91 by 22·45 metres and was finely decorated. Fifty-six lion heads, each a water-spout from the roof, were found, and the best of these now form one of the chief ornaments of the Palermo museum. The remains of other statues were also found in excavation and it is probable that the pediments and metopes were of an equally high quality. The town lay mostly on the spur inland from this temple.

[210 km.] The S.S.120 branches south beside the railway leading to **Cerda** and ultimately to either Agrigento or Enna and Catánia.

Hotel
3rd Class *Motel Aurim.*

[220 km.] You arrive at Términi Imerese.

Términi Imerese
Hotel
4th Class *delle Terme*
Bathing
Good, sandy bathing.

This is quite a large, lively town. It produces pasta – in the making of which the quality of the water is most important – famous even beyond Sicilian shores. This is on account of the mineral waters which spring here. Pindar praised them, and the ancients confirmed his judgment.

It was a colony of Himera and known as Thermae Himerenses. The Carthaginians, capturing it with its mother-city, occupied it, but its heyday did not arrive until the Romans, those lovers of good baths, came. The waters issue at a temperature of 108°F and are prescribed for arthritis. They can be drunk at the little spa beside the Hotel delle Terme.

The town is divided between an upper – *Città Alta* – and a lower quarter – *Città Bassa*; the upper is the prettier and more interesting, as well as the older, piracy having made it advisable formerly to live upon the heights. A steep, stepped climb and a winding road connect the two settlements. By the citadel is a *rock-shelter*. Prehistoric finds made there belong to the last phase of the Upper Paleolithic 'Gravettian' culture. Below the railway, close by the sea, some *Roman baths*, carefully excavated, rather dully evoke Términi's glorious past; better placed, and more suggestive, are the vestiges of the Roman *amphitheatre* and a *curia* in the public garden.

The chief treasure of Términi is a beautiful *triptych* of 1453 attributed to Gáspero da Pésaro. It shows the Madonna with Saints John the Baptist and Michael, and is housed in the church of Santa Maria della Misericórdia.

The seventeenth-century *cathedral* has four *statues* of 1504–6 incorporated in its façade; also a Roman *cornice* below the tower. Inside, the most interesting thing is a *crucifix* painted on both sides by Ruzzolone, in 1484, though in an archaic manner. It is in the third chapel on the left.

3 km. east of the town the ruin of a *Roman aqueduct*, carried on double arches, crosses the torrent-bed of the Barratina.

[224 km.] Trabia.

Hotel
4th Class   †*Lido.*

[235 km.] A turning left (2 km.) to **Altavilla Mílicia** from where one can best reach the quite impressive remains of the *'Chiesazza'* which belonged to a Basilian monastery, having been built in 1077 by Robert Guiscard as a thank-offering for the victory of Misilmeri.

Hotels (at the turning)
2nd Class   †*Lido Sporting*;
             †*Torre Normanna.*

[243 km.] **Santa Flávia** (the railway station is called Sólunto). In the village, a turning right leads round the headland, where there is soon an entrance to the ruins of *Soluntum* – again a marvellously situated place. Long thought to be the site of the Carthaginian town of Cafara which the Greeks called Soloeis or Solous and the Romans variously Soluntum or Solentum, this city is now known to have been founded by Timoleon (*c.* 350 B.C.) to replace the original Cafara, which lay some 7 km. to the south-west and had been destroyed in 397 B.C. The plan dates from this foundation although the buildings whose bases you see are Roman and fragmentary. The water-storage tanks have their interest, but the site, with its view of the coast, is everything: the medieval *castle* at **Sólunto** in the foreground, the famous vineyards of Casteldaccia beyond, then Cefalù, the mountains rising to Enna, and, sometimes, the shapes of the Aeolian Islands riding the far sea.

The road continues round the seaward side of the hill to **Aspra** – and on to rejoin the S.S.113.

Around this headland there are hotels.

Hotels

2nd Class	*Motel A'Zagara* (Aspra) :
	†*Zagarella* (Santa Flávia).
3rd Class	†*Baia del Sole* (Olivella).
4th Class	*Costa d'Oro* (Aspra).
Pension	
3rd Class	†*Guttilla* (Olivella).

[246 km.] **Bagheria** lies a little way off to the left of the road; once the easterly resort of aristocratic Palermitans and now well known for the cluster of seventeenth- and eighteenth-century villas gathered round what is really just a dusty, struggling town of a dingy, Andalusian sort. It has overspread the vineyards and citrus groves which once lent some privacy to the villa gardens – though here and there an elegant front rises gratefully above the squalor.

The *Villa Palagonia* is the most famous of all – a mere party house, a folly of extravagant design built in 1715 by the father of that Prince of Palagonia whom Goethe (as he records in his *Italian Journey*) encountered on the streets of Palermo, in full dress and attended by liveried servants bearing silver plates to collect money for the ransom of Christian slaves held by the North African Muslims. Brydone visited it during this prince's day and describes it as it then was:

The amazing crowd of statues that surround his house appear

at a distance like a little army drawn up for its defence; but when you get among them, and every one assumes his true likeness, you imagine you have got into the regions of delusion and enchantment; for of all that immense group, there is not one made to represent any object in nature; nor is the absurdity of the wretched imagination that created them less astonishing than its wonderful fertility. It would require a volume to describe the whole, and a sad volume indeed it would make. He has put the heads of men to the bodies of every sort of animal, and the heads of every other animal to the bodies of men. Sometimes he makes a compound of five or six animals that have no sort of resemblance in nature ... the seeing of them by women with child is said to have been already attended with very unfortunate circumstances; several living monsters have been brought forth in the neighbourhood. The ladies complain that they dare no longer take an airing in the Bagaria; that some hideous form always haunts their imagination for some time after: their husbands too, it is said, are as little satisfied with the great variety of horns.

The inside of this enchanted castle corresponds exactly with the out: it is in every respect as whimsical and fantastical, and you cannot turn yourself to any side, where you are not stared in the face by some hideous figure or other. Some of the apartments are spacious and magnificent, with high arched roofs; which instead of plaister or stucco, are composed entirely of large mirrors, nicely joined together. The effect that these produce (as each of them make a small angle with the other) is exactly that of a multiplying glass; so that when three or four people are walking below, there is always the appearance of three or four hundred walking above. The whole of the doors are likewise covered over with small pieces of mirror, cut into the most ridiculous shapes, and intermixed with a great variety of crystal and glass of different colours.

All this is now in a sad state of decrepitude, but it should be seen before it finally crumbles. The entrance is in the Piazza Garibaldi and the villa may be seen on application to the caretaker (see also p. 30).

The *Villa Valguarnera* (1721), off Corso Umberto, is the better, architecturally speaking, and the *Villa Butera*, called the 'Certosa' on account of its wax figures of historical personages clad in Carthusian habits, shows that poor Prince Palagonia was not altogether alone with his fantasies.

[253 km.] **Acqua dei Corsari**. Junction with the S.S.121 to Enna; exit from motorway.

[256 km.] As the S.S.113 runs by the sea into Palermo it passes the popular beaches of **Romagnolo** where some of the bathing establishments have restaurants. Among these the Spanò is famous for its Palermitan sea-food dishes; particularly the *pasta con sarde*, pasta with a sauce of fresh sardines, parsley and pine nuts, which is a Sicilian speciality. Altogether, we risk saying this is the best restaurant in Sicily.

[260 km.] Palermo.

PALERMO

Air
Flights from Rome, Milan, Naples, Malta, Tunis, Réggio di Calábria, Catánia, Trápani, Pantelleria, Lampedusa.
   Airport: Punta Ráisi, 35 km. Coaches to Alitalia Terminal (at Via Mazzini 59).
Sea
From Naples, overnight car ferry. Steamers to Cágliari, Tunis, Trápani, Ústica Island. Hydrofoil to Cefalù and Lípari in summer.
Rail
Connections over the island and mainland via Villa San Giovanni.
Bus
Most urban buses (including those to Monreale and other environs of Palermo) start from Piazza Verdi, Piazza XIII Vittione or the Central Station. Long-distance buses run to Cátania, Cefalù and Messina (from Piazza XIII Vittione), Enna, Caltanisetta and Agrigento (from near Central Station) and Trápani (Piazza Marina).
Taxi ranks
Stazione Centrale (*Map* **44**); Piazza Castelnuovo; Stazione Maríttima (*Map* **4**) – but the demand for cabs makes the main streets a better bet for cruising taxis.
Information
E.P.T. office, Piazza Castelnuovo 35 (*Map* **6**).
Azienda Autónoma, Villa Igéia (*Map* **3**), Salita Belmonte.
Tourist Information Offices, Airport; Via Emerico Amari 135; Stazione Centrale (*Map* **44**); Stazione Maríttima (*Map* **4**).
Tourist police, Largo dei Cavallieri del S. Sepolcro (or telephone 215 521 in an emergency).
C.I.T. office, Via Roma 320/322.

Library
American Library, Viale Enrico Parisi 4.
Consulates
United Kingdom, Via M. Villabianca.
United States, Via Vaccarini 1.
Puppet theatres (Opera dei Pupi)
Argento, Via del Pappagallo 10 (20.00 hours) ;
Cutícchio, Via Orológio 14 ;
Mancuso, Via del Médico 6.
Bathing
Bathing can be had at Romagnolo (p. 104), Mondello Lido (p. 141), Sferracavallo
(p. 152), Ísola delle Fémmine (p. 152) and from Aspra to Santa Flávia (p. 103).
Hotels

Luxury	†*Villa Igéia Grand Hotel*, Salita Belmonte (Aquasanta).
1st Class	*Grand Hotel delle Palme*, Via Roma 398 ;
	Jolly Hotel del Foro Itálico, Foro Itálico 22 ;
	†*Mondello Palace*, Mondello Lido.
2nd Class	*Centrale*, Corso Vittório Emanuele 327 ;
	Mediterraneo, Via Cerda 44 ;
	Metropol, Via Turrisi Colonna 4 ;
	Motel Agip, Viale della Regione Siciliana ;
	Ponte, Via F. Crispi 99 ;
	Sole (*Grande Albergo*), Corso Vittório Emanuele 291 ;
	†*Splendid Hotel la Torre*, Mondello Lido ;
	Touring, Via M. Stábile 136 ;
	Villa Lincoln, Via Archirafi 10.
3rd Class	*Bristol*, Via Maqueda 437 ;
	Conchiglia d'Oro, Mondello Lido ;
	Diana, Via Roma 188 ;
	Elena, Piazza G. Césare 14 ;
	Elite, Via M. Stábile 136 ;
	Firenze, Via Candelai 68 ;
	Liguria, Via M. Stábile 128 ;
	Moderno, Via Roma 276 ;
	Olimpia, Piazza Cassa di Risparmio 18 ;
	Regina, Corso Vittório Emanuele 316 ;
	Sausele, Via V. Errante 12 ;
	Stella Maris, Porto di Palermo ;
	Terminus, Piazza G. Césare 37 ;
	Torinese, Via G. Meli 5 ;
	Torretta de la Glara, Via Quintino Sella 1 ;
	Vittória, Via Maqueda 8 ;
	Wagner, Via Ammiráglio Gravina 88.
4th Class	*Bologna*, Piazza Bologni 2 ;
	Capri, Via Maqueda 129 ;
	Cavour, Via Manzoni 11 ;
	Corona, Via Roma 118 ;
	Del Massimo, Via Cavour 118 ;
	Ferrara, Via Roma 188 ;
	Gori, Via Gorizia 8 ;
	Itália, Via Roma 62 ;
	Minerva, Via Michele Amari 11 ;
	Novelli, Salita Santa Caterina 1 ;
	Odeon, Via Emerico Amari 140 ;
	Orientale, Via Maqueda 26 ;
	Paradiso, Via Schiavuzzo 65 ;
	Pátria, Via Alloro 104 ;

Posta, Via A. Gagini 107 ;
Pretória, Via Maqueda 124 ;
Quattro Canti, Vicolo Paternò 4 ;
Rosália Conca d'Oro, Via S. Rosália 7
San Remo, Via Maqueda 124 ;
Santa Lucia, Via F. Crispi 258 ;
Savóia, Via Bentivegna 38 ;
Sicília, Via Divisi 99 ;
Splendor, Via Lincoln 161 ;
Universo, Piazzetta Chiesa Cocchieri 4 ;
Verdi, Via Maqueda 417 ;
Vesúvio, Via Agrigento 4 ;
Villareale, Via Villareale 16.

Pensions

2nd Class *Ariston*, Via M. Stábile 142 ;
Esplanade, Mondello Lido ;
Villa Espéria, Mondello Lido.

3rd Class *Castelnuovo*, Piazza Castelnuovo 50 ;
De Ángelis, Via Lincoln 74 ;
Gardenia, Via M. Stábile 136 ;
Libertà, Via E. Parisi 10 ;
Lio, Via F. Guardione 76 ;
Lo Porto, Via Lincoln 101 ;
Millo, Via Roma 391 ;
Rizzico, Via Onorato 13 ;
Stábile, Via M Stábile 142 ;
Villa Azzurra, Mondello Lido ;
Villa Resi, Mondello Lido.

Restaurants

Hotel Villa Igéia, where the evening grill is really good ;
Spanò (Romagnolo), the best sea-food in south Italy ;
Al Gámbero Rosso (Mondello Lido), a nicer position than *Spanò*, and only just less good grub ;
Le Caprice (Via Cavour), conventional but good enough ;
Peppino (Piazza Castelnuovo), best of the more modest in price ;
Al Cassarò (Via Isnello), a bit 'typical' but entertaining and tasty.

Night-spots

Hi-Fi Whisky a Gogo, Villa Boscogrande, Via Tommaso Natale 91 ;
Charly Max, Piazza Leoni 9 ;
Cirano, Via Molise 5B ;
Grant's, Via Principe Paternò 80 ;
Le Mirage, Via Emerico Amari 148 ;
Life, Via Ausonia ;
Madison, Piazza Don Bosco 13 ;
Meeting Pipers, Via Empédocle Restivo 125 ;
Open Gate, Via Generale Arimondi 5 ;
Royal 68, Via Umberto Giordani 5 ;
La Torre, Piano del Gallo, Mondello (summer) ;
Le Terrazze, Viale Regina Elena, Mondello (summer).

Capital of Sicily and of its own province, and seat of the Sicilian regional parliament, Palermo is a growing city of roughly 600,000 inhabitants.

HISTORY

Prehistoric men inhabited the area of Palermo, but the town itself was established by the Carthaginian Phoenicians in the fifth century B.C. The Carthaginians occupied the Conca d'Oro as a check to the gradual expansion of the Greek colonies from the south and east of the island.

The Carthaginians perhaps called their own town Ziz – a word recalling the Arabic *aziz*, or 'beautiful'. The earliest references (fifth century B.C.) are Greek ones and they use the name Panhormos, tentatively translated to mean 'all-' or 'many-harboured' and perhaps having the connotation of a safe harbourage in all weathers. The Romans modified this name to Panorumus; under the Byzantines – perhaps in a Sicilian dialect – this became something like Balarma, and the Arabs in their turn called it variously Balármuh or Balarmúh, after which it finally became Palermo.

Its reputation for good harbours depended on the ancient configuration of the land which has now disappeared. Originally there were two streams running to the sea in deeply cleft valleys on either side of a spur, 100 feet high, where now the Palazzo dei Normanni stands (*Map* **41**). Both streams, the Papireto on the north and the Maltempo on the south, must have entered the sea at the head of deep, sandy inlets which formed the harbourages and were suitable for beaching boats. Over the centuries, these inlets and valleys have become filled in, mostly by heavy silting-up, and the streams themselves, becoming unhealthy drains running through the enlarged town, were diverted and channelled underground in the late sixteenth century.

Thus the most ancient town was an elliptical one in plan, more or less centred upon the present Archiepiscopal Palace (*Map* **37**). The western half of the Corso Vittório Emanuele (known as the Cássaro Vécchio) was always the city's main thoroughfare. The sea may have reached as far inland as the Via Roma. North of the Cathedral (*Map* **30**), and stretching to the sea – already in Byzantine times – was a newer growth of town called Neapolis (new town) from which the upper part was differentiated as the Palaia Polis (old town). The tracks of the Via del Celso, to the north of the Cássaro Vécchio, and of the Vie Biscottari and Chiara (unless, here, it was the Via Università) trace out the plan of Byzantine Neapolis; Palaia Polis occupying the Piazza della Vittória with the site of the

Palermo

N

Key on following page

Town Plan of Palermo

1 Museo Pitrè (Museo Etnográfico) (p. 136)
2 La Favorita Park (p. 136)
3 Villa Igéia and Azienda Autónoma
4 Stazione Maríttima and Tourist Information Office
5 Politeama Theatre (p. 112)
6 E.P.T. Office
7 Church of San Giorgio dei Genovesi (p. 133)
8 Church of Santa Zita and Oratório della Compagnia del Rosário di Santa Zita (pp. 134–35)
9 Museo Nazionale Archeológico (National Museum of Antiquities) (p. 118)
10 Church of Sant' Ignazio (the 'Olivella') (p. 118)
11 Oratório della Compagnia di Santa Caterina (p. 135)
12 Post Office
13 Church of Santa Maria della Catena (p. 133)
14 Porta Felice (p. 112)
15 Church of San Doménico and Oratório della Compagnia del Rosário di San Doménico (pp. 132 and 135)
16 Church of Sant' Agostino (p. 131)
17 Palazzo Chiaramonte and Sant' António Abate (p. 116)
18 Oratório della Compagnia di San Lorenzo (p. 135)
19 Church of San Francesco (p. 132)
20 Church of Santa Maria dei Mirácoli (p. 117)
21 La Zisa Palace (p. 137)
22 Church of La Pietà (p. 116)
23 National Gallery of Sicily (in Palazzo Abbatelli) (p. 120)
24 Church of La Gáncia ('Santa Maria degli Ángeli') (p. 129)
25 Santa Cristina la Vétere (p. 132)
26 Quattro Canti (p. 114)
27 Church of Santa Caterina (p. 131)
28 Church of Santa Teresa (p. 116)
29 Cappella dell' Incoronazione (p. 125)

30 Cathedral (Santa Maria dell' Assunta) (p. 125)
31 Church of San Giuseppe (p.115)
32 Palazzo del Município (p. 115)
33 Churches of La Martorana (Santa Maria dell' Ammiráglio)and San Cataldo (pp. 129–31)
34 Church of Casa Professa (p. 129)
35 Palazzo Aiutamicristo (p. 121)
36 Church of La Magione (p. 129)
37 Archiepiscopal Palace (p. 115)
38 Convento dei Cappuccini (p. 137)
39 Villa Bonanno Gardens (p. 115)
40 Porta Nuova (p. 115)
41 Palazzo dei Normanni (Cappella Palatina) (p. 121)
42 Tower of San Nicolò (p. 117)
43 Porta Sant' António (p. 111)
44 Stazione Centrale (Central Station) and Tourist Information Office
45 Church of San Giovanni degli Eremiti (p. 133)
46 Church of Santo Spírito dei Vespri (p. 134)
47 La Cuba and Caserma Tüköry Barracks (p. 137)
48 Villa Napoli and La Cúbula (p. 138)
49 Ponte dell' Ammiráglio (p. 138)
50 Church of San Giovanni dei Lebbrosi (p. 139)

A Route to Mondello Lido
B Route to Monte Pellegrino
C Route to Villa La Favorita, Pallavicino, Mondello Lido
D Route to Airport, Trápani via Castellammare del Golfo
E Route to Altarello, Baida, San Martino delle Scale
F Route to Monreale, Trápani via Álcamo
G Route to Altofonte (Parco), Piana degli Albanesi, Corleone, Agrigento
H Route to Palazzo di Favara, Santa Maria di Gesù
J Route to Messina, Enna, Catánia, Agrigento (via Bívio Manganaro)

Palazzo dei Normanni and the block of buildings north of the Cássaro Vécchio and opposite to the Villa Bonanno Gardens (*Map* **39**) in the square. The Via Scioppettieri and the Via Sant'António probably trace where the ring of the town was closed to the east.

Already in Byzantine times the land must have encroached on the sea and the harbours been driven eastwards, but the town did not grow farther until the Arabs made it their capital. To accommodate their administrative and military forces and to enclose a palace for the emirs, the Arabs built a new quarter, in the first half of the tenth century A.D., to the east of the old town. This was, and is still known as, the Kalsa (*el-Halisah* – the elect). It was separately walled.

At this period – a peaceful one for citizens, if not for their rulers – the first suburbs began to be built. The most southern of these comprised the Jewish quarter, which lay around or over the head of the southern harbour, lying north and east of what is now the Porta Sant'António (*Map* **43**), and a bazaar district called the *Harat-al-jedidah* ('new quarter') in the neighbourhood of that gate – both divided from the old town by the valley and stream. Opposite the north side of the town, across the other valley, a large settlement arose in a crescent running from the line of the Via Sant'Agostino and Via Bandiera as far north as the Piazza Verdi. This was called the quarter of the Schiavoni, or Illyrian merchants.

In the first part of the eleventh century, these quarters were walled into the town and a citadel was built on the promontory enclosing the northern harbour. It may have been on the site of a Roman castrum; now only the Piazza Castello marks its site. About this time the Amalfitan quarter may have begun to grow. This later housed the merchants from the Italian mercantile republics, but originally housed only those from Amalfi, who were the first to trade on any scale with the Arabs. This lay over the site of the ancient northern harbour – always the better and more important of the two – which was by then rapidly dwindling to much the same size as the present Cala. This mercantile colony grew in size under the Normans, and was incorporated into the circuit of the walls after the Sicilian Vespers, later being known as the Lóggia quarter – and now as San Pietro after the fishermen's patron, St Peter.

The Norman kings removed from the Kalsa to the upper fortress, beginning the building now known as the Palazzo dei Normanni, or Palazzo Reale, and the court settled a new quarter roughly corresponding with the western half of the Albergheria today. The

Muslims kept to the Kalsa and the Schiavoni quarter, which came to be called the *Sari-al-Qadi* – 'the Judge's bastion' – and was, as Siracaldi, still called so until the last century, when the great new growth of the city blotted this quarter out. The Norman kings also – imitating the emirs who had built the palace and gardens of La Favara under the slope of Monte Grifone, to the south of the plain – laid out a great park or pleasance, to the west of the city, in which they built pavilions, some of which stand today in the suburbs: La Cuba (*Map* **47**), La Cúbula (*Map* **48**) and the beautiful Zisa (*Map* **21**).

The population rose to something like 100,000 in the twelfth century, then declined through the drain of men impressed for the unending wars and from the scourge of the plague. By 1492 there were only about 65,000 inhabitants of Palermo; the town fell into neglect and all growth halted. There are, however, a few true Renaissance buildings in the city.

This dereliction must have made the easier that great rebuilding under the Spanish viceroys which, largely intact as it is, lends Palermo its special flavour.

The new port with a mole was built in 1567 and new fortifications put in hand, including the sea-wall along the Foro Itálico. Then, by 1582, the Cássaro was extended down to the sea at *Porta Felice* (*Map* **14**). The Via Maqueda was opened up in 1600 and the Quattro Canti corner (*Map* **26**) embellished in 1611.

After the unification of Italy, building began again on a scale hitherto unprecedented. Most of this nineteenth- and early-twentieth-century growth lay, however, outside the old town, and only the cutting, right through the town, of the Via Roma, and the rebuilding of various parts of the city bordering upon it, significantly altered its character. This street was begun before 1914 and completed after the First World War, its southern end being the newest.

The bombing of the port area in 1943 has necessitated considerable rebuilding, though the higher parts of the town on the whole escaped the worst of this. Slum clearance will eventually do away with much, if not all, of the old hugger-mugger of back streets which is so picturesque and characteristic of Sicilian life – but so very deplorable.

The city now centres upon the 'Politeama' (*Map* **5**) – really the theatre of that name, built in 1874 – and the two squares opposite to it which appear to be one: Piazza Ruggero Séttimo and Piazza

Castelnuovo. (On the buses, the names of these, as with that of the theatre, are differentiated to indicate the location of the stops over this rather complicated junction of many routes.) The modern residential, and the better business quarters – such 'uptown' centre as there is – now all lie north of the old town; industrial development mostly to the south – an expansion that has almost doubled the extent of the city. Modern Palermo can scarcely be said to have a centre at all, unless it is in the habit of people to walk up and down the Via Ruggero Séttimo of an evening – although the Palermitans make less of the *passéggio* than any other Italian or Sicilian citizenry.

An aspect of the city which is sometimes forgotten is its immediate neighbourhood. Into this, the life of the town has, of course, always spread its influence, if for no other reason than because it was its market and principal customer. In the seventeenth and eighteenth centuries, however, the patricians of Palermo took to building country villas at Bagheria and over the Piano dei Colli to the north. These were within easy coach-ride of their town *palazzi* and were frequently less summer residences than places in which to hold parties. When Queen Maria Carolina built La Favorita on the Piano dei Colli, she made it her retreat from the unpleasantness of exile and the coldness of the Palermitans towards her, and yet she was still – physically – in a position to dominate the Government. Nowadays, this does not seem surprising, but the present twenty minutes' journey by bus then took an hour or more by coach.

A last word: the imprecise bombing of Palermo in 1943 was the act of the American Air Force. Palermitans are polite about it, but the Allies are not entirely forgiven for these or other raids elsewhere on the island. And never, in all its history, has Palermo suffered such a physical catastrophe as that bombing.

PRINCIPAL SIGHTS

The quarters of the town of greatest interest to the visitor are concentrated within walking distance, within a radius of about a mile, centring on the Quattro Canti corner (*Map* **24**). Although a map is provided, to help the reader orientate himself on the ground, we describe first those quarters and streets, etc., on which the plan of the old town is largely based. Individual sights are then described under the categories: Museums, Palaces, and Churches and Oratories. The sights appear in alphabetical order under each heading. The chart facing p. 27 will give an idea of what not to miss if your time is short, both among these central sights and the sub-urban ones which are described in a separate section.

Buses are not very helpful in the old quarters, though they come in useful when returning from the perimeter to the centre, which all do at one point or another.

CENTRAL SIGHTS

Quattro Canti
Map **26**.

Officially called the Piazza Vigliena after the viceroy who, in 1611, built it as an adornment to the city of which it had become the centre-point. The four buildings forming the angles of this cross-roads of the Via Maqueda and the Corso Vittório Emanuele were built as though bevelled off to face one another diagonally, these blank walls being decorated with symbolic figures in a baroque and spuriously architectural setting. The four seasons are there, and four kings of Sicily; but, most significantly, also the four saintly patronesses of the four quarters (each lying behind its corner) into which the city was then almost equally divided: old Siricaldi, the quarter north of the Corso and west of Via Maqueda, now known as Il Capo, being represented by Santa Oliva; the Albergheria (p. 117), south of the Corso, represented by Santa Cristina; the Kalsa (p. 116) represented by Sant'Ágata to the east of Via Maqueda; and the old Amalfitani or Lóggia, nowadays San Pietro, to the north and east of the Corso Vittório Emanuele, represented by Santa Ninfa.

At that time Palermo was deeply divided into these quarters; and even a hundred years ago intermarriage between their inhabitants was rare, and immigrants from one to another considered as scarcely acceptable foreigners. The cult of Santa Rosália as patroness of the whole city was not introduced until 1642, and, as a few minutes' talk with a true Palermitan of today will reveal, she has not really succeeded in unifying the parishioners of its many districts – except vis-à-vis countrymen.

Piazza Pretória

This noble baroque square, just by Quattro Canti, is almost filled with an extravagant *fountain*. A pinnacle of figures rises from the centre of a great circular basin, raised in a kind of moat crossed by four bridges from a circular and balustraded platform, the whole peopled with a colony of white statues – tritons, river-gods, nymphs – altogether making a very fine effect though individually of inferior workmanship. It was built in the third quarter of the sixteenth century by two Florentines, Francesco Camilliani and Michaelangelo Naccherino.

The piazza is surrounded, on the east, by one side of *Santa Caterina* in the adjacent Piazza Bellini (*Map* **27**); across the Via Maqueda, by *S. Giuseppe* (*dei Teatini*) (*Map* **31**); and on the south side, by the *Palazzo del Municipio* (Municipality) (*Map* **32**) – formerly the Pretório, or governor's office, from which the square takes its name – all of them handsome buildings.

Cássaro Vécchio

This is the name for the western stretch of the Corso Vittório Emanuele, running from the Porta Nuova (*Map* **40**), by the Palazzo dei Normanni (*Map* **41**), to the Quattro Canti (*Map* **26**). It was the main street of the medieval town, while the section from the Porta Nuova to the Via Matteo Bonello was the central thoroughfare of the ancient town. Many fine *palazzi* front on to it.

The *Cathedral* (*Map* **30**) lies across its green, bordering the street, and the *Archiepiscopal Palace* (*Map* **37**) occupies the farther corner. Higher up, there is a garden on the southern side called the *Villa Bonanno* (*Map* **39**). The antique bits of masonry under its date-palms were Roman houses. A notable convent building faces the garden from the Cássaro, and the Norman palace dominates it from the west.

The street culminates with the surprising and imperial splendour of the *Porta Nuova* (*Map* **40**), built as a triumphal arch to celebrate the Emperor Charles V's personal capture of Tunis in 1535. It was struck by lightning and repaired in 1667, which accounts for the high baroque passages upon what is essentially a sixteenth-century Spanish building. The four giant telamons must be derived from those far smaller ones which decorated Hieron II's vast Altar of Zeus (p. 239) at Syracuse. Had the sculptor, Gaspero Guercio, seen a reconstruction of an equally huge Agrigentine one, we must have known of it.

In the courtyard of the Carabinieri barracks, beside the Porta Nuova, is the small twelfth-century *Church of La Maddalena*, now used as a memorial chapel to the Carabinieri war dead. You can ask to see it, and it is worth doing so.

Via Maqueda

A handsome street lined, for most of its length, by seventeenth- and eighteenth-century *palazzi*. The northern reach is the most altered – it has some good shops, though these are more concentrated along the street's northern extension, the Via Ruggero Séttimo. The southern reach, from the Quattro Canti (*Map* **26**) to the Porta Sant'António (*Map* **43**), hard by the Central Station (*Map* **44**), is very fine. Specially worthy of notice are the eighteenth-century *Prefettura* and *Palazzo Santa Croce* which are on diagonally opposite corners of the crossing where the Via Bosco and the Via Divisi join the Via Maqueda. The Palazzo Santa Croce has a lovely courtyard – it is usually worth while peeping through any open *palazzo* door that one can.

Cássaro Nuovo

This is the name for the eastern stretch of the Corso Vittório Emanuele, running down from Quattro Canbi to Porta Felice (*Map* **14**). The most easterly part of the Cássaro Nuovo was known as the Dead Cássaro, a name which the bombing of 1943 did its best to confirm. The gate itself has been restored to its appearance of 1637.

Quartiere della Kalsa

Until the bombing which, as one may see, devastated this area, it was a fisherman's and seaman's quarter and its womenfolk were renowned for their embroidery. Parts of it still have charm, being neat and clean in a sailorly, shipshape way, but too much now is simply the squalid and temporary refuge of the very poor awaiting rehousing.

But the Piazza della Kalsa is still handsome; the front of the *church* of *Santa Teresa* (*Map* **28**) is baroque and striking. It is by Giácomo Amato. A step along the Via Torremuzza, the *church of La Pietà* (*Map* **22**) by the same architect contains a rather moving *Deposition from the Cross* by Vincenzo da Pávia.

Best of all, now, despite damage and dilapidation, is the walk down the lower end of the Via Alloro, lined on either side with *palazzi* whose nobility is yet unbowed.

Piazza Marina and Palazzo Chiaramonte
Map **17**.

The Piazza Marina was once an arm of the sea, but so silted up by the ninth century that the Arabs reclaimed it when building the Kalsa quarter. Aragonese nobles celebrated great occasions by jousting here, and it was an execution ground. A fine banyan tree now grows in the garden of the square, and country buses make it their terminal.

In the south-west corner is the pleasant Renaissance church of *Santa Maria dei Mirácoli* (*Map* **20**); on the south side the *Palazzo San Cataldo*, a restored building which incorporates, along the side, some of its original, arched windows. A number of these reconstructions exist in Palermo and elsewhere on the island, the nineteenth-century Romantic Movement having fired their owners to a new appreciation of this period so despised by their forefathers.

The *Palazzo Chiaramonte* (*Map* **17**), also known as *Lo Steri*, the Hosterium, lies on the east side of the Piazza. It is currently closed, being – eternally, it seems – 'in process of restoration'.

This magnificent *palazzo* was begun in 1307 as the residence of the Chiaramontes, but became the palace of the early viceroys, and later that of the Inquisition. The size and Gothic grandeur tell of the short, happy period of the Aragonese kings of Trinacria.

Inside are two rooms with curious ceilings, painted by Simone da Corleone and Cecco di Naro in the latter half of the fourteenth century but in imitation of the Arab manner. In the right-hand court is the church of *Sant' António Abate* which has a fine façade. Its keys are with the Soprintendenza ai Monumenti at the Palazzo dei Normanni.

Quartiere dell'Albergheria

This quarter, south-west of Quattro Canti, is an area of cottage-hovels and old, decaying palaces, where there is a smell of horses from the *carrozze* stables. In the streets and *vicoli* there are markets, that in the Via Porta di Castro, the quarter's main thoroughfare, being the most extensive.

Dreadfully bombed in 1943, and really poor, however picturesque it may be – and, with its Saracenic flavour and occasional Gothic façades, this it certainly is – one cannot but welcome its clearance and rebuilding, already in progress. None the less, while it remains, it is well worth exploring. The Via Biscottari, continuing the Via Santa Chiara, and the Via Porta di Castro run, on the whole, east–west, and though the side streets are sometimes tortuous one should not get lost following them.

The *Tower of San Nicolò* (*Map* **42**) belonged to the fourteenth-century city-wall.

In the Via delle Mosche (Street of the Flies) Giuseppe Bulsamo, 'Count Cagliostro', was born in 1743. Of all plausible Sicilians – Italians regard plausibility as a pre-eminently Sicilian quality – 'Count Cagliostro' seems to have been the most convincing. Escaping from the island after the detection of sundry of his ingenious crimes, he travelled in the Levant and Near East, learning alchemy and kindred subjects from one Althotas at Rhodes. He then visited Malta where he curried favour with the Grand Master Manoel di Pinto, who had a taste for the heretical 'sciences', and obtained from him useful introductions to great persons in Italy. He married in Rome and, with his wife as assistant, thereafter journeyed throughout Europe imposing on the credulous with his love-philtres, elixirs, beautifying mixtures and so forth. His blandishments found particular favour with women, but in London he had great success with a new brand of freemasonry which he invented. His career of duplicity began to catch up with him when he was involved in the tragic confidence trick of the 'Diamond Necklace', played upon Marie Antoinette in 1785. From this imbroglio a gloriously impudent defence extricated him, but he was sent to the Bastille upon other charges. Released, he returned a third time to London, where he was soon in the Fleet Prison. Again released, he made for Rome where, in 1789, he was arrested and tried for heresy. Sentence of death was commuted to life imprisonment – his wife was sent to a nunnery – and he died in 1795 in the castle of San Leo.

MUSEUMS

Museo Nazionale Archeológico
In the Piazza dell'Olivella; Map **9**.

Open Tuesdays to Saturdays 09.00–16.00 (150 l.); Sundays 09.30–13.00 (free). Closed on Mondays.

This occupies a charming seventeenth-century former convent next door to the church of *Sant'Ignazio* (1598), or the *Olivella* (*Map* **10**), in which there is a shrine to the patroness of this quarter of the town. The church received a direct hit by a bomb but is now restored.

This National Museum is one of the most important in Italy and the chief museum of Greek art outside Greece. A certain amount of rearrangement is in progress, but the following notes may help a hurried visitor.

Ground Floor: Beyond the courtyard with the *triton fountain* are two rooms containing Punic sculptures and inscriptions, among Egyptian exhibits which are of considerable interest.

Across the larger courtyard are rooms holding the major finds from Sclinunte (Selinus) and Himera, with other Greek statuary. The huge terra-cotta decoration from a pediment of Temple C at Selinunte (p. 170) is still being assembled: a prancing *gorgon* guards the sanctity of the temple. Other fragments from the entablature of this temple are here. The *lion-spouts* from the temple at Himera are almost matched by those from Agrigento.

The *Sala di Selinunte* contains the four marvellous *metopes* from Temple E (p. 167) of the early fifth century B.C.: Herakles fighting with an Amazon (note his toes upon her foot – a wrestler's hold); Zeus and Hera, at their wedding, beautifully illustrate their relationship; Actaeon is here a ritual sacrifice – Artemis is the implacable force; Pallas Athene, too, is the irresistible goddess overpowering a Titan. The four panels, together, show how subtly the whole frieze of metopes was designed.

The earlier *metopes* (early-sixth-century) set in the large reconstruction on the side wall are from Temple C (p. 170): a quadriga; Perseus beheading the Gorgon, under Pallas Athene's patronage; Herakles meting out punishment to the dwarf Kerkopes. These very archaic and lively reliefs follow a traditional design from which those from Temple E have departed.

The other Selinuntine fragments in the room are of an equally high quality: the single, archaic metope of Europa riding the bull comes from a temple destroyed in the fifth century to make way for a more elaborate one.

In the next rooms, among assorted Etruscan objects from Chiusi is an *oinochoe* of unmatched magnificence, in bucchero-ware (sixth-century), which tells the story of Perseus and Medusa.

Upstairs: The large bronzes include the justly famous *Ram* (third-century B.C.) from the Castello Maniace at Syracuse, and *Herakles and the Arcadian stag*, an outstanding Roman work from Pompeii.

In a long gallery, many of the 5,000 votive figures in terra-cotta that were found in the Sanctuary of Demeter at Selinunte (p. 171) are arranged in a way that traces the chronological evolution of their design. Here is the goddess, once bought for a shilling, but, when placed in the temple, hallowed by her tremendous significance.

Next floor up: This is devoted to Palermo's extraordinary collection of *Greek vases* – some superb as works of art; others more interesting, perhaps, as records of life as it was lived then, or for their literary content – and a very well-displayed collection of West Sicily Paleolithic to Early Iron Age finds, including pottery from Sant'Ángelo Muxaro (p 175). Note the casts, etc., of the Paleolithic incised drawings from the Addaura caves – one of the most revealing documents of the far past in all the world is that of the bird-dancers.

Palazzo Abbatelli (National Gallery of Sicily)
Via Alloro; Map **23**.

Open 09.00–14.00, Sundays 09.00–13.00 (free). Closed Fridays.

This excellent example of quattrocento Sicilian building has been restored and now houses a superbly arranged *art gallery* containing many exquisite and important works of art. The entrance is through a remarkably fine doorway.

The Palazzo was designed by Matteo Carnelivari for the master-pilot of Sicily, Francesco Abbatelli, and built between 1488 and 1495. Late Catalan-Gothic here crosses with the Italian Renaissance. It was for long occupied by nuns and much altered internally, then bombed.

The *ground floor* is chiefly occupied by sculptures. Of these Francesco Laurana's *bust of Eleonora of Aragon* and the *Madonna della Neve* (1516) by a follower of his (possibly the young Antonello Gagini still working in his master's idiom) stand out as masterpieces. The bust is so reticent that it is scarcely a portrait; rather than making a statement about the sitter, it makes one about stone and sculpture, and only evokes the lady as her beauty might have lingered in Laurana's memory. Another *Bust of a Gentlewoman*, attributed – with reason, one would say – to Laurana, fades even more into the stone, becoming a reverie. On this floor too is a gorgeous Hispano-Moresque *vase* of the fourteenth century – and a huge fresco of the *Triumph of Death*; the artist is unknown, but it is dated 1445. This is an overpowering work in which Death, upon a dying horse, rides both over the living and the dead, whom he has shot with his arrow. The victims are the great of the earth; the rich variously disturbed, apprehensive and unconcerned; but a group of the poor seem to supplicate death – the painter's (perhaps socialistic?) meaning escapes us, but not his extraordinary quality.

Upstairs, one's admiration grows from room to room. Not all exhibits are of Sicilian origin. There are Tuscan paintings from the late fourteenth and early fifteenth centuries and some fifteenth- and sixteenth-century Flemish paintings, of which Mabuse's 'Malvagna' triptych is the pearl. But the discovery of painters of the calibre of Tommaso di Vigília, the Master of the Políttico of Trápani and Marco Bastaiti is worth any journey you may have made to reach Palermo.

Suddenly you come into a corner room in which is hung Antonello da Messina's *Virgin of the Annunciation.* If one were vouchsafed a vision of the Madonna it must surely be like this, shining, remote, yet actual. This painting is in extraordinary emotional depth; a loving portrait and a personal tribute by the painter to a wonderful, serious and desirable young woman, shown at the instant of deifica-tion. Her gentle face is bathed in the light of the grace of God shining from her blue mantle. Her hands are so stereoscopically painted that they had to be small or else that gesture of surprise and gratitude would have dominated the picture and the face would have faded. This it does not do: it all but blinds with its beauty. Surely this could be the greatest painting in the world? It is difficult after this to respond to the less visionary excellence of the three panels from a triptych, also by Antonello: SS. Girolamo, Gregory and Augustine.

The gallery is being extended to house works from the seven-teenth and eighteenth centuries.

PALACES

For **Palazzo Abbatelli**, see previous page

Palazzo Aiutamicristo
Via Garibaldi; Map **35**.

Built to the design of Matteo Carnelivari in 1490, it has a Catalan-Gothic façade and a courtyard worth seeing. It was here that the Emperor Charles V lodged on his victorious return from Tunis in 1535.

Palazzo dei Normanni, or Palazzo Reale (Cappella Palatina)
At the west end of the Corso Vittório Emanuele; Map **41**.

Open during church hours, closing between 12.00 and 16.00. The staterooms are open daily from 09.30 to 13.30 and from 15.00 to 18.00 in summer; winter 09.00–16.00; Sundays and Festivals 09.00–13.00. Free

Originally the landward fortress of the Arabs, it was rebuilt by Roger II and his successors to be their chief palace. It has been much altered and the central tower, the *Torre di Santa Ninfa* (or the 'Pisan' tower), though its windows have suffered alteration, is now the most substantial part of the exterior where Norman work can still be seen. It is improbably topped by the green copper dome of the observatory.

The palace is entered from the terrace through a seventeenth-century *courtyard*, in the walls of which, in some places, the fabric has been cut back to reveal the decorated Norman work beneath.

A stair mounts to the gallery off which opens the palace chapel – the *Cappella Palatina*. The *mosaics* on the outside of the chapel are modern. On one of the left-hand columns of the gallery is an inscription in Latin, Greek and Arabic, making reference to the famous water-clock that Roger II caused to be constructed.

The chapel was built by Roger II, between 1132 and 1140. One seems to enter a medieval reliquary whose colour and rich ornamentation is all on the inside. The form of the church is basilical; the choir being raised above the general level, while, at the west end, a raised dais, its back and sides enclosed by a marble balustrade, makes a platform for the royal throne – God and the kings confronting each other, at a higher level than ordinary humanity, down the avenue of pillars of *cipollino* and granite. Above, the ceiling – a triumph of Arab stalactitic decoration – is interrupted by a *cupola* so mounted over the sanctuary as to light the church's heart differently, and almost as if miraculously, as the sun's position changes through the day. The whole church is rich, and of exquisite workmanship in every detail – the lower walls inlaid with marble slabs and tesserae, the *ambo* (or pulpit) and the great paschal candlestick, the floor itself – but, above all, its glory is the effect of the mosaic-covered walls where a host of brilliantly coloured figures crowd upon the shimmering, glowing gold of their background.

These mosaics have been very much, and sometimes drastically, restored at many periods. The mosaics on the right of the sanctuary are the oldest: the Transfiguration in the centre; the Baptism on the left; on the right the Raising of Lazarus. Higher up, two panels balance each other both by their subject-matter and symbolism; the

Flight into Egypt and the Entry into Jerusalem. Other scenes in the church depict Old Testament stories and incidents from the lives of St Paul and St Peter – to whom the church is dedicated.

The decorated *ceiling* of the nave, and the interior of the *dome* are more precious than even the best mosaics here. The use of muqarnas stalactitic forms to decorate the semi-dome of a niche has been found to go back to the eleventh century, though possibly not much before 1090, in the Algerian Kingdom of the Zirids. Then here (dated at 1132) and at Fes, in the Kairouyyin Mosque (placed at between 1135 and 1142/3) comes the technique, not only of organizing the forms over a rectangular area but also of filling the coving of domes. Linking examples must once have existed and since disappeared (this ceiling was not the only one in this palace), for although the internationalism of the eleventh and twelfth centuries is one of the most significant aspects of the age, it is not very probable that two major examples of the manner, one in wood, as here, the other in stucco, as at Fes, should appear all but simultaneously quite so far apart. Very noticeable in a number of Norman churches in Sicily is the variety in the construction of squinches by which a square support (and in one case a rectangular) is converted to the circular base of a dome; the forms invented to this end are extremely close to those used in Sicilian stalactitic work (here, Monreale, La Zisa) and in contemporary (Almohad) examples in Morocco and Western Algeria. Which was the germ of which, or where the notion was first really developed, must remain a mystery; but the connection exists between architecture and decorative motif and its existence points perhaps to Sicily as the source of this very beautiful and sophisticated style. The ceiling has been a good deal restored and repainted – the remaining original Arab areas show that it was covered with worldly scenes of girl musicians, drinkers, huntsmen and the like; also that haloes were added to many of the figures at the order of Ferdinand II in an effort to de-islamize this jolly, infidel heaven, garlanded about as it is with Cufic quotations from the Koran and verses in praise of the king.

Not only the royal dais speaks here of kingly pride, and one cannot help but feel that all the skill and money lavished on this chapel were to make it quite as worthy of the king's estate as of God's – and yet the longer you stay here, the more the religious mystery of the place overawes you. Whatever King Roger had in mind, his architect and his craftsmen made this a fitting temple for some God: as you linger in the gloom, the light from the windows slowly seems to grow stronger and the glowing of the gold-leaf, imprisoned behind the glass of the tesserae, to wax – until one can see how, at the culmination of a long, Byzantine service, the congregation would come to feel themselves bathed in the unearthly light of Heaven itself.

A beautiful bronze *door* leads to what was a narthex, but has since become the *baptistery*, to reach the *sacristy* where, behind a grille, a treasury of precious caskets seems almost tawdry after the one you have just quitted. The archives are also kept here.

Also on this floor of the Palazzo dei Normanni is the office of the Soprintendenza ai Monumenti.

On the floor above are the former *Royal Apartments*, of which the most interesting is the *Sala di Re Ruggero*. It is a small room, but perfectly preserved in its vaulted, Norman form. The floor and walls are faced with inlaid marbles and bands of tesserae; rich mosaics fill the vaults and the whole effect is one of sumptuous, golden formality into which has crept something earthy and humorous and at variance. The *taste* of it is elusive; a key to this lies, I think, in the cross-fertilization there was between the Byzantine and Islamic arts. The marbled walls derive from Greco-Roman palaces, via Byzantium, but we know them better, now, from a few rich mosques of a still later date, from the halls of *medrassa* and our knowledge of such palaces as the Alhambra, el-Badi at Marrakech or el-Asi at Hama. The mosaics represent a Byzantine taste and technique, yet they were executed (1179) by Sicilians and based upon designs traditional to Islamic woven fabrics, brass-ware, etc. The endearingly clumsy drawing is Sicilian. The introduction – so surprising and exuberant – of a pair of centaurs: you are reminded that the Classics were studied at this extraordinary court when their very existence had been forgotten elsewhere in Europe. This little room cocoons the living spirit of Norman Sicily.

Other parts of the Norman palace, now disengaged from subsequent rebuildings, can be visited with the permission of the Soprintendenza ai Monumenti; the *armoury, dungeons* and *treasure-chamber*, etc. The *chamber* in which the Sicilian Assembly meets is shown you when it is not in session – a huge, neo-classic salon heroically decorated by Giuseppe Velesquez with frescoes in praise of Herakles. In another room are *portraits* of the viceroys of Sicily; fortunately, as portraits, they are of doubtful veracity, all having been painted by Fernando de Acuña.

Not open to the public is the Observatory on top of the palace. From it, Giuseppe Piazzi discovered Ceres, the first asteroid known to us, on January 1st, 1801.

CHURCHES AND ORATORIES

For **Cappella Palatina**, see under Palazzo dei Normanni (above).

Cathedral (Santa Maria dell'Assunta)
Map 30.

This building of eccentric though imposing appearance seems to typify all that is unexpected and individual about Sicily. Sturdy Norman shapes from the far north, imposing an alien conception of discipline upon the luxurious and Oriental intellectualism of Byzantium, while still relishing the ingenious, mathematical precision of Arabia: these are the secrets of the Sicilian Norman style.

The cathedral was built by Archbishop Gualtiero Offamílio in 1185 and preserves its original, glorious proportions. To ferret out this building, one should walk round the eastern end, where the *apses* and the two *towers* – as indeed, the western two also – are practically unaltered twelfth-century work. By continuing along the north side, where the blue and white inlay of tiles is in a strange and distinguished taste and there has been less adaptation, one can look again at the south side and disentangle the original work from the additions.

Opposite the north-west corner of the cathedral, across the street, and entered round the corner, is the *Cappella dell'Incoronazione* (*Map* **29**). It still contains some frescoes, although it was damaged in 1860. From its high loggia, of the sixteenth century, the newly crowned kings of Sicily used to show themselves to their people. (Keys obtainable from the Soprintendenza ai Monumenti at the Palazzo dei Normanni.)

The west front of the cathedral, very fine indeed, dates from the fourteenth and fifteenth centuries; it is joined by the span of two symbolic Gothic arches to the surprising *belfry* – surprising, mostly, because it was restored in a highly arbitrary way in the nineteenth century. The Normans themselves tended, however, to give rein to their streak of fantasy when building *campanili*, as the four other towers show. The baroque *dome*, added 1781–1801, is simply misconceived.

The south side is most notable for the wide Gothic *porch* added in the fifteenth century. The left-hand column supporting the arches is an Arab one, perhaps a relic of the mosque into which the earlier, basilican church on the site had been converted. It bears an inscription from the Koran. The beautiful *doorway* into the church is by Antonio Gambara – 1426; the *doors*, of 1432, by Francesco Miranda recall the Siculo-Norman manner, and above the centre one, in a niche, there is a small Byzantine Madonna – a relic of the early basilica? Or an archaistic work?

Inside, one is struck by the breadth as well as the airy length, and the plainness, of this royal building. Nothing remains of its Norman splendours save tombs of the kings and this spatial glory.

The six *tombs* of the royal Normans and Hohenstaufens lie in the double *chapel* to the left of the entrance from the southern porch. Crowded together as they have been, the four porphyry, canopied sarcophagi are still most moving. In design and conception, in the use of red porphyry, they link the Roman Empire and the Byzantine with modern Europe in a proud, impressive, yet unselfconscious way.

The ashes of Henry VI, Holy Roman Emperor (d. 1197), lie in the front tomb on the right; beside him, front left, his son Frederick II of Hohenstaufen, Holy Roman Emperor and 'Stupor Mundi' (d. 1250), together with Peter II of Aragon (d. 1342) – a curious economy: or hero-worship? The two tombs at the back, which were brought from Cefalù and have characteristic mosaic work on the canopies, are those, left, of Roger II (d. 1154) and, right, his daughter Constance, Queen of Sicily, wife of Henry VI and mother of Frederick. On the left wall of the chapel is the tomb of Duke William of Aragon (d. 1338), son of Frederick II (of Aragon); on the right-hand wall, an antique sarcophagus incorporated into the tomb of Constance of Aragon (d. 1222), Frederick of Hohenstaufen's first wife.

The various *sculptures* by Antonello Gagini (1478–1536) which adorn this church, set as they are against a simple though appropriate background, make an excellent introduction to this great, but far too little-known, artist's work.

The *statues* on the pillars of the nave are from a former high altar, as are the three *reliefs* in the second chapel from the west in the northern aisle, the *statues of apostles* in the choir, and the *relief of Christ* upon the altar. In the southern transept are other altar statues by Gagini; and in the inner chapel, entered through the Sacristy, is a lovely *Madonna*. The beautiful restraint and fullness of form which, especially, the nave figures of Saints Agatha, Nympha, Domenicus, Stephanus, Laurentius and Damianus exhibit, remind one of Pisano. Indeed, there always appears to be a certain archaism in the best Sicilian art, unless this is, in fact, simply a deep inherited respect for those plastic fundamentals which Greeks, Arabs, Byzantines and Normans had alike understood in their time. This is great sculpture; Antonello, pupil of the greater Laurana, was the master among his remarkable family.

The *bas-relief* of the Passion, mounting a large Crucifixion in the northern transept, is by Fázio and Vincenzo Gagini – so much less good, more mannered and more conventionally of its period than anything of their father's. The wooden *Crucifixion*, above, is a remarkable work of the fourteenth century.

There is one other important sculpture in the cathedral: Francesco Laurana's *Madonna* in the second, most easterly, chapel of the northern aisle. Though his pupils are also thought to have worked on it, it has nevertheless all the authority of a master's work. It is dated as 1469, securely in the midst of the Quattrocento, that period of purity and serenity in Italian art which is perhaps as perfectly represented by Laurana's own purity and serenity as by any other's. Such a reticent grace as his is rare in any art.

Santa Rosália, the most popular saintly patron of Palermo, is honoured in the easternmost chapel in the southern aisle. Unfortunately the *coffer* of silver (1631) in which her relics are housed is seldom on show. Santa Rosália is of obscure provenance. Puzzled by this obscurity, Brydone sought diligently to find out more about her 'who has become (as she remains) so capital a personage in this part of the world'. He discovered an epic poem written in the Sicilian dialect and learned,

that St Rosália was niece to King William the Good. That she began very early to display symptoms of her sanctity. That at fifteen she deserted the world, and disclaimed all human society. She retired to the mountains on the west of this city; and was never more heard of for about five hundred years. She disappeared in the year 1159. The people thought she had been taken up to heaven; till in the year 1624, during the time of a dreadful plague, a holy man had a vision that the saint's bones were lying in a cave near the top of the Monte Pellegrino. That if they were taken up with due reverence, and carried in procession thrice round the walls of the city, they should immediately be delivered from the plague. At first little attention was paid to the holy man, and he was looked upon as little better than a dreamer; however, he persisted in his story, grew noisy, and got adherents. The magistrates, to pacify them, sent to the Monte Pellegrino; then lo the mighty discovery was made! – the sacred bones were found, – the city was freed from the plague, – and St Rosália became the greatest saint in the calendar.

This is as much as I can discover also. Her festival (July 15th) is still a great holiday, the jubilations taking up several days with street illuminations and firework displays of an unequalled extravagance and gaiety.

In the cathedral *Treasury* is the Empress Constance's crown. It was taken from her tomb when this was opened during its removal from Cefalù, with fragments of her silk damask robe and pieces of jewellery. The crown is really a velvet cap within a golden circlet – most Byzantine.

In the *crypt* there is another Antonello Gagini: the sculptured *tomb* of his patron, Archbishop Giovanni Paternò (d. 1511) – a curious, high relief from which the head alone is brought into the round – a notable portrait.

Also here is the *tomb* of Frederick of Antioch in which is employed a sarcophagus of earlier date than the kneeling figure.

Here too, among the tombs of other archbishops, is that of the founder Gualtiero Offamílio, who died in 1190. This odd name represents an Italianization of 'Walter of the Mill' and he was an Englishman; not a nice or admirable one either. John Julius Norwich has much to say about him and his doings in *The Kingdom in the Sun*, as, too, about his fellow-English bishops and canons who generally bedevilled the Sicilian Norman court.

Church of Casa Professa
The Jesuits' church: in Via Ponticello, off Via Maqueda; Map **34.**

Built 1564–1636, it was badly damaged by bombs in 1943 and has been reconstructed. A church of splendid proportions. The *belfry* is built upon the square tower of the fifteenth-century *Palazzo Marchesi.*

Attached to the west of this church is the *Biblioteca Communale*, a library founded in 1760. It contains specimens of early printing and a quantity of manuscripts.

Church of La Gáncia (Santa Maria degli Ángeli)
In Via Alloro; Map **24.**

In the shade of the high wall of this fifteenth-century church's courtyard one feels less in Sicily than in Spain. Inside is a *Nativity* and a *Marriage of the Virgin* (in a stucco frame by Serpotta) by Vincenzo da Pavia; and, in a chapel, *reliefs* by Antonello Gagini and two *medallions* by him on the piers of the choir. The ringing of the bells of this church sounded the call to the abortive revolt of April 1860 led by Francesco Riso.

Church of La Magione
In the Piazza La Magione; Map **36.**

This Norman church is plain and masculine even for that masculine style of architecture, but of unusually spacious proportions. It was founded in 1150 by Matteo d'Aiello, Roger II's notable chief secretary, for a Cistercian convent, and dedicated to the Trinity. In 1193, Henry VI gave convent and church to the Teutonic Knights of Jerusalem for their hospice and chapel. From them it gets its name.

One is grateful that its bombing provided the opportunity to restore it to its Norman form.

Church of La Martorana (Santa Maria dell'Ammiráglio)
In the Piazza Bellini; Map **33.** *See also Church of San Cataldo (p.* 131).

This church was founded in 1143 by George of Antioch, Roger II's grand admiral, and it is one of the earliest Norman churches in Palermo. It was presented in 1433 to a convent, founded in 1194 by the Lady Eloisa Martorana, which adjoined it.

It was here in 1282, after the Sicilian Vespers, that the barons and the mayors of the cities met and decided to offer the crown of Sicily to Peter of Aragon.

In the sixteenth and seventeenth centuries, the building was enlarged by incorporating the atrium into the church, which meant pulling down the old narthex that had before connected the church to the beautiful *belfry*, which happily still stands before the door.

Inside, the later addition is at a lower level than the older part of the church. Its baroque decoration – the frescoes are by Borremans (1717) – make it seem rather like a drawing-room; but there are on the walls, preserved from the old narthex, two original, though much-restored, Norman *panels* in mosaic. The one represents the founder Grand Admiral at the feet of the Virgin, the other King Roger II crowned by Christ. The figure of the admiral has been shockingly badly restored at some time; compare this mosaic with that of Theodore Metochites offering the church he likewise founded – the Kariye Camii at Istanbul – to the Saviour. Norwich suggests that the figure of Roger is a portrait; the only one we have. A 100 l. coin dropped in a slot-machine illuminates these and the other mosaics. On the right – to the south – there is a most beautiful twelfth-century *door* of Arab workmanship. Outside are a few *arches* left from the twelfth-century cloister of the convent.

Up the steps in the old church one enters a different atmosphere, composed of a sturdier attitude towards religion and a proper sense of architecture. The *mosaics* are by Greek Byzantine artists. The scenes on the walls show the *Nativity*, the *Dormition of the Virgin* and the *Apostles*. In the cupola is *Christ, with angels, evangelists and prophets*. The central apse has been rebuilt – on the altar is an *Ascension* by Vincenzo da Pávia, of 1533 – but on either side the apses hold mosaics; *St Anne* and *St Joachim*. The *transennae* in front of these apses, and the inlaid *paving*, are particularly fine. The admiral was lavish with this small but jewel-like offering to the Madonna. Lord Norwich has much more, fascinating too, to say about this church.

Since 1953, the church has been given to the Uniate Greek Church and shares cathedral status with the old church at Piana degli Albanesi. The offices said are therefore according to the Greek rite; the priests, bearded and long-haired, wear the tall Greek hats and soutanes of a different cut from the Roman. (The small church on the same platform, see below, is San Cataldo.)

Church of Sant'Agostino.
Map 16.

This church occupies the corner of Via Sant'Agostino and Via Maestro d'Acqua. Its odd, late-thirteenth-century *doorway* of lava mosaic and the fine *rose-window* above it are of the fourteenth century. Serpotta stuccos grandly, graciously, but by no means altogether reverently, adorn the interior. This was remade in 1675 and Giácomo Serpotta (1656–1732) decorated it between 1711 and 1729; it is therefore a work of this wonderful sculptor's frivolous maturity. The whole church with its fourteenth-century *cloister*, its two almost primitive *Madonnas* on the south wall, the sumptuous *cupboards* in the sacristy and the enchanting *organ* (eighteenth-century), seems to suggest Christian Palermo as it set out to be – grave and Augustinian – and as it ended up, profane, sensual, elegant, though ultimately sad. None the less, Serpotta's work is superb.

Church of San Cataldo
In the Piazza Bellini and standing on the same platform as La Martorana;
Map 33.

On the eastern side of this church can be seen a small section of the Roman *city-wall*.

Built in 1161, this church has been restored to its early Arabo-Norman aspect. Its exterior is more worthy of attention for its form and detail than the stripped interior (which is usually shut; apply at La Martorana if you wish to enter it) although the *pavement* is beautiful, as are the proportions of the whole; and the interior of the domes most interestingly constructed.

Church of Santa Caterina
In the Piazza Bellini; Map 27.

Built 1566–96. The interior decoration is a good example of Sicilian baroque. However ornate it may be with its marble veneer, there is a kind of austerity about the background; upon this, the sculptured decoration is concentrated – itself bold, and repeating again the contrast between plain and decorated passages. The curves so typical of baroque are nearly always, in Sicily, more restrained by strong straight lines and plain passages than elsewhere, save in Spain – whence, of course, Sicily received the strongest influences at the time. Giacomo Amato, Andrea Palma and Gaetano Lazzara designed this, the second executing the main chapel, and the third the transepts and side chapels. They were aided by several other hands.

In the right-hand transept is a noble *statue* of Saint Catherine of Alexandria by Antonello Gagini, of 1534.

Church of Santa Cristina la Vétere
In the Cortile dei Pellegrini to the left, facing the Cappella dell'Incoronazione; Map **25.**

This little church was built by Walter of the Mill in 1171. It has recently been restored to its plain beauty of structure, but perhaps because of its plan – a 'central' one – you seem badly to miss the original decoration which must have lined it sumptuously with colour and rich textures.

Church of San Doménico
In the Piazza San Doménico, in Via Roma; Map **15.** *See also Oratório (p.* 135*).*

Off the Via Roma opens the Piazza San Doménico with the surprising and ornate *Colonna dell'Immacolata* built after the style of the Neapolitan *guglie* by Giovanni d'Amico in 1727 and topped by a Madonna by Giovanni Battista Ragusa.

San Doménico was rebuilt in 1640, though its façade belongs to 1726. Chapels in its rather splendid interior are ornamented by statues by Antonello and others of the Gagini family and school. The church is used as a modern Sicilian Pantheon – a use which never seems conducive to a warm religious atmosphere. It was here that Ruggero Séttimo convened the rebellious Sicilian parliament in 1848, and a suitable setting it seems for the histrionic liberals of that time (not, though, that the Sicilian parliamentarians were liberals, exactly).

Séttimo and Francesco Crispi are buried here among many others whose fame did not reach so far as theirs.

Church of San Francesco
Off the Via Paternostro, in a small piazza; Map **19.**

This was built in the thirteenth century (1255–77) like most Italian churches dedicated to St Francis of Assisi – its *doorway* with the zigzag decoration belongs to 1302, a period when devotion to the saint was at its zenith.

Inside, the baroque decoration has been removed since it was doubly damaged, by earthquake in 1823 and bombing in 1943, and one sees again the pleasing simplicity of its original shape to which the beautiful chapels of the next two centuries make the happiest of additions. Besides the eight Serpotta *statues* in the nave, the fourth chapel in the northern aisle, called the *Capella Mastrantonio*, was carved by Francesco Laurana and Pietro de Bontate (1468) – a superb Renaissance work; and in the westerly chapel there are two *Madonnas* by Doménico Gagini. In the southern aisle, the fourth chapel holds the marvellously delicate *tomb* of Elisabetta Omodei, who died in 1498. The *choir-stalls* of 1520–24 are very fine.

Church of San Giorgio dei Genovesi
In the Piazza San Giorgio; Map **7**. *If closed, key at No.* 17.

This was built by the Genoese colony in Sicily, Giorgio di Fáccio being the architect. Built between 1579 and 1591, it is a fine and noble church of the Italian Renaissance, a manner of which one sees little that is as pure as this in Sicily. There is too a satisfactori-ness in its being all of a piece, design, execution and furnishing, most of the last being that originally commissioned for it.

Church of San Giovanni degli Eremiti
In the Via dei Benedettini; Map **45**. *Closed on Fridays.*

Built – or rather adapted from the much larger mosque that it was built to be – by Roger II in 1132. A small, romantic church in a pretty cloistral garden, the delicate arches of which are Norman too, though belonging to the very end of the twelfth century. This is at once the nearest building to any Sicilian–Arab one extant, and the most famous Siculo-Norman church in Palermo. Now deconse-crated, it is yet not merely a museum; the interior, under the two small cupolas, has an elegant nave and three narrow apses.

Church of Santa Maria della Catena
At the sea end of the Corso Vittório Emanuele, close to the Porta Felice; Map **13**.

The Cala harbour used to be closed at nights with a chain stretched across it at water-level (a common device in the fifteenth and sixteenth centuries, still practised in the form of submarine nets during wartime), and from this the church takes its name – *catena* – 'chain'.

The church is late-fifteenth-century and the architect was Matteo Carnelivari. It has an arched *porch* which makes an odd and successful combination of late Gothic and Renaissance styles. Its *doors* are by Vincenzo Gagini. The widely proportioned interior is elegant and satisfying.

Church of Santo Spírito dei Vespri or Church of the Vespers
In the old cemetery of Sant'Orsola, Via del Vespro; Map **46**.

Built between 1173 and 1179, a small and most severe-looking church founded by Archibishop Offamílio – one might almost think as a penance for the richness of his cathedral, so strict and puritanically Norman is it.

It was the church of a Cistercian monastery – hence the strictness and severity of its design. The interior is as plain and heavy as north-English Norman, or Welsh, a very provincial style compared to the grandeurs of Palermo. Yet there are passages of exterior decoration which betray the Sicilian passion for richness.

The east end of the church is designed to be a sanctuary separate from the scheme of the main body.

It was here that an Angevin Frenchman insulted a Sicilian's bride as the couple left their nuptial Mass at the hour of Vespers on March 31st, 1282, Easter Tuesday – an insult which provoked a tumult that sparked off the volcanically successful rebellion of all Sicily against the tyranny imposed by Charles of Anjou: the massacre of the Sicilian Vespers.

Church of Santa Zita
Via Squarcialupo; Map **8**. *See Oratório below*.

Rebuilt between 1586 and 1603, it was badly damaged in the bombing of 1943. It retains a *tomb* by Antonello Gagini – that of António Scirotta in the second chapel to the left of the choir. Gagini also carved the *arches* of the apse and the *chapel* on the right of the choir. All these works belong to 1517–27 and were saved from the earlier building.

Oratório della Compagnia del Rosário di San Doménico
Via Bambinai; Map **15.**

Open The custodian lives at No. 16 and very much prefers to let one in only between 10.00 and 12.00.

The treasure of this seventeenth-century chapel is its altarpiece by Van Dyck: the *Virgin of the Rosary* with St Dominic and the four patronesses of Palermo – a painting from the Spanish Low Countries commissioned for Spanish Sicily. The other paintings on the walls are by Pietro Novelli, Lo Verde, Stomer, Luca Giordano, all of whom are put in their proper place by being hung in Van Dyck's first-rate company. Moreover, the incomparable Serpotta was let loose upon the walls.

Oratório della Compagnia del Rosário di Santa Zita
Next to the church of Santa Zita; Map **8.**

Serpotta again, and at the top of his amazing form. For all the rococo frilliness of the whole effect, the eye is constantly arrested by the vivid simplicity with which Serpotta states the facts of a leg, a neck, a rounded shoulder. Here the *reliefs* of New Testament history and that of the naval battle of Lépanto brilliantly demonstrate Serpotta's versatility.

Oratório della Compagnia di Santa Caterina
Via Monteleone; Map **11.** *The resident custodians will let you in if you ring.*

The pretty little courtyard and tiny vestibule so diminish one's sense of scale that upon entering this small chapel one is struck by its spaciousness – enough, it seems, to contain all heaven descending upon its walls in the lovely shapes of Serpotta's stuccos. How well adapted was his work to the decoration of rooms of this size!

Oratório della Compagnia di San Lorenzo
Via Immacolatella 5; Map **18.** *Ring at the door for admission.*

A masterpiece belonging to the last decade of the seventeenth century, Sicilian rococo at its best, and Serpotta at the height of his powers, this chapel is not to be missed. Extravagant, riotous and unfalteringly graceful, the white stucco figures descend in a cloud to the beautifully rich-coloured church furniture.

Caravággio's last painting (1609), a great canvas of the Nativity, used to hang over the altar, but was stolen in 1969. One hopes it may be recovered; it is a painting filled with appeal for help to combat despair; beautiful; disturbing.

SUBURBAN SIGHTS

Museo Pitrè and La Favorita

Lying on the Piano dei Colli, north of the city, on the Via La Favorita, leading to Pallavicino village and Mondello Lido; Map **1** *and* **2**. *All buses to Mondello pass the entrance.*

Open Daily. 09.15–13.00 and 15.00–18.00. A small entrance fee except on Sundays. Closed on Fridays. La Favorita is closed for the present.

The Villa la Favorita was built in the chinoiserie manner, in 1799, by Queen Maria Carolina as a retreat and a diversion during her husband Ferdinand II's first exile from Naples. The park was laid out by Ferdinand at the same time.

The Museo Pitrè or Museo Etnográfico now occupies the stables and service-block which stands beside the *Palazzina Cinese* itself.

The *palazzina*, washed in earthy reds and painted with imitation Chinese decoration, is very pretty and capricious, and it is good to see it being carefully restored, but sad that it is likely to be a long time closed because of this restoration.

The décor and furnishing of the upper rooms is rather too insistently charming to seem livable-in – it has the air of a too-elaborate joke: in its elaboration it reveals the appalling tedium of an exiled court and, in its smallness, a rather desperate attempt to achieve an intimacy impossible in the formal palaces of Naples, Caserta and Palermo.

There is a cumbersome lift by means of which the food, cooked next door, was hoisted to the servant-less dining-table on the first floor – one of the saddest contraptions anywhere to be seen. The ground-floor halls, decorated to simulate Pompeian ruins, are among the prettiest conceits to have come out of the eighteenth century. Nelson presented the royal couple with the *prints* on the ballroom walls. He was then living with Sir William and Lady Hamilton in the near-by Villa Palagonia.

The Museo Pitrè or Museo Etnográfico was founded in 1909 as a collection of Sicilian folk-art and to illustrate the popular customs, costumer and usages which were fast dying out. Among ex-voto paintings, painted carts, kitchen-ware and marionettes, there are several state and private carriages. This collection effectively illustrates the popular as against the aristocratic Sicily of which one sees so much.

La Zisa
Map **21**.

For the time being one must ignore this unique and most important monument. Years ago it was closed for restoration and some work was begun; since then – more open to damage by weathering than before – it has been allowed to rot. The 'competent' authorities in Sicily provoke one to violence.

Convento dei Cappuccini
Outside the Porta Nuova, in the Via dei Cipressi; Map **38**.

The convent is an old one, much altered at various times. Its interest lies in its *'catacombs'*, semi-subterranean passages along the walls of which, stacked in coffins, laid in niches or propped against the walls in ranks, are some 8,000 naturally mummified bodies of Palermitans who died before 1881, when interment here was discontinued. One enters by the door marked 'Catacombe'; tip the guardian.

The bodies are grouped in order of their temporal dignity – ecclesiastics, dons, nobles, women – and all quite extraordinarily dusty. The flesh has dried on the bones, the skin turned to parchment, and the expressions of each, distorted in the process of de-hydration, now lie about the living. These things are terrible as caricatures, yet amazingly beautiful; their dead and rotting clothes especially so. When a body finally falls apart it is often piously bundled into a bag of sacking from which protrude its death's-head and its very marvellous hands. The Palermitans used regularly to visit their dead here.

La Cuba
In a yard of the Caserma Tüköry (a barracks), No. **100** *Corso Calatafimi; Map* **47**. *You apply to the sentry and the officer of the guard sends a soldier to conduct you; no cameras allowed. Buses* 8 *or* 9 *from Piazza XIII Vittione*

This small but impressive shell of a pavilion belonged to a palace built by William II (1180) and called La Cuba from the Arabic for a dome – *kubbeh*. It was one of several such palaces – pleasances or pavilions – which the Norman kings built for themselves in a great park which stretched over this area, suitable settings for their Oriental manner of living.

It looks rather lost with goal-posts painted on its front, roofless and with its entrance blocked; but it has all the virtues of Norman architecture. Originally, it stood in an artificial lake and contained only the one high room decorated with niches ornamented with stalactitic forms in stucco. Boccaccio laid his 'Sixth Tale of Day Five' in La Cuba.

La Cúbula

*In the garden of the Villa Nápoli; Map **48**. Best entered under the archway of No. 375 Corso Calatafimi (a big new block) and the iron grilled gate to the right; a custodian or gardeners will let you in. Buses 8 or 9 from Piazza III Vittione.*

This arched and square-set pavilion belonged to William I's park (1160) and is remarkable for its wide *dome*, the decoration of which has, alas, now disappeared. As a garden kiosk it seems rather heavy, a fault to which Norman domestic architecture seems slightly prone, but it should be remembered that so much of the charm of these buildings lay in the contrast between the austerity of the exteriors and the richness of the interiors; these garden houses must have had a fantasticality of their own in their luxuriant setting of trees and ponds and avenues of which its present garden setting is a faded, if charming memory. The ruinous, eighteenth-century *Villa* incorporates the arches of the smaller *'Cúbula Soprana'* on its north-eastern side.

Ponte dell'Ammiráglio
*Beside the Corso dei Mille; Map **49**.*

This bridge crosses the old bed of the River Oreto, now diverted. A narrow bridge carried on arches, it was built in 1113 by the Grand Admiral George of Antioch. The fact that it was in use until this century – upon it Garibaldi's Thousand met the first Bourbon resistance to their entry into Palermo (May 27th, 1860) – is a testament to Norman engineering; yet it is also remarkable for the aesthetic excellence of its design. Not less remarkable is the squalor which governmental indifference allows to surround this monument.

Church of San Giovanni dei Lebbrosi (St John of the Lepers)
A little hard to reach, east of the Corso dei Mille; Map **50**.

Founded in 1070 by Count Roger, it is consequently one of the oldest Norman churches extant although it was not completed until the twelfth century, when a lazaretto was added to it. It has recently been restored to its original state, barring the internal decoration. Small and severe, despite its domes, it is a beautiful example of the architecture of the period. The *campanile* was added, in suitable style, in 1934 and the excavated bases of walls in the vicinity belonged to an Arab building which the Norman replaced.

It is hoped that the key will be found (see p. **29**) and given to a near-by guardian, or try the Soprintendenza ai Monumenti. You might also complain about this building's leprous surroundings.

Palazzo di Favara or di Mare Dolce
In an unpaved back-street south-west of the town, the Vicolo Castellacei, off Via Emiro Giafar (No. 19 *for the keys) and under the lee of Monte Grifone (Route Exit H). Though hemmed in by other buildings, it is recognizable by the Norman decoration along its parapet. Bus* 11.

This palace was originally built as a country pleasance by the emir Giafar between 997 and 1019. It was surrounded, on three sides at least, by a vast artificial lake with a large island in it, and by an extensive park, and was probably the Normans' model for their own park closer to the city. It was in fact rebuilt by Roger II. What remains is part of one wing of his palace. It contains the restored *chapel* (for which, like the garden, you need the keys). Walk round the left hand of the buildings and into the rural squatter-like cottages which surround what was once the central courtyard of the palace – conservationists will be saddened, lovers of the picturesque less so.

Here Frederick II spent most of his comparatively penurious childhood – that strange, brilliant child growing up under the tutelage of Cardinal Cencio Savelli, later Pope Honorius III, and falconing on the hills beyond the gardens. A contemporary description of him at thirteen (translated and quoted by Georgina Masson in *Frederick II of Hohenstaufen*) says:

neither small nor taller than one would expect of his age ... robust limbs and a strong body, with which his vigorous spirit

can achieve whatever he undertakes. He is never idle, but passes
the whole day in some occupation or other, and so that his
vigour may increase with practice, he fortifies his agile body
with every kind of exercise and practice of arms ... He loves
fast thoroughbred horses: and I believe that no one knows
better than he how to curb them with the bridle and then set
them at full gallop ...

To this is added a regal majesty and majestic features and
mien, to which are united a kindly and gracious air, a serene
brow, brilliant eyes, and expressive face, a burning spirit, and
a ready wit. Nevertheless his actions are sometimes odd and
vulgar, though this is not due to nature but to contact with
rough company ... He is intolerant of admonitions, and judges
himself capable of acting according to his own free will, and
considers it shameful for himself to be subject to a guardian
and to be considered a boy ... transgressing with the freedom
customary to kings. However he has virtue in advance of his
age ... he is well-versed in knowledge and has the gift of
wisdom ... In him, then, the number of the years do not count,
nor is there need to await maturity, because as a man he is full
of knowledge, and as a ruler of majesty.

In the year of this description he came of age and led a force over
the island to reclaim his royal ownership of the demesne of Sicily,
which had been annexed by others; and he was married nine months
later. By the time he was seventeen he had asserted his authority
over the whole of the Holy Roman Empire.

Behind the palace lies a huge *citrus grove* which covers the former
lake and the island. The garden-side walls of the palace have been
less defaced than the outer by centuries of squatters and you can see
the cemented lower walls which held the waters of the lake, and
walk on the island where there are date-palms. This is the nearest
we can get to Norman Palermo – and in the lemon-scented evening
it can seem very close indeed. (A driver who took me there was
ginger-haired and had fair, freckled skin and Norman features – of
Frederick's own type, and a type not infrequent in Sicily even now.)

The uncompleted ring-road round the city halts end-on to the
garden, a part of which will be sacrificed to continue it. The road is
needed, but not well planned, thus still further damaging – out-
raging – the poetry which once made Palermo a most special place.

The spring of Mare Dolce, flowing from under the hill of Monte Grifone at the top of the garden, is now mostly piped to the city water-supply, and the double-arched structure which sheltered the stream that supplied the garden is now a ruin, blocked up; a quarry devours the hill and ugliness closes in on all sides. If the Government cannot rescue La Favara it does not deserve the position of responsibility to which it has climbed; Italia Nostra, HELP!

Environs

MONDELLO LIDO
About 10 km. north of the city (Route Exit A), and the favourite Palermitan seaside resort. Buses 14 or 15 from Central Station, 6 from Piazza Verdi. (For hotels, see under Palermo.)

As the sandy beach stretches for 1½ miles its popularity is not surprising. At the southern end, *Monte Pellegrino* rises above **Valdesi** village and at the northern end, *Monte Gallo* above **Mondello** proper, where there is a medieval *watch-tower*.

MONTE PELLEGRINO
About 5 km. to the north (Route Exit B), this mountain forms the western headland of the Conca d'Oro. To ascend it, take bus No. 12 from Piazza XIII Vittione which continues across it to Valdesi on Mondello bay.

The mountain is 1,969 feet high and rich in prehistoric sites. It was called Heirkte in Greco-Carthaginian times and during the first Punic War was held as a fortress for three years by Hamilcar Barca against a Roman siege (247–245 B.C.). The sanctity of the mountain and the pilgrimage of its name are due to Santa Rosália, the Norman princess* (p. 127) who retired to a hermitage on these heights. The cult of Santa Rosália dates from the seventeenth century, as does the zigzag *Scala Vécchia* which mounts from Le Falde between the Primo Pizzo (where stands the huge 'Castello Utveggio') and the Pizzo Grattarola.

The *Santuário di Santa Rosália* clusters around a *cave*, converted into a chapel to the saint in 1625. The trickles of water seeping down the walls are believed to have miraculous properties. The *statue* is

* There is no historical record of such a lady.

by Gregório Tedeschi, the *painting* of the saint's crowning is by Núnzio la Mantia.

A path leads in a half-hour walk on to the *Semáforo*, lying just under the summit. The colossal *statue* some distance to the northeast of the summit is, of course, Santa Rosália. Although now largely motor-borne, the pilgrimage here on July 11th–15th and September 4th are still events, the earlier being the bigger.

The coast road east of Monte Pellegrino passes Addaura, from which the caves take their name. They lie up the spur which forms, at its end, the *Punta di Priola* and can be visited only with the permission and aid of the Soprintendenza alle Antichità at Palermo. Any date given to the incised drawings on the walls of these caves is as yet provisional, but they seem to be Paleolithic rather than early Neolithic; and they have the *feel* of hunters' art elsewhere. They are well reproduced, with other finds from the caves, in the Museo Nazionale Archeológico (see p. 118).

BAIDA AND SAN MARTINO DELLE SCALE

Route Exit E. Bus 23 to Baida. Pullman excursion buses to San Martino go on Sundays and holidays from Piazza Verdi.

The road passes **Altarello** (4 km.). Here, in the Via Lóggia, stands the *Palazzo dell'Uscibene*. This ruined hall belonged to a Norman palace situated within the precincts of the park in which La Zisa and La Cuba stood. It has niches in its walls decorated with seashells in stucco, a tantalizing hint of much delightful embellishment that has vanished from surviving buildings of the period.

At 5 km., it passes **Boccadifalco**, 'the falcon's beak', so called from the crag on which the village stands and commands the pass into the beautiful upland *Valle del Paradiso*.

From Boccadifalco **Baida** is 2 km. off to the right, under the 3,445-foot peak of *Monte Cúccio*. This hamlet is the descendant of a tenth-century Arab one (called 'white' – *baidhâ*) which the Benedictine monks of Castellaccio annexed when they were driven from their hilltop by the powerful Manfred Chiaramonte. Here they built a new monastery between 1377 and 1388, but this foundation was declining by 1499 and Archbishop Paternò took the building over as a summer palace for the bishops of Palermo. Since 1595 it has belonged to the Observantine order. The late-fifteenth-century *church* with a slightly later *doorway* contains a beautiful *John the Baptist* by Antonello Gagini.

8 km. farther up the Valle del Paradiso, among pine forests, is **San Martino delle Scale**, a hill resort. The *monastery* itself was perhaps founded by St Gregory in the sixth century, but was re-built in 1346 and altered at various times, then enlarged by Viceroy Marvuglia in the late eighteenth century. It is now a college and orphanage. There is a Zoppo di Ganci painting of the *Magi* in the church.

Hotels (at San Martino delle Scale)
3rd Class   *Ai Pini.*
4th Class   *Miramonte.*

MONREALE

8 km. south-west of Palermo (Route Exit F) and 925 feet up. Bus 9 from Piazza XIII Vittione. By car you can continue on to Partinico (see Palermo to Trápani, Route 1).

Population
Over 23,000.
Hotels
2nd Class   *Carrubella Park Hotel.*
3rd Class   *Il Ragno.*
4th Class   *Savóia.*
Restaurant
The *Carrubella* has a superb position and furnishes the town with its first respect-able restaurant.

Cathedral

The whole reason for Monreale's existence is the cathedral which William the Good built there during years of concentrated work from its foundation in 1172 or 1173 until 1186, when the doors were put in place, the detail of decoration perhaps taking another twenty years to complete. The town grew up around it and remains today a 'cathedral town' in the strictest sense. When first built, the cathedral and the monastery attached to it, with, perhaps, some neighbouring royal buildings, stood upon the edge of the royal park.

And what a church it is! It was one of the wonders of the world in its day, and has remained so ever since. When you arrive in the cathedral square you are less struck by its beautiful exterior than by its tremendous *presence*. If there is an example of the mystic idea that beauty exists in an eternal present, this is it: this cathedral was born, like Pallas Athene, fully mature and in all its beauty, strength and power – and at an instant which has not yet ceased to tingle with the joy of the event.

The exterior is comparatively plain and massive: one tower is incomplete; the *west porch* is eighteenth-century; the long *portico* on the north side is by Gian Doménico and Fazio Gagini, and therefore of the later sixteenth century. Bold almost to harshness, the decoration on the west front – of blind interlacing arches in lava and limestone supported by light columns of white marble – makes very worth-while the small pilgrimage northwards, under the arches holding up the *Cappella del Crocifisso*, to see the apses, on which this motif is repeated with still greater authority and effect.

The bronze *doors* in the western porch are by Bonanno da Pisa, 1186; those in the northern porch date from 1179 and are by Barisano da Trani. By these latter it is usual to enter the church.

Interior: more than three times as long as the Cappella Palatina (p. 121), the interior measures 335 feet by 131 feet – upon entering, one opens one's eyes wide in wonder. It is as if, after Cefalù and the royal chapel, Norman ideas of what churches should be had blossomed into a flower as surprising and simple as that of a great cactus. And, too, it was a final and lucid statement of Norman assurance which needed no elaboration, only size – and to be signed in gold.

The *columns* of the nave are all of Roman origin, and all save one of *cipollino*. Ceres and Persephone appear on the antique capitals. The *ceiling* had to be replaced after a fire in 1811, and this was done over-exuberantly – but that over the choir is original.

The dazzling *mosaics* over the arches of the nave tell – from the eastern end of the southern wall, across the western door, and returning from west to east on the northern wall – the story of the Creation and Old Testament. In the aisles, above the beautiful marble *dado*, the mosaics show Christ's teaching, scenes of the miracles and the Passion, and others of the teaching of SS. Peter and Paul fill the transepts and choir and close the cycle. SS. Peter and Paul stand in the side apses while, in the great central one, rising above the saints, angels and the enthroned Madonna, is Christus Benedicens. This figure is perhaps less spiritually imposing than the earlier one at Cefalù – and relies on its blue bulk for its right to dominate the whole – but it is nevertheless the one inescapable feature of the church: the power of God directing the works of men.

The mosaics of Cefalù are the earliest; those of the Cappella Palatina are a little later, and these come some forty years later still – a period representing at least a whole generation of artists. There is, consequently, a marked development in style. Whereas Cefalù is very Byzantine, and much of the ornamentation of the Cappella Palatina is too, although the artists seem to be feeling their way towards a less rigid adherence to traditional Byzantine forms, here at Monreale their pupils and their pupils' pupils have created a far freer and altogether more Western interpretation of their art. Mosaic is necessarily an inflexible medium lending itself best to the making of simple and graphic statements, yet here at Monreale the budding humanism of the age has prompted an indigenous generation of artists to force their little stones to obey a fresh invention and a new and subtler sense of symbolism. Mosaic can hardly be pushed farther in this direction; after this one must turn to fresco and the fluidity of brushwork, although this is to sacrifice that directness of impact and that lambent quality of mosaic which was so well suited to religious illustration. A quite unusual feature, here, is the use of an undulating landscape flowing, as it were, in syncopated rhythm upon the drum-beat of the arching.

Among the saints in the centre apse is St Thomas à Becket, martyred only about eight years before the mosaic was made. He stands in the lower, right-hand rank of saints; the middle figure. His presence here is a little odd since William II's wife was Joan of England and his father-in-law therefore Henry II, who had wished to be rid of the turbulent priest. St Thomas was prime champion of the Church's claim to the right to rule the kings and to maintain its liberty of action in their kingdoms, and their mutual opposition to this was something that united the ruler of England and Norman Sicily: but, interfering as the archbishop had been in life (he had meddled in Sicilian affairs also), he was now safely dead and canonized, and vastly revered throughout Roman Christendom as a result of the Church's able propaganda on his behalf. Yet another explanation suggests itself: a surprisingly well-substantiated suggestion is put forward by Hugh Ross-Williamson that Becket's death was in fact that of the 'witch king' – or rather that he was sacrificed in Henry's place as a surrogate. The Normans were, of course, pagans before they came south into France, Britain, Italy and the Levant – and were barbarians in the old Greek sense of the word. There is a lot that is still mysterious about them, and some quality in their works – even here where everything Norman is so highly coloured by Islamic and Christian influences – touches off a tingling excitement in us, the source of which we do not know how to define. Is there, under all this Oriental and intellectual passion for the Christian story, a secret and chthonic undercurrent which Normans, Britons and most likely the Sicilians too, could understand as giving another dimension to their religion, but of which we have by now forgotten all meaning? Yet, in a beautiful mosaic above the royal throne, William II offers his cathedral to the Virgin – but, for him, was she all Virgin as we know her, or in part Persephone also?

King William I, the builder's 'Bad' father who died in 1166, lies in a porphyry sarcophagus in the *chapel* south of the choir. There William II is also buried, in a white marble sepulchre of 1575. In the northern chapel, beside the choir, lie the rest of William I's family, his wife Margaret, and his sons Roger and Henry; these tombs are reconstructions dating from 1846. Here also is an inscription marking the place where the body of St Louis of France rested on its way from the disastrous Tunisian crusade back to Paris.

In the *Treasury* are precious things; and the view from the roof of the church is a stupendous one.

Cloisters

The twelfth-century cloisters of the Benedictine monastery adjoining the south of the cathedral are almost as famous as the church itself. There is a separate entrance on the south side of the cathedral square.

This very large cloister is arcaded on all four sides: 216 slim pairs of columns, of very varied design and each having an elaborately carved, unique capital of marvellous workmanship, carry as many pointed arches. It has gone rather too far for beauty and lacks the architectural setting which could have made sense of so much repetition and so wide a space. What *is* beautiful, though, is the Arabic *fountain* which stands in a colonnaded enclosure of its own in the south-west corner.

Behind the monastery is a little garden *belvedere* with a delightful view over the Oreto Valley to the hills and the sea.

In the courtyard of the *seminary* (No. 1 Via Arcivescovado), some remains of William II's palace can still be seen. It is best to ask to go into the building.

ALTOFONTE (or PARCO)

12 *km. along the Piana degli Albanesi (p. 289) road (Route Exit G).*

A copious spring at the top of the hill on which this little town stands, as well as its desirably beautiful view made this an ideal site for the royal hunting-lodge palace which Roger II built here on the very edge of the great royal park. In 1307 the place was turned into a Capuchin monastery which its abbot, Cardinal Scipio Borghese, rebuilt in 1618. Under all this – or rather under the remains of all this – there is still the Norman palace chapel and some surrounding fabric of Roger's building. To see this, you enter the arched doorway left of the *Chiesa Madre*, in the town's only square, and ask at the sacristy, on the right as you enter. The *chapel* has a single nave and is broad and high, a beautiful space off which only one apse opens, the lateral ones being suggested by niches.

CHURCH OF SANTA MARIA DI GESÙ

4 *km. to the south-east of Palermo (Route Exit H) on the slopes of Monte Grifone, in the Via Santa Maria di Gesù, which is a continuation of the Via Guadaqua. Bus 10.*

This church dates from 1426. It is best known for its marvellous morning view, but the place is charming and also contains the arcaded *tomb* of one António Alliata by Antonello Gagini (1524) – the urn from which has been moved to the vestibule of the sacristy – and the lovely Gothic *Cappella la Grua* with faded Spanish frescoes of the late fifteenth century.

ÚSTICA ISLAND

Population
Over 1,250.
Hotels
2nd Class †*Grotta Azzurra* (San Ferlícchio district).
3rd Class *Cottage Hotel* (Mezzaluna district) ;
           Diana ;
           Patrice ;
           Stella Marina.
4th Class *Isola Bella.*
Pensions
3rd Class *Ariston* ;
           †*Clélia.*

A three-hour sail from the Stazione Maríttima (*Map* **4**); daily in summer; winter on Mondays, Wednesdays, Fridays and Saturdays.

Hydrofoil also during summer. The lonely and much-weathered crater of a long extinct volcano, this restfully pastoral island can have been inhabited only in peaceful times. Efforts are being made to promote it as a tourist resort – and a very good one it could make. For the present, however, the accommodation is simple though pleasant, and no nicer place in which to lie in the sun and enjoy the clean sea could be imagined.

The skin-diving and fishing is admirable; also good quail-shooting in season.

A Tourist Village is planned for 1972.

PALERMO TO TRÁPANI

Route 1 (Route Exit F.) By the S.S.186 (Monreale – p. 143 – is a short diversion off this road) then the S.S.113 after Partinico to Álcamo, Calatafimi station (for Segesta, a diversion of 6 km. in all) and Trápani (122 km.). **Route 2** (Route Exit D.) By the S.S.113 via Sferracavallo and the coast, continuing on the 187 to Castellammare and Trápani (102 km.), Érice being a diversion off the road 15 km. longer.
Rail Fairly frequent trains. The journey by *rápido* takes 2 hours 15 minutes. (Segesta, 1 hour 15 minutes) and, by *diritto*, 3 hours 15 minutes.
Bus Buses generally take the S.S.113 via Segesta; Castellammare is best reached by train.

ROUTE 1

Accommodation en route At Partinico; Álcamo.

Leave Palermo by the Corso Calatafimi, branching left (5 km.) if you do not want to ascend to Monreale (3 km.) as directed. (Older rebels may care to make the pilgrimage to Montelepre, the bandit Giuliano's centre of operations. To do this you should leave Palermo by the Via Dante to its end in a T-junction, turn left and half-right in the Piazza Principe di Camporeale, up the Via Noce and continue on to Montelepre, 25 km.; rejoin the S.S. 113 at Partinico (34 km.).)

[29 km.] **Partinico.** This distressingly poor town of over 25,000 inhabitants was the birthplace of Giuliano, the bandit whose fame and glamour has now been eclipsed by that of the more serious and intellectual Che Guevara, but who does not deserve to be forgotten.

It has now become famous for Danilo Dolci's heroic campaign to get a dam built despite the opposition of vested criminal interests.

Hotel
4th Class   *Monte Cesaro'.*

[68 km.] **Álcamo,** a town founded by Frederick II in 1233, contains some quite interesting churches.

Hotels
4th Class   *Centrale;*
             Miramare.

[85 km.] From Calatafimi station Segesta is on the right.

SEGESTA

History

Sometimes it seems as if the Greeks of the west chose their city sites with an even sharper eye for their natural beauty than the Greeks of the fatherland – and it may well be so, since most of the cities of Greece have been where they are since time immemorial, whereas, to a certain extent, the colonial Greeks could pick and choose as they liked.

What is extraordinary, however, is that Egesta (Segesta) was not a true Greek city, nor was its temple – a marvellous Doric building – the work of Greeks, although its architect could have been a Greek.

The Elymians, the people who built it, and who also occupied Érice (p. 157) and Trápani (p. 153), claimed to be of Trojan and Achaean (that is, Mycenaean) descent. They appear to have settled in this part of Sicily in the twelfth century B.C. and they may have been right, up to a point, in making their claim. Their 'Trojan' origin could have been a way of saying that their homeland had been in Hellenized Asia Minor and their migration forced on them by the great upheaval that ended the Mycenaean era. They rapidly adopted Greek ways after the eighth century B.C. despite the continual warfare which they waged against Selinunte from 580 B.C. onwards. (See History of Syracuse, p. 212.) In 409 B.C., the Elymians' ally, Carthage, destroyed Selinunte, but this was done at the price of their own independence. Segesta was saved by Carthage from an attack by Dionysius of Syracuse in 397 B.C., but, in 307 B.C., Agathocles of Syracuse slaughtered, it is said, 10,000 of the citizens, enslaving the rest, only to repeople it with Greeks and call it Dikaeopolis. Again it came under the patronage of Carthage (and reverted to its old name), but, during the first Punic War, the Segestans murdered the Carthaginian garrison by treachery and made themselves the allies of Rome, suffering, in consequence, a Carthaginian siege. The town was finally destroyed by the Arabs in the tenth century A.D.

Very little now remains except the superb unfinished temple, standing on one spur, and the theatre, standing on another and a higher one of Monte Rontanelle.

Temple

This stands nearly 1,000 feet above sea-level – its dedication is unknown. It is a Doric peripteral hexastyle* and dates from the second half of the fifth century B.C. The peristasis of 36 columns, each 30 feet high, stands upon a stylobate measuring 200 feet by 86 feet. The entablature and pediments are intact. The metopes, in a manner a little old-fashioned for its date, are longer than their height and, indeed, all the horizontal lines of the building are emphasized in one way or another.

The pillars are smoothed ready for fluting, a process which was normally done after erection, but here work on the building was abandoned before this was begun. The surfaces of the steps of the stylobate, though they have been given the slightly convex curve which would help lighten the effect of the temple while also seeming to settle it firmly on the hillside, retain the bosses, intended to have been chiselled away, by which the stones were hauled from the quarry and into position. The cella – the sanctuary – which was to have stood within the peristyle, was never built.

Without the dark cella, one is more prone than ever to stand within the colonnade of its pillars and look outwards at the ravishing landscape surrounding – which is exactly contrary to the builders' conception of a temple. Temples were often, as here, placed upon commanding heights, though this was often because they contained treasuries and were best set in defensible positions – or as a symbolic tribute to the deity's authority. The temple itself

* Readers are reminded of the Glossary of Architectural and Archaeological Terms on p. 315.

was regarded as a casket containing the holiness of the deity and that of the various sacred objects – from the image itself to the votive offerings. Sacrifice to the deity was made on an altar standing before the door of the cella, but quite apart from the temple. A temple, in fact, was inward-looking and no matter what skill and expense was lavished on its exterior, this only redounded the more to the honour of what lay within.

To a great extent each temple was designed as a self-sufficient unit having no reference to its site, but only to its purpose. It was Athenian architects who discovered both the need to design buildings to accord with their sites and the art with which to do this within the limits of traditional design, and, considering the appositeness of this temple to its setting, Professor Lawrence suggests that the architect was in fact an Athenian. Hence the emphasis upon the horizontal in the building: from the front, contrasting it with the height behind and below; from the side, carrying it out like a prow from the slope of the spur.

The survival, even in ruin, of so many Doric temples where all else save foundations of later buildings have disappeared, is due to the fact that their builders underestimated the strength of the stone they built with. The earlier temples of Greece had been built of wood, which dictated both the form and much of the engineering that went to the construction of stone Doric temples. It was not until the fourth century B.C. that the Greeks learned that they had been building at a quite unnecessary cost in money and effort to ensure the stability of a stone structure. Upon this discovery, the Doric order was abruptly replaced by the far lighter Ionian, at a decided loss to the grandeur of the temple building; and to our cost, since too few Ionian temples – most particularly so in Sicily, so beautiful too in their different ways – have survived those vicissitudes of time and history which the over-extravagantly built Doric temples have managed to withstand.

Theatre

Lying near the summit of Monte Bárbaro, at 1,362 feet, the semi-circular *cavea* is 207 feet in diameter and has 20 rows of seats, the whole cut out of the rock. It is Hellenistic in date. Only the base of the *scena* remains, but the wonderful view towards the Gulf of Castellammare is spread before you, altered only in detail from early times: the woods that once covered the mountains have dwindled, and a part of Calatafimi shows, where no town used to be; a road and a railway wind through the valley where there was only a track, but none of this in any way diminishes this most moving of places in which to have sat through the day listening to poetry whose beauty too is undiminished.

There is a Tourist Board café near the temple at which refreshments can be bought.

[122 km.] You reach Trápani.

ROUTE 2

Accommodation en route At Sferracavallo; Ísola delle Fémmine; Cínisi; Balestrate; Álcamo Marina; Castellammare del Golfo; Érice.

Leave Palermo by the Viale della Libertà and at the roundabout of Piazza Vittório Véneto keep straight on by the Via Resuttano. Do *not* join the motorway to Punta Ráisi airport.

[12 km.] **Sferracavallo**, a port and lido.

Hotel
3rd Class   †*Bellevue del Golfo.*

[14 km.] A right-hand branch-road to **Ísola delle Fémmine**, a lido.

Hotels
2nd Class   †*Saracen Sands.*
4th Class   *Scogliera Azzurra.*

A big new hotel is to open in 1972 which will offer facilities for thermal and sea-bathing cures.

[32 km.] A turning left to **Cínisi**.

Hotels
3rd Class   *Madonia.*
4th Class   *Itália.*

[33 km.] A turning right for **Terrasini** where two second-class hotels and a Tourist Village are shortly opening.

[51 km.] **Balestrate.**

Hotel
4th Class   *Del Golfo.*

[59 km.] **Álcamo Marina,** a lido.

Hotel
4th Class   *La Battigia.*

[65 km.] **Castellammare del Golfo.** A less engaging place than one hopes.

Hotels
3rd Class   †*Punta Nord Est.*
4th Class   *Autostelle A.C.I.* ;
            Terme Segestane (Ponte Bagni).

[88 km.] A turning right leading, in 23 km., to **San Vito lo Capo.**

Hotels
2nd Class   †*Cala' mpiso.*
3rd Class   *Capo San Vito.*
4th Class   *La Conchíglia.*

[94 km.] A turning right, 7·5 km., to Érice (see p. 157).

[103 km.] You reach Trápani.

TRÁPANI

Air
Connections with Palermo, Pantelleria (airport at Chinisia and Lampedusa).
Sea
Steamer connections to Pantelleria and Egadi islands and occasionally from Palermo, Genoa, Cágliari, Tunis.
Rail
Palermo, Agrigento (direct).
Bus
Connections to Palermo, Érice, Mazara, Álcamo and towns on these routes.
Information
E.P.T. office, Corso Itália.
Tourist Information Office, Piazza Saturno.
Bathing
Bathing can be had at Lido di San Giuliano. Or continue 7 km. along the north-east coast-road to Pizzolungo (for its hotels, see under Trápani).
Hotels
2nd Class   *Nuovo Russo,* Via Tintori 6 ;
            †*Tirreno* (Pizzolungo).
3rd Class   *L'Approdo* (Pizzolungo) ;
            Vittróia, Piazza Vittório Emanuele.
4th Class   *Aosta* (Casa Santa) ;
            Miramare, Via Serraino Vulpitta 4 ;
            Moderno, Via Tenente Genovesi 20 ;
            Sole, Piazza Umberto I.

Pensions
3rd Class   *Aristón,* Vico Palazzo Senatorio 4 ;
                Maccotta Via degli Argentieri 4 ;
                Messina, Corso Vittório Emanuele 87.
(The sensible tourist who enjoys quiet will stay at Érice (p. 157), or at Pizzolungo
for the bathing also.)

The nearest point of the island to Africa, once a Phoenician base
against the Greeks of eastern Sicily, and later an important link
between the island and Spain, Trápani is a provincial capital with a
population of 80,000.

This is not one of the towns on most visitors' sight-seeing lists
and contains nothing of especial interest; yet its older parts make
it a delightful and very Sicilian place where good buildings of
various periods stand shoulder to shoulder along the streets of the
old town. It has grown enormously and hideously on its inland
side, and the huge gaps which bombing tore in the solidity of the
old quarters are filling up with tall new blocks.

Here the land runs out to sea in a long flat promontory curved
like the blade of a scimitar. The old town occupies its base; the
ancient one – Drepanon – was probably farther up its length.

Tunny fishing (*la mattanza*), which takes place in June off the
coast here, is being pushed these days as a tourist attraction. But
since the great fish are trapped in corrals of netting, harpooned and
bludgeoned to death by the fishermen before they are hoisted
aboard, the method is less attractive than effective. A tunny fish is
incised among the prehistoric drawings on Lévanzo Island. There
is still a certain ritualistic character to the *mattanza*; it is directed by
the chief fisher, or Raís, whose title is of Arabic origin.

HISTORY

Drepanon was an Elymian city and the port for Eryx. Samuel
Butler and Robert Graves think the *Odyssey* was written here – by
a princess. The topographical arguments for this view are ingenious
and the controversy has a Baconian charm.

This may have been the site of that almost legendary, ill-fated
Heraklea which Dorieus founded. Not an easily defensible site, in
remote times settlements here may well have come and gone with
some frequency.

The port of Drepanon became a full-blown city when Hamilcar Barca brought people down here from Eryx in 260 B.C. Catulus (not the poet) took it for the Romans in 241 B.C.

Its still evident, late-medieval prosperity derived from its convenience as a port linking Tunis with Anjou, Naples and Aragon in the thirteenth century. Tunis is only just below the visible horizon, and the town's close connection with Africa goes back to Carthaginian times. The King of Navarre, Theobald, died here in 1270 of fever contracted when crusading against Tunis. There is a story that good John of Procida conferred secretly with the organizers of the revolt of the Sicilian Vespers at the end of the cape, and Peter of Aragon in fact landed here in 1282 when he accepted the Sicilian throne after the Vespers. Charles V – whose interests again took him campaigning against Tunis in 1535 – made good use of this base.

PRINCIPAL SIGHTS

Church of San Doménico
By Via Garibaldi.

Fourteenth-century.

Município
Via Torrearsa.

An enchanting piece of civic pride, 1696.

Church of Collégio
Corso Vittório Emanuele.

This has a fine baroque *façade* (1636) and sumptuously carved eighteenth-century *cupboards* in the sacristy by Pietro Orlando. Here the twenty famous and beautiful *misteri* – wooden statues of the eighteenth century – are kept; they are carried in the Good Friday procession round the town.

Il Palazzo
Southern sea-front.

A fourteenth-century palace, several times enlarged.

Church of Sant'Agostino
Off Via Torrearsa.

Templar church with fourteenth-century *door* and *rose-window*.

Church of Santa Maria del Gesù
Among the rebuilding of the San Pietro quarter.

It has a Renaissance *south door*; a traditional sixteenth-century *west façade*; a very beautiful Andrea della Róbbia *Madonna* inside; and a *baldacchino* by Antonello Gagini, of 1531.

Palazzo della Giudecca
Eastern quarter, old ghetto.

A sixteenth-century Spanish plateresque building with five windows and an embossed tower.

Walking through the streets you will see numerous other lesser buildings of the fourteenth, fifteenth and sixteenth centuries, many with doorways of a noble simplicity.

Environs

Sanctuary of the Annunciation and Museo Nazionale Pépoli
Once outside the town, this large sanctuary is now in the suburbs, 2 miles to the east of the centre. Trolley-bus No. 1 (black letters).

Open (museum) 09.30–16.00 Tuesdays to Saturdays; 09.30–13.00 on Sundays and holidays; closed on Mondays.

Founded in 1315 but rebuilt in 1760 – excepting the front doorway, the rose-window and the northern door. Inside, the *Cappella dei Pescatori* (of the Fishers) has a graceful fourteenth-century *arcade*; the *Cappella dei Marinai* (of the Sailors) is Renaissance; sixteenth-century *doors* behind the High Altar lead to the *Cappella della Madonna* itself. The figures on the inner arch leading into the sanctuary are by the Gaginis; its grille is late-sixteenth-century. The Madonna so much venerated here is a beautiful fourteenth-century Pisan-school one.

In the adjoining convent is now the *Museo Nazionale Pépoli*. On the ground floor are some pedestrian Gaginis, though there is a really fine *St James the Great* by Antonello (1522). The *stoop* of 1486, from the Annunziata, on the stairs, is much admired. Upstairs is a dull Titian of the *Stigmata of St Francis* and various things salvaged from churches. The big canvas, on the stairs, of *Jupiter hailing Napoleon* is, I think, one of the world's funniest paintings, unconsciously. But what makes this collection well worth visiting are three medieval paintings: the *polyptych* of the Virgin with saints from which the Sicilian 'Maestro del polittico di Trápani' takes his name; the wonderful *Pietà* of Roberto di Oderísio, a Neapolitan (1380); and the *Madonna Enthroned*, attributed to a Palermitan painter (*c.* 1450). There is also a quite interesting archaeological section.

ÉRICE

Population
Over 1,600.
Information
Azienda Autónoma, Via G. F. Guarnocchi 17.
Hotels
1st Class   *Jolly.*
3rd Class   *La Pineta.*
Pensions
3rd Class   *delle Ortensie;*
             Edelweiss.

14 km. north-east of Trápani, Mount Eryx is still pretty impregnable. The infrequent buses take an hour to climb it; No. 2 trolley-bus takes you in ten minutes to the cable-railway (insist on being put off at the right spot, you will miss it otherwise), but the cable-car goes only hourly between 08.00 and 19.00. Either way, the views as you ascend are tremendous.

So surprisingly high a hill – 2,454 feet – standing alone as it does, Mount Eryx is a positive invitation to myth and mysticism. Apart from its long association with Aphrodite (see p. 71), the mountain acquired a legendary fame both for being impregnable and for the watch it kept over Carthage and, later, Tunis; a sharp lookout, it was said, could count the ships that put out from there (on a clear day, for otherwise Cape Bon is lost in the haze). Pyrrhus took the city, though, and in 260 B.C. so did Hamilcar Barca, who destroyed it. The Roman consul, Junius Pullus, seized it in 248 B.C. and was there besieged by Hamilcar, while Hamilcar was blockaded by another Roman army below him – a stalemate that was ended by the

Roman naval victory at Drepanon. Tiberius and Claudius restored (and made too fine) the temple. For the Arabs this was *Gebel 'Hamed* – 'Mahomet's mountain' – and when Count Roger besieged it he dreamed of St Julian, so renaming it Monte San Giuliano when he took it. It is still called by this name locally, though it was renamed Érice in 1934 during Mussolini's imperialistic revival.

Small doubt but that this is an ancient place – one enters it by the Porta Trápani and from here the *walls* as far as the Porta Spada have a Cyclopean base, here and there repaired by the Romans. The towers, and most of the wall, are medieval. A certain mountain grimness clings to the town, and this is not materially relieved by some Norman and Gothic windows and doors.

Chiesa Madre (*dell'Assunta*) stands on the right inside the Porta Trápani. It was founded in 1314, two years after the lookout-tower, which acts as its campanile, was built. Its great *porch* belongs to 1426. Inside, it is impressively gloomy, but there is a *Madonna* by Francesco Laurana.

The *Church of San Giovanni Battista* has a good thirteenth-century *doorway*, and a couple of Gaginis inside.

The *Museo Communale Córdici*, in the Municipality, is notable only for Antonello Gagini's *Annunciation*, one of the best of that master's works, and a Roman *head of Aphrodite*, displayed among some prehistoric finds. The *Castle* is situated at the easternmost and highest point of the mountain, overlooking a precipitous drop. The castle is romantically medieval and among its masonry can be seen many fragments from the temple of Venus Erycina, or Aphrodite of Érice, on the site of which it stands. Within is a *pavement* and a *piscina* belonging to the temple. Of the real shrine of the myth nothing whatever remains.

It does not matter which way you look from Érice, the view will be stupendous; and it is in these dizzy views – clouds streaming up the valleys so very far beneath you, larks so much higher than you are, shadowy glimpses of Africa – and in the murmuring of the bees at the flowers in the castle gardens that you must seek Aphrodite Erycina. Night falls mysteriously here, creeping up from below to isolate the height, and about this, too, there is a numinous awe.

EGADI ISLANDS

Sea
From Trápani, the excursion is a charming one whether by hydrofoil, daily steamer or hired boat.

Favignana

Hotels
2nd Class   †*L'Approdo di Ulisse* (Calagrande).
4th Class   *Egadi.*

Favignana is the most populous and prosperous, having an important tunny-fishing industry. There are some prehistoric *caves* here (see below).

Lévanzo

Pension
3rd Class   *Paradiso.*

Lévanzo has important Paleolithic cave-paintings in the Grotta della Cava dei Genovesi and elsewhere. Neither these nor those on Favignana can be visited unless by permission of the Soprintendenza alle Antichità of Palermo, with whom arrangements to view them should be made.

Maréttimo

Maréttimo is the smallest of the inhabited islets. If Butler and Graves are right, this is the model for Ithaka in the *Odyssey*.

Le Formiche: these tiny islets are called 'the ants'.

PANTELLERIA ISLAND

Population
c. 10,000.
Air
From Palermo, Trápani, daily.
Sea
Motor-boat three times a week; hydrofoil twice weekly in summer, from Trápani.
Hotels
2nd Class   †*Punta Fram;*
              †*Punta Tre Pietre.*
3rd Class   †*Miryam;*
              Turistico Residenziale (Blue Marino).
4th Class   *Di Fresco.*
Pension
2nd Class   *Mediterranea.*

Rising to a weathered cone, 2,743 feet high, lonely and darkly volcanic in the sea, this island is treeless, producing zibibo grapes and little else. The rocky bathing is fine and some of the volcanic manifestations scattered about have their interest. A disastrous history, as is only to be expected of a naturally defenceless island lying between Carthaginians and Romans, Muslims and Christians, a prey to Turkish rovers in the sixteenth century, culminated in the inordinately heavy bombing and shelling from the sea between May and July 1943, the Allies being persuaded that it had been strongly fortified against their attack, which it had not. The little town is still largely cracked or ruinous, but pretty, barrel-vaulted cottages dot the gentler slopes. It is not, to my mind, a light-hearted place although, when completed, ambitious plans now underway for more 'tourist village complexes' may help make it more so. Augustus exiled his daughter Julia here, poor woman.

PELAGIC ISLANDS

Air
From Palermo or Trápani, daily, to Lampedusa only.
Sea
From Trápani via Pantelleria to Linosa and Lampedusa, weekly; from Porto Empédocle (p. 176) to Linosa and Lampedusa, weekly.

Lampedusa

Population
c. 4,500.
Hotels
2nd Class   *Baia Turchese.*
4th Class   *Martorana.*
Pension
3rd Class   *Giardina.*

Non-volcanic, about six miles long by two at its widest, cliff-ringed except for where the shelf of rock which it is slopes south-east into the sea and there are beaches, this bare island is rather like Malta, which it resembles, too, in vegetation, the bulk of which is of cultivated varieties. The island had a troubled history, the sadder for being so obscure. It was uninhabited when in 1551 Charles V's great fleet, mustered to attack Dragut of Djerba, foundered here. It was finally colonized in 1847, from Naples, and Mussolini used it as a place of exile for his political opponents. Fishing and canning, sponge-fishing also, are the principal industries, together with early vegetables. A nice if rather a lonely place, there are plans for developing a tourist trade.

Linosa

Population
c. 500.

A quiescent volcano and a rather grim place of fishermen and some farmers and, currently, some unlovely exiled *mafiosi*. It abounds with mice and cats gone wild, living on its scrub-lands.

Lampione is uninhabited.

TRÁPANI TO AGRIGENTO

Route S.S.115, turning on to the 118 to enter Agrigento. 187 km.
Rail More convenient than by bus, although not a main line and even a *rápido* is very slow.
Bus Local buses are inconvenient since the route crosses provincial borders and the more convenient services generally connect the towns of each province with its capital rather than link one capital to another. The best method of transport for the tourist is to join the almost daily tourist buses – the *Nastro d'Oro* of C.I.T. (see p. 34) or Europabus. Castelvetrano or Selinunte are, however, the first places where their route coincides with that described below.
Accommodation en route At Marsala ; Mazara del Vallo ; Castelvetrano ; Marinella ; Sciacca ; Ribera ; Porto Empédocle.

Extensive salt-pans lie to the west after you leave the town; the little windmills are for crushing the salt. Later, the road passes above Lo Stagnone bay and the salt islands of the same name enclose a lagoon in which lies the island of San Pantaleone which was *Motya*. This is far more easily visited from Marsala.

[31 km.] You reach Marsala.

Marsala

Population
Over 80,000.
Hotels
2nd Class *Motel Agip.*
3rd Class *Stella d'Itália.*

This is a drowsy town world-famous for its wines, which, it is pleasant to find, are not all the sweet ones that it is best known by. The bathing here is very pleasant from sandy beaches.

The early history of Lilybaeum is referred to in that of the Aeolian Islands and Syracuse. It was founded as a Phoenician town in 396 B.C. at the very end of Capo Boeo, to the town's north-west – the westernmost extremity of Sicily. It was the heir of the already ancient Phoenician 'counter' at Motya, which Dionysius of Syracuse had destroyed the previous year.

The Arabs appear to have used it more than Trápani as a port for Africa and its present name derives from their *Mars-al-Allah* or *Marsa Ali* (alternatively, 'the harbour of God' or 'of Ali'). When Trápani subsequently became the more useful port, Marsala declined, and Charles V almost wholly blocked its harbour to protect the town from African pirate raids.

Garibaldi landed his Thousand here (see History) and the town was gravely damaged by bombing in 1943.

The large export trade in local wine was founded by an Englishman called John Woodhouse in 1773. The Anglo-Sicilian firms of Woodhouse and Ingham-Whitaker are prominent here.

The *Cathedral*, in the Piazza della Repúbblica, has an uncompleted baroque front. It is dedicated to St Thomas of Canterbury and there is a fine *statue* of St Thomas the Apostle inside by Antonello Gagini (1516). The treasures of the cathedral are eight sixteenth-century tapestries of the capture of Jerusalem, but they are rarely exhibited.

In the Archaeological Zone, which is to be thoroughly excavated – situated north-west up the avenue to the cape –, there is a *Roman house*. This is the only part of the excavations made on the site of Lilybaeum left exposed. There is one good figurative mosaic and several geometric ones which, as so often, prefigure the motifs of Islamic art, one suggesting particularly Arab marquetry work.

The church of *San Giovanni*, which is near the above, covers a grotto 'of the Sibyl', likely to have been a water-cult shrine. The church of the *Cármine* has a rather fine *tomb* attributed to Doménico Gagini (1475).

Motya (Mozia)

The excursion to the site of Motya on the island of San Pantaleone is best made by boat from Marsala (8 km.), and permission must be got from the agent for Colonnello Lípari, Via Garraffa 74.

The harbour of the island town, three of the gates, necropolises and the foundations of some houses have all been found during excavations. In the small *museum* are archaeological finds from the site; these include a group of two lions attacking a bull which, if its provenance is not Mycenaean, is much under Mycenaean influence. Motya was destroyed by Dionysius of Syracuse in 397 B.C. Before that it had been a growing and important Phoenician colony for 400 years, the more sophisticated, perhaps, for being so close to Carthage. As it has never been rebuilt since its destruction, further excavation now planned is expected to reveal more about the Phoenicians than is at present known or likely to be discovered elsewhere.

[53 km.] The main road by-passes Mazara del Vallo.

Mazara del Vallo

Hotels
2nd Class	*Hopps Hotel.*
4th Class	*Mediterraneo;*
	Villa Giovanna.

An important, lively fishing-town sprouting baroque domes and *campanili* from many churches, Mazara was a frontier-post colony of Selinus, suffering the same fate as its founder city (see History).

Euphemius the Byzantine, who called in Arab aid in the hope of becoming emperor, discovered his mistake when his allies took this town for their own in A.D. 827. Count Roger captured it in 1075, and it was here that the first Norman council of Sicily was held in 1095.

The *Cathedral* is beside the pretty Piazza della Repúbblica (statue by Marabitti), and, though founded by Count Roger, is no longer Norman. Original work of 1073 can, however, still be seen on the exterior of the apse. It contains a *Transfiguration* by Antonello Gagini (1530) and a *tomb* by Doménico (1485).

San Niccolicchio, a cube of an eleventh-century Norman church set on a platform above the Molo G. Caito, is on the port. Roofed with glass to indicate its original vaulting, this restored building is most impressive, particularly so the blind arching of the three apses at its rear.

In the Piazza Mokarta are bits of the ruined *Norman castle*, also built by Count Roger, the more impressive for including a fine arch.

The *Museum* contains Roman antiquities of no great importance, but is housed in a former *Palace of the Knights of Malta*, who used

Mazara as a link port with Malta when going overland to Palermo, their nearest civilized centre and seat of the Spanish viceroys on whom they were in many ways dependent.

[55 km.] *Madonna dell' Alto* (or *Santa Maria della Giummare*). This church stands on an eminence beside the ring-road section of the S.S.115, near its eastern end. It was built as a Basilian convent by Julietta, Count Roger's daughter, in 1103. Recent restoration has disclosed a fair amount of its original fabric and a thirteenth-century *fresco*. It is well worth a few minutes' halt to see.

[65 km.] A mile off to the right is **Campobello di Mazara**, a wine-producing centre. In the *parish church*, there is a *crucifix* by Fra Umile da Petralia, the fifteenth-century Sicilian sculptor whose rare works are quite lovely.

From here the Strada di Tre Fontane leads south for 2½ km. to the Báglio Ingham farmhouse, beyond which a column drum has been abandoned, on its way to Selinus, in a field on the left. Turn right, and in a few minutes you reach the *Rocche di Cusa* quarries. These have never been worked since the destruction of Selinus in 409 B.C. and the whole process of the Greeks' quarrying can be seen here. Note the state in which the column drums (for Temple G) were transported. They were dressed for erection on the temple site and fluted in position.

[73 km.] You reach Castelvetrano.

Castelvetrano

Population
Over 31,000.
Hotels
1st Class   *Jolly*;
                Selinus.
4th Class   *Belvedere*;
                Ideal;
                Impero.

This sleepy, dusty town, shaken by the earthquake of 1908, is in some ways the best point from which to visit Selinunte (14 km.), to which there is a branch railway line and very occasional buses.

The neighbourhood produces wine and the town, furniture. It holds one treasure, the *Ephebe of Selinunte*, in the Município. This is a fine bronze of the first half of the fifth century B.C. Though in its rather attenuated form and elegance it departs from strict tradition, it exhibits both its own and the subject's strength only from side view. This treasure was stolen in 1965, but recovered in 1969; only when they lost it did the local authorities realize its worth, and now it may prove difficult to persuade them to let you see it.

In the baptistery of the church of *San Giovanni Battista* there is a good *statue* of the Baptist by Antonello Gagini (1522).

A current sight of the town is the *courtyard* (off Via Serafino Mannone) where the body of the bandit Giuliano was found in 1950, although Gavin Maxwell believed he was killed at Monreale and the corpse dumped here. As a place of pilgrimage it is a sorrowful sight, for Giuliano became a symbol of the individual's rights against tyranny of all sorts – governmental, civic or *mafioso* – and here he lay dead.

Environs of Castelvetrano

Some 3 km. west of the town stands the twelfth-century church of the *Santissima Trinità di Délia*. The caretakers of the property on which it stands let one in. A most beautiful and interesting church, it is a square enclosing a Greek cross in plan, with three apses. Stylistically, it is most interesting for its external decoration, which is confined to the upper half, almost identical on the north, west and south. The archaistic tombs it contains belong to the owners' family, the two brothers who restored the church so faithfully in 1880 lying in the regal sarcophagus in the centre. The church suffered some slight damage in the earthquake of 1968.

North and over to the west of Castelvetrano lies the area that was so terribly struck by earthquake in 1968. **Salemi, Santa Ninfa, Gibellina, Partanna** and **Santa Margherita di Belice** are either totally or largely ruined, but beginning now to be rebuilt. The country palace which figures as 'Donnafugata' in *The Leopard*, which was at Santa Margherita, is no more; one is glad Lampedusa did not live to suffer its loss.

Sometimes it seems that nature is implacable in its hostility to the Sicilian poor, but while scandal after scandal attaches to the misuse of money set aside for post-earthquake reconstruction, their worst enemies are seen to be their better-off compatriots.

[82 km.] After Castelvetrano the S.S.115 bends left and a branch road (S.S.115D) runs ahead 5 km. southwards to Marinella Lido and Selinunte. After the station, a right fork leads to the acropolis, after passing the group of Temples E, F and G, while the left fork runs into the fishing village and tiny beach-resort of **Marinella Lido**.

Hotel
4th Class   †*Lido Azzuro.*
Pensions
3rd Class   *Costa d'Avorio;*
             Miramare.

SELINUNTE

This now quite deserted city-site has a particular charm. It is, however, less spectacular than most, both in its position and its ruins. Although a part of Temple C has been reconstructed and Temple E has recently been almost rebuilt, the most moving and impressive sight remains that of the giant skeletons of the other temples lying as if an earthquake, with one fell blow, had laid them low – as in fact there is good reason to believe was the case.

The visitor should be warned about the sharks of Marinella who dog one about the ruins and roads, even by motor-cycle, trying to peddle antiquities. These are sometimes genuine – terra-cottas of Demeter among them – but most are fakes made from originals stolen from a museum some time ago; the 'bronzes' are brass with verdigris clumsily fudged up to deceive the unwary. However, some obstinate bargaining on your part will get you what can be very pretty souvenirs, for once at small cost to your pocket, and at least you will not break the law against the export of antiquities, since you carry home fakes.

History

To a slight eminence here, between the mouths of two rivers, the people of Megara Hyblaea sent out a colony in or about 628 B.C. Megara Hyblaea lay just north of Syracuse and was not able to expand locally; in desperation, therefore, it ventured to establish this daughter city so far westwards that its frontiers had constantly to be maintained against Carthage and Segesta. But the great plain on the edge of which it lay was in itself prize enough for the venturing, and while the city was able to defend itself it prospered exceedingly, as the size and number of the temples demonstrate.

The Selinuntines waged an intermittent but long-lasting war against the Elymians of Segesta, who sought to oust them from this plain. After the Greek victory at Himera, in 480 B.C., the Selinuntines allied themselves with Syracuse against Carthage, a grouping which made the Carthaginians the readier to come to the Segestans' aid when asked to do so in 409 B.C. Hannibal, son of Gisco, is reputed to have brought an army of 100,000, with which he took the city by assault before either Agrigentum or Syracuse could come to the rescue. The city was laid waste. An attempt at resettlement under Hermocrates, an exile from Syracuse, was short-lived, the Carthaginians again driving the settlers out in 250 B.C. To this revival belong the foundations of houses that have been excavated over the acropolis top and the quite elaborate defences that guard its northern edge.

The site

Marinella – now quite a brisk little seaside resort – lies on a slight plateau, on the western edge of which, undefended, the eastern group of temples was clustered. Between this and the city proper lies the valley of the Gorgo di Cottone river, whose mouth is so silted up that only a shallow mere indicates where there was once a harbour. The acropolis plateau, crowned by the columns of Temple C, lies to seaward; the plateau on which the city stood is to its north, divided from it by a lower saddle. To the west of these runs the valley of the ancient River Selinus – now called the Modione – in the mouth of which was the town's principal harbour, though neither this nor the other was ever a good one. Across the Selinus – so called from the Greek *selinon*, 'wild parsley' (*selinum*), which flourishes along its banks – stands a large sanctuary of Demeter Molophoros. Some way farther west again, near the sea, the necropolis spreads.

Eastern temples

Temple E will be the first to attract your attention. It was the last to be built and was long thought to be perhaps the finest classical Sicilian temple of the mid fifth century B.C. Now that its columns, entablature and pediments have been raised from the ground where their pieces used to lie stretched out, almost in order, the column

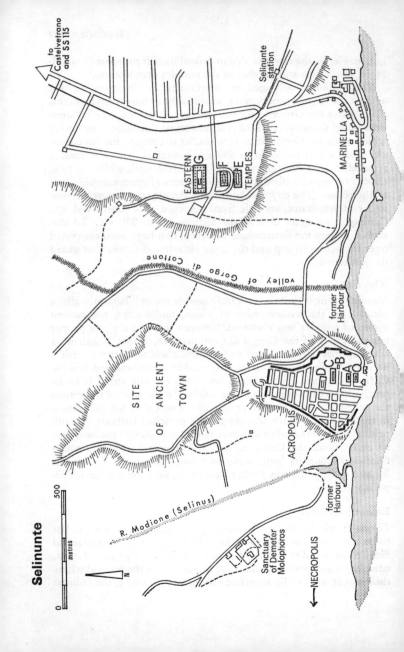

Selinunte

to Castelvetrano and SS 115

Selinunte station

MARINELLA

EASTERN TEMPLES

G
F
E

Valley of Gorgo di Cottone

former Harbour

SITE OF ANCIENT TOWN

ACROPOLIS

C
B
D
A

former Harbour

R. Modione (Selinus)

Sanctuary of Demeter Molophoros

NECROPOLIS

N

metres
0   500

drums like sections of sliced cucumbers or the bones of skeleton fingers, the result is not a disappointment. It was always rather long for its width (220 feet by 83 feet) and I venture to suggest that it was not designed in isolation, but to hold its own somewhat as a balance, across Temple F, to the vast Temple G. It is quite marvellous that this lost beauty could have been restored to us 1,164 years after its total collapse.

From this temple the set of four metopes in the Palermo museum was taken. It may have been dedicated to Hera.

Temple F dates from 560 B.C. and is the oldest of this group. It was prostyle and had a double row of columns at one end, with fourteen in single file along the sides.

Temple G was begun about the middle of the sixth century B.C. and left unfinished in 409 B.C. It was too big and ambitious: measuring 371½ feet by 177¼ feet, it was the next largest temple in Sicily to the Olympieion at Agrigento. The stylobate comprises 1¾ acres; the columns – some were never fluted – measured more than 53 feet, each drum weighing roughly 100 tons. This too was prostyle and the vast cella was divided into three aisles, the central one of which was probably open to the sky. The pronaos, on the east, led into the avenue of columns forming these aisles – the naos – and the shrine itself was in an adytum at the far west of the cella. The western end shows modifications in line with advancing fashion, the eastern being archaic and the western classic. The huge, unshaped blocks, lying to the west, came from the quarries at Cusa (p. 164) but were never used. The temple was probably dedicated to Apollo.

Acropolis

Open daylight hours; 200 Lire entrance fee; car park. The streets on the small plateau have mostly been laid out on a grid plan, the central dromos keeping west of the temples and the principal crossing running east–west between them. This lay-out may date only from Hermocrates' revival, but, since Akragas was also arranged thus, Woodhead suggests that it is not necessarily unwise to credit the western Greeks with the use of this 'Hippodamian' scheme a century before Hippodamus is said to have invented it. It does fit with the temples, and it may well be a sixth-century plan.

The ruins of a small *archaic temple* are met with first; then the stylobate only of *Temple O*; then the stylobate and some columns of Temple A.

Temple A, with 36 columns, measured 132 feet by 52¼ feet and was hexastyle peristyle; the cella was raised a step higher than the pronaos and, within, there was an adytum, again a step higher. It appears to have had a propylaeum to its east. Like Temple O, it was built between 490 and 480 B.C. and these were the last – and probably showed the best workmanship – of all the Selinuntine temples.

Temple C, part of the north colonnade of which was re-erected in 1927, stands beyond the principal cross-street and on the highest part of the plateau. It dates from mid sixth century, and the three archaic metopes in the Palermo museum belonged to this temple. The temple measures 208¾ feet by 78¾ feet; it had 42 thick columns, some of which were monolithic blocks 28 feet high, and, as had already become customary, the corner ones were made thicker than the others to counteract the optical illusion which otherwise would have made the weight of the pediment appear to have splayed the corner columns outwards. This temple's fall during an earthquake can be roughly dated, since, in falling, it crushed the Byzantine village which had clustered in the ruins. This bears out the estimate made 150 years ago by young Charles Cockerell, who, by comparing the state of the exposed surfaces of the stones with those that had been protected, gauged it to have been about the eighth or ninth century A.D. Paulus Diacunus records an earthquake in Sicily in A.D. 797.

To the east of Temple C – most Greek temples opened eastwards – lie the remains of its sacrificial altar.

Between Temple C and the cross-street is the base of the small *Temple B*, simply a cella preceded by a pronaos – a structure called a prostyle aediculum which is the ancestor of our chapels, as the pronaos was the ancestor of the narthex.

Temple D abuts on the central dromos. It possibly dates from a little earlier than Temple C, between 570 and 554 B.C. It had 34 columns, measured 183¾ feet by 77½ feet and was hexastyle peristyle in form.

Site of ancient town

The residential parts of the city, on the larger and higher plateau to the north of the acropolis, have been little explored. To its north, on the slope below, is a *necropolis* used from the foundation to the sixth century B.C.

Sanctuary of Demeter Molophoros

Across the Selinus (Modione) river and opposite the saddle between the city plateaux, stand the remains of the Sanctuary of Demeter Molophoros (the place is locally called *La Gaggera*). In a high-walled enclosure stands the cella or 'megaron' surrounded by no peristyle. Its date is around 575 B.C. and it is of interest to specialists because of its cornice and roof construction. Demeter Molophoros – the name means 'apple-bearer', that is, 'fruitful' – may have been the mother who gathered her children in death: the great necropolis of Selinunte stretches from here along the coast for several miles. Occasional tombs and piles of bones are to be seen. The huge collection of 5,000 votive figurines of Demeter (now in the Palermo museum) was gathered from this immediate neighbourhood, and they are still being found.

Enter from round the south-eastern corner – the corner itself was occupied by a small enclosure dedicated to Hecate Triformis* – where are the remains of the pillared propylaeum. A small altar, then a large one, stand on the near side of a water canal crossing the front of the megaron itself. A little to the north, off to the right before you enter the propylaeum, was a small, roughly square temenos with a temple to Zeus Meilichios.

The instructive quarries of *Rocche di Cusa*, where the temple stones were cut, lie about 12 km. west over sand-dunes – a wearisome walk. They are best visited from Campobello (p. 164).

[85 km.] The S.S.115 crosses the *Belice river*, the ancient Hypsas which entered the sea through wide marshes – now drained – and formed the natural boundary between Greek and Phoenician Sicily.

[97 km.] **Menfi**, a small town among the *latifonde* – hereditary estates. The *baronial palace*, now the Municipio, incorporates a polygonal *tower* from a Swabian castle. The town's grid-plan lay-out dates from 1658, a landowner's creation. Danilo Dolci has done good work here, tackling crippling poverty.

* Triformis – 'triple'; the goddess entire.

[119 km.] You reach Sciacca.

Sciacca

Population
Over 32,000.
Information
Azienda Autónoma, Corso Vittório Emanuele 84
Bathing
Good and sandy.
Hotels
1st Class   *Grande Albergo delle Terme*
2nd Class   *Garden*;
    Motel Agip.
3rd Class   *Fazello*;
    Monte Kronio (Monte Kronio).
4th Class   *Nuova Itália.*

Sciacca is a thermal centre (once *Thermae Selinuntinae*) and a fishing port. A sprightly town, summer nights in its Piazza Scandaliato, high above the port and faced by the grand front of the *Município*, are everything one feels they should be in a place of this sort, but all too rarely are in fact. If you are travelling by local bus, this is a good place to stop the night as it is connected with the larger towns in all directions.

Sciacca was an important place in later medieval times and seat of the turbulent Spanish family of Luna, who feuded outrageously – and, even for Sicily, old-fashionedly – with the Perollos during the fifteenth and sixteenth centuries. The town stands, as it were, on a stairway leading to the sky and is surrounded by a towered wall of 1336 in which the very grand north-western *Porta San Salvatore* was built during reconstructions to the fortifications in the sixteenth century. It is worth while driving around up to the upper levels to see this unspoiled town's fascinating mixture of Saracenic domesticity with a European gloss.

The *Cathedral* (centre), while retaining its handsome Norman east end, has four Gagini *statues* on its west front; and, inside, there is a *Virgin* attributed to Francesco Laurana.

The *Church of Santa Margherita* (1342) has a beautiful *side-door* by Doménico Gagini.

The *Church of Santa Maria della Giummare* (upper town) is a Norman sanctuary with a castellated front and a pleasant mixture of additions from all periods since its building. The *frescoes* are by a local eighteenth-century painter, Mariano Rossi.

The *Church of San Nicolò* (west) is a primitive twelfth-century church, in bad repair.

Casa Arone (centre) is a very fine fifteenth-century palace, though the *Steripinto* (west) is a still finer palace of the same period.

Environs of Sciacca

8 km. to the north-east of Sciacca lies **Monte San Calógero**, also a thermal station where the grotto into which the hot vapour flows has been hollowed out and stone channels and seats carved in pre-historic times, though anciently Daedalus was given the credit for these works. Specially equipped speleologists and archaeologists recently found evidence of Copper Age (third millennium B.C.) human and grain sacrifices placed far into the caves whence the volcanic vapour flows, in hopes to placate such terrifying under-world powers.

20 km. inland from Sciacca lies **Caltabellotta**, a high medieval town where the peace that eventually ended the War of the Vespers was signed.

The *Chiesa Madre* is Norman in parts and has a portal with pointed arches. It was built in 1090 by Count Roger. Inside is the *Madonna della Catena* by Gagini; and a *St Benedict* of the Gagini school.

The *Castello*, only one tower now remaining to watch a marvel-lous view, was the last place where, in 1194, Queen Sibylla and her son, William III, were known to be alive; what Henry VI did with them is not known, but he could hardly have let them live.

In *San Lorenzo* there is a rather splendid group of the *Deposition*, the figures being made of painted terra-cotta – by Antonino Ferraro, 1552.

[131 km.] Ribera. A landowner's seventeenth-century foundation, this time made by the Prince of Paternò and called after his wife's family. It was the birthplace of Francesco Crispi in 1818.

Hotels

2nd Class	*Miravalle.*
4th Class	*Itália;*
	Palma.

[143 km.] A turning right leads (6 km.) to the site of *Heraclea Minoa*.

The town stood on a cliff-girt promontory above the entrance to the Halykos river – now called the Plátani. The headland is made of marl and clays, very subject to landslides, which probably led to the abandonment of the town in the first century B.C. Below the cliffs extend marvellous wide beaches backed by woods.

The road to the ruins passes the lower courses of *walls* on its left and crosses their path some 80 yards before you arrive at the *Antiquarium*, through which the site is entered. (Open daily 09.00–17.00, Sundays 09.00–13.00.)

The town was founded as a daughter colony of Selinunte in the sixth century B.C., most probably to check the growing power of Akragas. At first it was simply called Minoa and it is possible that this was the name of the place or of an earlier, perhaps existing settlement on the site. Diodorus is the ancient source for the legend telling that Daedalus, having fled from Crete and taken refuge with and service under King Kokalos of Camicos in Sicily, was pursued there by Minos of Knossos, this expedition leading to Minos' death and failure. Landing at the mouth of the Halykos river he built a city – or, an alternative legend has it, after his death his followers built it. Diodorus tells also how Theron of Akragas found Minos' tomb here in the early fifth century B.C., describing it as an underground tomb-chamber with a temple to 'Aphrodite' built above it – an uncommon form, the only known example of which has been unearthed at Knossos.

So much of the Selinuntine colony of Heraclea, and that of its later Akragantine owners, has slipped away that it must be uncertain whether the excavations now in progress (and interesting to see) will ever disclose evidence of a former Minoan or Mycenaen settlement here. One lives in earnest hopes it may. Minoa passed to Akragas in 508 B.C., but after the disasters of 409 B.C. it was depopulated and destroyed, then given by Dionysius of Syracuse to Carthage under treaty. It was then called Ras Melkart. In 345 B.C. it was restored to the Greeks and democracy, by Timoleon; but he too agreed, if its people should be free to leave it, to cede it back to Carthage to be the Punic frontier town. It was about Timoleon's time that Heraclea was added to its name, some new colonists from Cefalù being worshippers of Dorian Herakles (though both Greeks and Carthaginians identified Herakles with Melkart, so one wonders if, especially as it now began to be a bi-racial town, local devotion to this god was not six of one and half a dozen of the other). The abominable Agathocles took it around 300 B.C., about the time of its greatest prosperity. It suffered badly in the first Punic War, after Hanno landed here and made it his base for the relief of Akragas, and fell to Rome in 210 B.C. In the slave revolt it became a shadow of itself and had to be repeopled, but then did well enough, even at the time of Cicero's visit; then was suddenly abandoned before the end of the first century B.C.

The *Theatre* – looking very odd under its plastic covering which protects the friable rock – belongs to the end of the fourth century B.C. It was soon enlarged, but fell into disuse, perhaps after the slave revolt, and late Republican Roman buildings in places overlie it.

As yet the *walls* are the only other sight of much interest to the layman. They have their own history of rebuilding, extensions, and so on. Known from aerial photography is the lay-out of many streets dating from the time of the Roman resettlement in the second century B.C.

Back on the 115, you will find a left-hand road leading (43 km.) to **Sant'Ángelo Muxaro**. The river valley going up towards this glorious citadel-hill is lonely and very beautiful. If you respond to the poetry of myth and landscape, push your way upstream to Camicos (though you must lose the river after **Cattólica Eraclea** going by **Raffadali** and **Sant'Elisabetta**). Sant'Ángelo Muxaro has been tentatively identified as Camicos, city of King Kokalos; later tombs of an Oriental, Minoan or Mycenaean type, with contents seeming to reflect a memory of models of a similar Cretan inspiration, have been found.

The tombs lie around the south and west sides of the remarkable hill, as you arrive at the steepest climb – a bit difficult to find; best to enlist a child to guide you to the *'tomba del príncipe'* (the helpful proprietor of the café at the top of the piazza speaks some English).

The lower tombs in the cemetery, rock-cut, belong to early Sican people, but the higher tombs are later (from the eighth century B.C.) and unique; larger, circular, 'beehive'-roofed, some with a funeral bench round them and containing pottery unlike any other in eastern Sicily. Some golden objects were also found here; a surviving bowl with a decoration of bulls walking in procession in its interior is in the British Museum. These tombs were used until the middle of the fifth century B.C.; they are not Mycenaean, but they echo that past in an uncanny way, particularly so the big one (28 feet in diameter) which was converted into a *chapel of Sant' Angelo* by the Byzantines – the 'tomba del príncipe' itself.

Daedalus, so the very ancient legend tells, built King Kokalos a new fortress defendable only by four men. Kokalos had his capital formerly at *Inkyon*, which was quite possibly at Monte della Giudecca (north-east of Cattólica), and his new city was called Camicos, thought now perhaps to have been here – and one might well think it feasible so to fortify this sharp hilltop that very few defenders could hold it. Kokalos reigned in the second millennium B.C., the tholos tombs here came very much later: puzzles remain, but one would like to believe.

Evening is the best time; you meet herds of goats with pipe-playing boys herding them – the archaeological evidence points towards what you will hardly need scientific proof of: you are persuaded that you have followed great Daedalus and august Minos to King Kokalos' fabled city.

[177 km.] Porto Empédocle is an ugly industrial port, the chief sulphur port of Sicily and, indeed, of all Italy. Its *mole* was built between 1749 and 1763, much of the stone being quarried from the ruins of Agrigento. A steamer plies once a week to the islands of Linosa and Lampedusa.

Hotel
4th Class   *Kennedy.*

[187 km.] Agrigento.

AGRIGENTO

Rail
Connections with Palermo, Catánia, Trápani.
Bus
Services to Palermo, Sciacca, Marsala, Trápani, Gela (connections to Syracuse), all starting from near Railway Station. Local buses to Porto Empédocle, San Leone, etc. from Piazzale Roma.
Information
E.P.T. office, Piazza Cavour 19 (*Map* **9**).
Azienda Autónoma, Piazza Vittório Emanuele.
Tourist Information Office, Piazzale Roma (*Map* **7**).

Bathing
Bathing available at San Leone Lido, where there are one or two modest hotels.
Hotels

1st Class	*Jolly*, Piazzale Roma 1 ;
	Villa Athena.
2nd Class	*Della Valle*, Via dei Templi ;
	Del Viale, Piazza Cavour ;
	Jolly Colleverde, Passeggiata Archeológica ;
	Mediterraneo, Via Setto Bibbirria ;
	Nuovo Amici, Piazza Stazione.
3rd Class	*Bella Nápoli*, Piazza Lena 6 ;
	Belvedere, Via San Vito 20 ;
	Paris, Via Imera 57.
4th Class	*Atenea*, Vicolo Pancucci 1 ;
	Gorizia, Via Boccerie 39.

Restaurant
Le Caprice, at the beginning of the Passeggiata Archeológica, entertaining as well as providing good eating.

A provincial capital of rising population, the upper part of the 'modern' town is old, picturesque and interesting, though over-tall post-war building now masks almost all view of it from the valley. None the less, the chief interest here lies in the ruins of the great Greek city it once was, its temples and beautiful museum.

HISTORY

The ancient city was six times larger than the modern, yet its buildings did not cover the entire area bounded by its walls. This occupied what, in fact, is a shelf of land, 3 km. inland from the sea and lying in the fork of two rivers – the ancient Akragas on the east and the Hypsas on the west, now called the San Biágio and the Sant'Anna respectively. From the north of this shelf rises a steep-sided ridge, its northern side being almost precipitous. This ridge has two high points: the Rupe Atenea, 1,152 feet high, and, slightly less high, Monte Camico, the hill now crowned by the older town. Since the shelf is protected on the east, south and most of the west sides by an abrupt escarpment, the whole made an ideally defensible area, given enough men to defend a wall 12 km. long.

An enormous confidence in the colony's future was shown by the Gelans who, in about 582 B.C., moved thus far westwards to establish the settlement of Akragas. They had for some time previously maintained a trading post at the mouth of the river, where there is now the San Leone Lido, and knew the potentialities of the site. These included a rich hinterland for which the city would provide a natural outlet.

Their confidence was not misplaced; from the start, the colony grew in power and wealth. This appears to have been due in part to the ability of Phalaris, the tyrant who reigned from about 565 to 549 B.C. If the original colonists settled upon the acropolis heights of the Rupe Atenea and Monte Camico they had by the end of Phalaris' reign begun to build in the centre of the shelf, where, under the excavations of a Hellenistic quarter near San Nicola (*Map* 13), traces of sixth-century B.C. buildings have been found. Phalaris waged war with the Sicans and pushed the colony's eastern border to Licata. It was Phalaris, too, who probably planned the walls which link the acropolis and the Rupe Atenea and the eastern and southern sides of the shelf. He died by assassination, and has left a probably undeserved bad name. The legend of his roasting victims in a bronze bull may indicate both ruthlessness in his character and devotion to a Rhodian bull-cult. But even ancient historians were not altogether satisfied with this story of most un-Hellenic behaviour.

Between the end of Phalaris and the advent, in 488 B.C., of Theron, the other great tyrant of Akragas, the colony appears to have consolidated its gains. Theron pushed its territory across the island to the north coast by uniting it with Himera after driving out the Himeran tyrant, Thrasyllus.

This new and threatening power of Akragas was the immediate cause of the Carthaginians' attack in 480 B.C. Thrasyllus' son-in-law, the tyrant of Rhegium (Réggio di Calábria), joined forces with the Carthaginians and Elymians against Akragas and her ally Gelon, tyrant of Gela and Syracuse, the greatest Greek power in the island. The Greeks' great victory off Himera won them seventy years' comparative peace, and heralded a golden age for the whole of Greek Sicily.

Pindar, who was around forty at the time, visited Akragas with Theron as his patron. For him he wrote the second and third Olympian Odes. About the city itself he had already written in 490 B.C.: 'Lover of splendour, most beautiful of mortal cities, that lives upon the hill of fine dwellings, above the banks where the sheep graze beside the river.'

Based upon its production and export of corn, oil and wine, and its sulphur mines, Akragas attained a legendary prosperity. Stock-breeding was another of the colony's profitable lines, and, in particular, its horses, so often victorious in the Panhellenic games, were famous. The most intimate contacts we have with this luxurious period are the very beautiful coins struck in the fifth century B.C. Often they show Zeus' eagle and Poseidon's crab, and the city's own victorious four-horse chariots (quadrigae).

The brilliant Empedocles was born in Akragas during this period. I quote from Bertrand Russell's *History of Western Philosophy* (Allen and Unwin, London, 1962):

> The mixture of philosopher, prophet, man of science, and charlatan, which we found already in Pythagoras, was exemplified very completely in Empedocles, who flourished about 440 B.C. ... he was a democratic politician, who at the same time claimed to be a god ... he was supposed to have worked miracles, or what seemed such, sometimes by magic, sometimes by means of his scientific knowledge. He could control the winds, we are told; he restored life to a woman who had seemed dead for thirty days; finally, it is said, he died by leaping into the crater of Etna to prove that he was a god ... since only fragments of his writings have survived, his poetic merit must remain in doubt. His most important contribution to science was his discovery of air as a separate substance. This he proved by the observation that when a bucket or any similar vessel is put upside down into water, the water does not enter into the bucket.

Among other things, Empedocles established the Italian school of medicine, influencing both Plato and Aristotle, and distinguished the elements of earth, air, fire and water, adding to them, as primitive substances, 'Love' and 'Strife', which, he considered, had alternating periods of ascendancy.

The victory of Himera supplied the victors with numerous slaves, the basic ingredient necessary for large public-building programmes. Nine temples were built at Akragas, as well as aqueducts and a fountain, famous in the ancient world, which has now disappeared.

After Theron's death, tyranny gave way to a lasting democratic regime; but there was continued rivalry between Akragas and Syracuse from which Syracuse gradually emerged as the greater power. Akragas fell to the Carthaginians and was thus involved in Carthage's struggle with Rome. The Romans attacked the Carthaginians in the west of Sicily; the fighting centred on Akragas, which was taken by the Romans in 262 B.C., sacked and the entire population sold into slavery.

The Romans, however, needed the city, so it was garrisoned and to some extent repeopled. Then it fell to the Carthaginians in 255 B.C., but was eventually recaptured by Rome in 210 B.C. It must by then have been a sorry place; three years later the population received an enforced influx of colonists, and Augustus later sent a further contingent of settlers.

The Pax Romana was bringing prosperity back, however. Agrigentum – as Rome called the city – was a lively place. Sicilian corn was of the greatest importance to Rome, and Agrigentum was a major corn-dealing centre. During the governorship of the notorious Verres it was also the centre for the collection of the corn tax. Little or nothing remains of Roman Agrigentum save the foundations of the 'Hellenistic Quarter'. When Porto Empédocle was built in the eighteenth century, giving the city a good port for the first time, the moles were largely constructed from the standing ruins of the ancient city which would of course by then have been more Roman than Greek.

After the collapse of the western Roman Empire, Agrigentum seriously declined. Gradually, the town withdrew to the Camico hill, from where it is only now extending again. The ridge along the southern edge of the shelf on which the Greek temples are built became a cemetery, and is pitted over with grave-pits and hypogea. Time, and a shaking or two by earthquake, brought all the temples slowly down, excepting only the one called 'Concord' (*Map* 22) which in the sixth century A.D. was converted into a church and palace by San Gregório delle Rape, bishop of Agrigento – a transformation which preserved it marvellously well until the church was dismantled in 1745.

Agrigentum fell to the Saracens in A.D. 829 and was delivered from them by Count Roger in 1087, when he refounded the bishopric. The town's name has gone through several changes: Akragas; Agrigentum; the Arab Kerkent or Gergent; the Italian Girgenti, which was changed by decree in 1927 to Agrigento.

PRINCIPAL SIGHTS: VALLEY OF THE TEMPLES

The Valley of the Temples, as the anciently occupied shelf below the modern town is called, is indeed a valley as two tributary streams run south from the Rupe Atenea area and east to join each other and the Sant'Anna (Hypsas) river at the south-east corner of the ancient city. From the valley, it looks as if every building in the present town were built to command a ravishing view of farmland, olive and almond orchards, on the far side of which Doric temples stand in line, and the wide plain stretches to the sea beyond. This site is so keenly beautiful that Pindar's praise of it cannot have been overdone, nor was Polybius wrong to have written: 'Agrigentum is superior to most other cities ... in its strength and above all in the beauty of its site and buildings.'

The S.S.118 makes its way through the present town and winds across this valley and through the enlarged opening, where the *Porta Aurea* – Gate IV of the city – stood; there it joins the S.S.115, the main road which follows the south-west coast of Sicily from Trápani to Syracuse. A road (*Passeggiata Archeológica*) has been built from just below the slope of the town, turning east off the S.S.118 and running round within the circuit of the walls to rejoin the S.S.118 by Gate IV, where there is a *posto di ristoro* which cannot be recommended for anything more solid than the welcome beverages it sells.

This site is so big – at least two miles square – that it is hard to recommend ways of seeing it. Buses from the Piazzale Roma or the top of the Via Francesco Crispi, leading out of Piazza Stazione, run to Porto Empédocle or San Leone, at about half-hourly intervals, and pass San Nicola (*Map 13*) – where the National Museum is, with other sights – and the Porta Aurea, which is a good centre for the temples themselves. If you are driving it is less wearisome; but best of all is to walk.

The various sights to be visited in the valley are listed in their topographical order, from the farthest point east, then by the south to the Sant'Anna river on the west, and, retracing tracks back to the Porta Aurea, and up the central road to San Nicola.

Chapel of San Biágio
Map 11.

The chapel stands on the easternmost spur of the Rupe Atenea; a car can be driven to within a couple of hundred yards of the chapel, after which it is a scramble up, and another down, to the sanctuary over the eastern face of the ridge. The building is a fifth-century B.C. *temple* ruin converted in the Byzantine period into a *chapel*. The foundations of the temple, which was larger than the

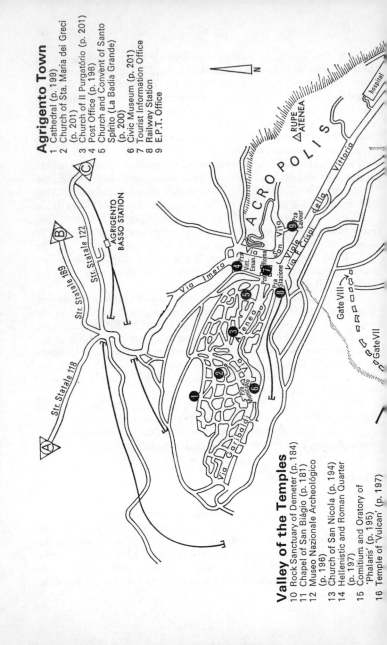

Agrigento Town

1 Cathedral (p. 199)
2 Church of Sta. Maria dei Greci (p. 201)
3 Church of Il Purgatório (p. 201)
4 Post Office (p. 198)
5 Church and Convent of Santo Spirito (La Badia Grande) (p. 200)
6 Civic Museum (p. 201)
7 Tourist Information Office
8 Railway Station
9 E.P.T. Office

Valley of the Temples

10 Rock Sanctuary of Demeter (p. 184)
11 Chapel of San Biágio (p. 181)
12 Museo Nazionale Archeológico (p. 196)
13 Church of San Nicola (p. 194)
14 Hellenistic and Roman Quarter (p. 197)
15 Comitium and Oratory of 'Phalaris' (p. 195)
16 Temple of 'Vulcan' (p. 197)

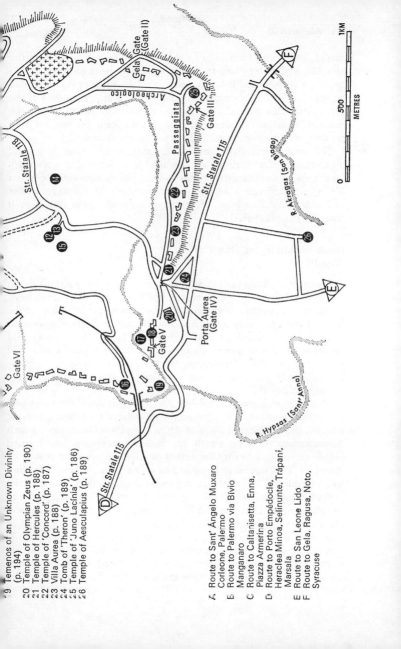

19 Temenos of an Unknown Divinity
   (p. 194)
20 Temple of Olympian Zeus (p. 190)
21 Temple of Hercules (p. 188)
22 Temple of 'Concord' (p. 187)
23 Villa Aurea (p. 188)
24 Tomb of 'Theron' (p. 189)
25 Temple of 'Juno Lacinia' (p. 186)
26 Temple of Aesculapius (p. 189)

A Route to Sant' Angelo Muxaro
   Corleone, Palermo
B Route to Palermo via Bívio
   Manganaro
C Route to Caltanisetta, Enna,
   Piazza Armerina
D Route to Porto Empédocle,
   Heraclea Minoa, Selinunte, Trápani,
   Marsala
E Route to San Leone Lido
F Route to Gela, Ragusa, Noto,
   Syracuse

chapel, have been excavated to the east of the building. Here the pronaos, with two pillars, stood before the entrance to the naos. No peristasis surrounded it and it belongs to the form of temple called 'in antis'. It dates between 480 and 460 B.C. Some fragments of the sima, from this temple, bearing very fine lion-heads, are in the museum. Conversion necessitated cutting a door in the west end and reconstructing the eastern wall with a single apse in it.

The temple was dedicated to Demeter, and it stood in a small precinct made by cutting back the hillside and levelling a platform on the slope. Between the chapel and the hill lie two small, circular *altars*, in one of which is a hollow (or bothros) – a typical feature of chthonic ritual furniture; characteristic vessels were found in it when it was excavated.

Rock Sanctuary of Demeter
Map **10**.

The guardian of the temple will show you the path and steps down eastwards, from the upper precinct, leading from the tip of the spur.

When discovered a few years ago, the natural caves which are the basis of this sanctuary were choked with rubble containing quantities of votive offerings and terra-cotta busts of Demeter and Persephone. These were mainly Greek, dating from the fifth and sixth centuries B.C., but among them were sub-Mycenaean proto-historic finds going as far back at least as the beginning of the eighth century B.C.

Walls belonging to a ruined structure, which are themselves preceded by a precinct, stand before the mouths of the principal caves; they are pre-Greek, although of a type – and workmanship – which demonstrates to what extent the Sicans hereabouts had learned Greek techniques before the actual establishment of the colony of Akragas. This structure consisted of a porch-like entrance leading to an inner and higher entrance, made through two doors, to the caves themselves. Across the lower level, water ran in channels from the third cave. This was fed into a complex system of basins and channels throughout the building and precinct. These seem to belong to a comparatively late date – true Greek or even Roman – but perhaps trace a course whose origins go back to the earliest days of this water-cult. A few steps to the north of the sanctuary, under a tangle of creepers lying at the corner of a terraced field by the path, this sacred water is now piped into a tank, and you may be glad to drink its cold, clear flow. This is a wonderful place, seeming inherently sacred even now.

Walls

To follow the course of the *walls*, walk south from the sanctuary and round the farmhouse to cross the fields in the dip beyond, east of the cemetery, where you will easily find the circuit breasting the rising ground beyond, at the head of the first valley. Before that, however, in the dip under the cemetery wall, you come to:

Gate I

The now low wall of its northern shoulder projects obliquely so that the defenders could threaten the attackers' shield-less side; of the other side, which would have had a tower, nothing remains.

Beyond, still by the cemetery wall, there is the base of a V-shaped bastion which was built into this valley that threatened to constitute a natural breach in the city's defences; each of the outer angles which this made with the line of the walls was fortified by a tower, of which now only the foundations are to be found.

Continuing by the line of the walls, or reached from the Passeggiata Archeológica by the farm track on the left that leads through it, you come to:

Gela Gate (Gate II)

Set at the head of a gully running 100 yards into the city-shelf side. The sides of this were cut back and crowned with walls and towers, those on the north bearing continuously upon the attacker's right, that on the left concentrating its strength upon a larger tower near the gate from which the defenders could be well above and behind the front ranks of any column that reached so far, thus partly circumventing the protection of their shields.

This gate was one of the principal ones of the city, and the rock walls near by have yielded many finds of a type associated with chthonic deities, Demeter and Persephone again, and Hades. These date in the main from the fifth century to the Roman period. 'City of Persephone', Pindar called Akragas – and we begin to understand why.

The wall-side path and the road (from which a branch leads into the San Biágio valley) now rise to the tip upon which the Temple of 'Juno' stands, the most southerly point of the town. The attributions of the temples to several Roman divinities date from the eighteenth century. They are either poorly substantiated or unsubstantiated except in the case of the Olympieion and the chthonic shrine, but since the temples have become famous under those names everybody seems content to retain them.

Temple of 'Juno Lacínia'
Map 25.

This is certainly an erroneous attribution. Like all Sicilian temples, it is Doric and, in this case, of peripteral hexastyle form. Its stylobate measures 125¼ feet by 55½ feet and this is raised upon an artificial platform. Nine of its thirty-four columns and most of the cella have fallen. Its style dates its building between 460 and 440 B.C. The Carthaginians' destruction of the city in 406–405 B.C. is here vividly marked by the red stains of fire on some of the stones. The oolitic limestone of which the Akragan temples are built is difficult to work, and is much weathered on the south-east sides of the columns against which the sirocco blows. The Romans restored this temple, replacing its former marble tiles with terra-cotta ones, but all this work has been tumbled by earthquake. The Romans also built the ramp up to the temple's eastern entrance, outside which lies the base of the altar.

Each temple once stood in its sacred enclosure or temenos – a sanctuary in fact. These were often bounded by a stoa or covered portico and embraced subsidiary shrines, altars to various aspects of the deity, images and treasures, stores for ex-voto offerings, etc. Here the line of temene must have been almost, if not quite, continuous from this point along all the length of the southern wall.

Gate III

This lies just west of the Temple of Juno. It has been much mutilated by subsequent works, particularly by hollowing out the graves of the Byzantine cemetery which begins here.

Beyond this gate, to the west, the wall was cut from virgin rock. The inner side is hollowed out with Byzantine grave recesses, and the rampart road pitted with them. It is worth while taking whatever opportunity offers to get a glimpse of the impressive outer side of the wall along this stretch. Next westwards stands the Temple of 'Concord'.

Temple of 'Concord'
Map 22.

This fine building dates from 450 to 440 B.C., the culminating phase of the Doric order. It is a peripteral hexastyle; has 34 columns, 22½ feet high; and the stylobate measures 129½ feet by 55½ feet. The cella is formed doubly in antis, the shrine proper – the naos – being the eastern half, which was placed back to back with the western – opisthodomos – though they were not contiguous. A stairway led from either side of the cella to the roof. Notice that while all the columns are of the same thickness, they are spaced more widely towards the corners – entasis to counteract the optical illusion of an outward fall which the building would otherwise give. San Gregório delle Rape (of the Turnips) cut the arches in the cella walls to open aisles when he converted this temple into a church in the sixth century A.D. He also walled in the intercolumniations, as can be seen in the cathedral of Syracuse, and dismantled the walls separating the pronaos from the opisthodomos. Other niches, etc., obviously not Doric, belong to this conversion also; but not the upper openings in the inner pediments. Raised upon its platform, it is not altogether easy to see this temple as thoroughly as it deserves; while the loss of the entablature along the sides, together with the preservation of both pediments, gives a false sense of weakness to some views. This is an example of a temple built without regard for its site.

One may be a little disappointed by the coarse texture of the stone of which these temples are built – and its colour, too, is not really pleasing. It is therefore best to try and imagine them as they were built to be: coated with a fine plaster of ground marble which must greatly have sharpened the impact of their forms, designed to get a maximum effect from the light and shadow of sunshine upon them, as all Doric architecture was. Moreover, the plaster casing was painted. One need not suppose this coloration to have been garish or bizarre, for every indication suggests that it was conceived integrally, both with the architectural forms and the carved passages such as metopes and pediments – this in a way that we have lost all notion of.

Villa Aurea
Map 23.

Westward again lies the modern Villa Aurea where on the opposite side of the road an early Christian and Byzantine cemetery has been extensively excavated. There is an interesting *hypogeum*, partly constructed of an earlier wall and cistern, and a curious '*street*' sunk between close-set grave-pits which remind one of the niches in the Cappuccini catacomb at Palermo.

South of the walls – outside the city – lie further grave-complexes belonging to the centuries preceding those upon the north of the ridge.

Temple of Hercules
Map 21.

This stands west of the Villa Aurea and almost over the gate through which the S.S.118 passes out. It belongs to the late sixth century B.C. and is the earliest of the series; a peripteral hexastyle measuring 220 feet by 83 feet with 38 columns. Its cella was roofless and had pronaos, naos and opisthodomos, both the latter in antis and having a stairway between them. The eight erect columns were restored thus by Sir Alexander Hardcastle in 1923. The temple of Herakles at Akragas once contained a famous image of the god which Verres attempted, but failed, to pilfer; and a fresco by Zeuxis of the day-old Herakles strangling the serpents. The ruins show evidences of the fire of 405 B.C., and also of Roman restoration. Something can be seen of the *altar* to its east.

Porta Aurea (Gate IV)

The name is a modern one, but there is no doubt that this was the city's main gate and an unusually large and well-defended one.

Subsequent alterations, by Byzantine as well as modern roadbuilders, have all but obliterated the remains of the original one. A road passed right through the city from the acropolis and out by this gate to the Emporium, as the Romans called the city's port at the mouth of the Akragas river.

Tomb of 'Theron'
Map 24.

This is a funerary monument (nothing to do with the tyrant) belonging to the last years of the Roman Republic. It stands a little way outside the Porta Aurea.

It is elegant and Greek, having been built – like the Oratory of 'Phalaris' (p. 195) – in the manner of the Greeks of Asia Minor, a fact which suggests a close link between the Greek communities of the Roman world.

Temple of Aesculapius
Map 26.

Situated some distance away south of the S.S.115 and east of the Porta Aurea – take the first track going south – this small temple stands on the bank of the San Biágio.

As there is not only a mineral spring near by, but the position corresponds well enough with Polybius' description, there is little doubt about the ascription of this temple to Aesculapius, that rather mysterious and ancient god who was probably Pallas Athene's son and the bright twin of dark, oracular Erechtheus, and who became the divinity of healing.

Technically, the construction of this building is interesting. Because of the instability of the alluvial soil upon which it is built, a platform of masonry much larger than the temple was constructed. Upon this the stylobate was built with crepidoma of three steps leading to the temple proper. This is Doric of the second half of the fifth century B.C. It is in antis, with naos and pronaos. There is the beginning of a stairway in the pier between pronaos and naos; various elements from its ornamentation are in the museum. The building evidences an elaborate use of entasis, which suggests that its architect was perhaps an Athenian.

The priests of Aesculapius evidently had a considerable practical understanding of psychosomasis and the merits of faith-healing. Patients slept in the temenos and their treatment was apparently dictated by rudimentary, though psychological, interpretations of the dreams they supposed the god had sent them there.

This temple contained a statue of the god by Myron. It was stolen by the Carthaginians and returned after the capture of Carthage by Scipio Africanus, only to be stolen again by Verres.

West of the Porta Aurea, through a gate beside the car park, and inside the wall, is the Temple of Olympian Zeus.

Temple of Olympian Zeus
Map **20.**

The base of an archaic shrine stands before the vast mound of great stones to which this temple has been reduced. The half of a *capital*, which is the first one sees of it, lying at a tilt among this colossal rubble, is tremendously impressive. This was the site – and the fate – of the largest wholly Greek temple in the world.

It was begun after Himera (480 B.C.) and left incomplete at the time of the disaster of 405 B.C. The pile of blocks thrown down by earthquake would have been much higher had not its stones been used for the building of Porto Empédocle.

The area has been so extensively excavated that one is confronted with a bewildering maze of pits, and apparently unrelated foundations, impossible to elucidate in words and tedious to work out in detail. None the less, it is easier to get some idea of the temple if you know that it is preceded, on the east, by a huge *altar* (54·50 metres by 17·50 metres), on the west of which can be seen the substructure of the stairs which led to the altar-platform. All the confusion to the south-east of this, apart from the archaic and self-explanatory foundations of the shrine mentioned above, belonged to Roman and Byzantine buildings, and also to a fortification of a later date. Once one has climbed on to the stylobate, where the Atlas-like telamon lies in the centre of the cella, a better idea of things emerges.

A heptastyle temple of such an unheard-of size required a different construction to any in the Doric canon. To meet its requirements – remember that at the time the Greeks were building with needless weight because they underestimated the strength of their stone – a compromise was devised by its architect, Theron, by which, in place of the usual columns of the peristasis, great buttresses were built all round, being rectangular pilasters on the inside but shaped into half-columns on the out. These were linked by a wall in which there were probably rectangular apertures. Neither the height of the columns nor that of this wall is known, but if the giant telamon figures of men holding a weight upon their arms (they are bent above their heads in the position in which masons carry blocks upon their shoulders) were used as additional support for the vast architrave, and stood one in each of the intercolumniar apertures, some idea could have been got of the harmonious proportions into which these could have been incorporated. The temple measured 369 feet by 184½ feet; the height of the columns, which were 14½ feet thick at the base (a man could stand in each flute), has been suggested as about 55 feet, and the overall height of the building at something like 100 feet or more. The reconstruction in cork of this temple in the National Museum is not quite satisfactory, but it gives a general and likely idea.

Within, the cella appears to have been formed by linking huge four-sided pillars, placed in line with the pilasters, with a light curtain wall. It had pronaos, naos and opisthodomos, and in place of the usual peristyles were wide corridors between the outer and inner walls. The cella itself was unroofed.

Diodoros tells us that, in the tympana of the pediments, there were sculptured scenes from the Gigantomachia and the Capture of Troy. The metopes on the east and west end may also have borne sculptures. And the whole was coated with marble-dust cement.

The weather-beaten figure of a telamon now lies in the middle of the cella floor, where it was reconstructed from fragments in the last century. These figures measured 25½ feet high. One complete and the upper parts of three more are housed in the museum.

As can be seen from this recumbent figure, built of blocks of a depth to correspond with that of the courses of the walls, everything about this temple was on too great a scale ever to have been monolithic. Single blocks of sufficient size to span the inter-columniations could not be raised or moved from the quarries, even by the gangs of Carthaginian slaves whose labour started the building. The half-columns were built of many blocks; the echinus of the capitals was made in two and the abacus in three. The U-shaped grooves in many of the blocks are thought to have acted as built-in pulleys and handles for facilitating the hoisting of the blocks by rope.

South-west of this temple is a large postern in the wall. The buildings whose remains lie west of the temple stretch to the limit of the temenos surrounding the temple and were connected with its service. A sacred way, coming from the agora, ran along the north of the temenos of Zeus and, turning south at the north-west corner of this, it was lined on its eastern side by a stoa marking the limit of the temenos. There were shops on the opposite side of the street, and a cistern below it. At the southern end of the stoa there seems to have stood a small fifth-century B.C. temple, destroyed in 405 B.C. and later converted to some other use. From this the stoa was continued, followed by the street, westwards along the southern side of the Temenos of the Chthonic Divinities (*Map* 18). Where the stoa ended, the street passed out of the city by Gate V.

Between the east–west stretch of the stoa and the fortifications of Gate V a partly paved platform carries the remains of two or three small temples belonging to various periods. These have only recently been excavated – indeed the whole Temenos of the Chthonic Divinities is still in process of being cleared.

Temenos of the Chthonic Divinities
Map 18.

This platform above the escarpment of the city's shelf and over the ravine through which flows the joined stream of the tributaries of the Hypsas, draining the Valley of the Temples, must be one of the loveliest places in Sicily. Across the ravine stands a farm where wheat and barley are threshed in the antique way, horses being driven round a circular pavement to tread out the grain, a life as old as Akragas – and older still, old as the cult celebrated upon this platform.

On its northern side are concentrated the oldest shrines and altars. Traces of a pre-Greek sanctuary have been found here, including a large prehistoric hearth or altar, and stone implements. The archaic Greek structures appear to have been set up alongside Siculan ones – another clear indication of the synthesis of religions which is demonstrated at the Sanctuary of Demeter, as indeed it is everywhere in Sicily.

The archaic buildings grew haphazardly at various times. There are eight altars for public worship, some placed singly, some in pairs, of which one is round and the other square. One enclosure of three chambers, and one of two, each having a pair of altars, were for the performance of secret rituals. There are also three primitive shrines. Two of these have a short pronaos leading to a pilastered pronaos before its simple naos. Here and there are many bothroi, such as those at San Biágio, and trenches, called favissae, in which obsolete cult-objects were stowed.

In the middle of the sixth century B.C., a proper temple was started upon the east centre of the area – the earliest known in the city – but work was soon abandoned, and although restarted on an overlapping site, this too was abandoned. The foundations of the two cellas of these, the one partly superimposed on the other, show that the earlier would have followed the plan – pronaos, cella with adytum – of the older shrines, and the later the more conventional Doric arrangement of pronaos and naos. Both, like San Biágio, lacked a peristasis.

A third temple was then begun, a little to the south of the others, and was finally completed some seventy years after the first project was begun, or soon after 480 B.C. This has for long been dubbed the *Temple of 'Castor and Pollux' (the Dióscuri)* (*Map* **17**) and its very effective-looking few standing columns were erected in 1836, somewhat in the manner of an artificial and ornamental 'ruin', and, as it turns out, are made up of fragments belonging to a number of different buildings. The actual temple, of which only the trenches cut in the rock to hold the foundations remain, was a hexastyle peripteral with thirteen columns along its sides.

Yet another temple was built in the Hellenistic period to the south of the last. To this belong the tumbled column-drums strewing the platform, as also the well-preserved altar to its east. Bits of ornament from this are incorporated in the 'Dióscuri' reconstruction.

Results of the current excavations may modify the chronology of these later temples.

Gate V

This stands south of the altar of the Hellenistic temple. Recently excavated, it is composed of a re-entrant in the line of the wall, a dipylon having two gates, one behind the other. Again, it has a tower on the east, against the shield arm, while it facilitates a defensive attack against the uncovered right of any attacker. Its carriageway is blocked by a fall of masonry from the side walls which appears to have happened in antiquity since there are traces of a rubble wall of Roman date, which had been carried across this obstruction.

Outside stood a mill, and a kiln where terra-cotta ex-voto figurines were moulded for offering at the sanctuary.

Temenos of an Unknown Divinity
Map 19.

Lying to the west again of the Temenos of the Chthonic Divinities, above the junction of the tributary stream and the Hypsas, this consists of the foundations of a walled enclosure (forming the parapet above the valley, which here needed no other fortification), which sheltered two or three small shrines that could be archaic, a circular altar and some other precinct buildings.

From this point one must either retrace one's steps to the Porta Aurea or take the arduous though delightful footpaths across the railway to the Temple of 'Vulcan' (*Map* 16) and the remaining western stretch of the walls. As few people do this, we interpolate here a description of the sights clustered around San Nicola, back on the S.S.118.

Church of San Nicola
Map 13.

Built in the thirteenth century, the Church of San Nicola was a Cistercian foundation of the time of Frederick II. For all its impressiveness, this is the oddest building, for not only is the Gothic mingled with Norman Romanesque, and the great door consorts strangely with the body of the church, but the façade is of direct classical derivation.

Inside, a cornice runs around three sides of its single nave vaulted over with three pointed barrel-vaults. On the sides of the nave are blind arcades upon heavy piers, those on the eastern wall being bracketed out *à la Romanesque*. A former western aisle composed of four deep chapels has been sealed off, and the choir has been restored as an anteroom connecting with the vestiges of the old cloister and other monastic buildings re-used for sundry purposes.

It is still a church and harbours a crucifix called 'Our Lord of the Ship' which has its own festival on September 1st, kept in accordance with its own traditional rites and forms. The rest of the former convent was semi-ruinous until its incorporation into the beautiful new museum. It retains some good Gothic details.

San Nicola now houses the justly famous, second-century A.D. 'Phaedra' *sarcophagus*, discovered in the eighteenth century. Its exceptionally fine carving on all four sides was never completed, which makes it technically interesting.

On the north face, the scene depicted is the nurse revealing Phaedra's love for her stepson, Hippolytus, shown preparing for the hunt with his companions. On the west side, Phaedra is shown distracted at Hippolytus' rejection of her. On the south face, roughed out only, is a boar-hunt; and on the east, also unfinished, the death of Hippolytus thrown from his chariot. In style, the carving reflects the Roman admiration for Greek art and could be called 'classicizing'.

Comitium and Oratory of 'Phalaris'
Map **15.**

Scratch the surface of the fields of Agrigento – just a hair's breadth deeper than a hand-plough cuts – and you discover something revealing from the past. Having built the new museum behind the Church of San Nicola, the archaeologists prudently cleared the site of the garden and approach before these were laid out, only to find the cavea of a small Hellenistic (second-century B.C.) assembly-place built like an intimate theatre with nine semicircular rows of seats divided, rather strangely, though coolly, by water channels. It is thought to be a *comitium* for public meetings.

The Oratory of 'Phalaris' stands across the Comitium from San Nicola. Its fanciful name describes what is in fact a heroön built, like the Tomb of 'Theron', in the manner of the oriental Greeks in the late second century B.C., in memory of a lady. This whole area was a sacred precinct, perhaps of the chthonic divinities, and has been used since the seventh century B.C.; this memorial shrine was built in association with the cult, by the lady's son. The Church of San Nicola also succeeds to the venerable holiness of the site.

It occupies the site of an earlier building and has two storeys; from a lower chamber a stair leads up to what was a small prostyle tetrastyle temple with four columns supporting an archaistic, Doric trabeation across its front.

In the Middle Ages it was converted into a chapel, when a dome was added, a pointed window cut in the west wall and the doorway arched.

Museo Nazionale Archeológico
Map 12.

Open Weekdays 09.00–15.00, 150 l.; Sundays and holidays 09.00–12.00, free.

This new and lavish museum contains a wonderful collection of local finds, well, if rather confusingly, set out. The confusion is not in the ordering of exhibits, but in the building's curious and not uninteresting plan. If you want to look at things systematically you should study the plans in the entrance lobby.

Otherwise, there is charm in the labyrinthine quality of the place: unexpectedly disclosed as marvels, wonders rise before the random stroller to delight him. I find this, of all the museums, the most vividly and immediately illustrative exhibition of Sicily's far past – at least to an unscholarly visitor like me. One should pry about, not to miss anything, and be sure to visit both levels of the centre and western wing.* Prehistoric finds are near the entrance. In the central gallery with V-shaped cases the exhibits are drawn from the old collections of Baron Giudice and the Civic Museum, mostly things of unknown local provenance, though many of them, the Attic vases in particular, of an extraordinarily high quality. In the great western hall is a complete, reassembled *telamon* from the Olympieion, so much vaster-seeming, erect, than his supine fellow on the site. Here too, on the lower level, are three more telamon heads, a model ground plan of the temple and a fine torso which is all that remains of its other sculptural decoration. Opening off the northern gallery in this hall is the chamber containing the finest sculptures from Akragas: the intensely beautiful, compact *ephebus* (*c.* 470 B.C.); the tender, saldly damaged figure of *Aphrodite bathing*, and a vigorous *torso*, both Hellenistic and the latter perhaps Praxitelean. In the southern gallery are many beauties of which the terra-cotta *head of Kore* is absolutely outstanding; it is a statement about the miracle of faith. One room contains lion-head spouts from various temples; they repeat their numinous message in every large Sicilian museum. In the eastern wing are more prehistoric rooms of local finds and others from the interior of the island, among them things from Sant'Ángelo Muxaro. There is a strange stone *goddess* in phallic form, which is one way to reconcile paternity

* A large gallery of exhibits of more scientific than general interest can be seen on application to the Director.

with the absoluteness of the Goddess. Also shown are the more important exhibits from the ruined Museo Diocesano (p. 200); do not miss the twelfth-century *reliquaries* of Limoges enamel and the Byzantine enamel, portable *altar*, the placatory gifts to the cathedral, Norwich suggests, of Bishop Gentile who took years to tear himself away from the court at Palermo to come and visit his provincial see of Agrigento. A beautiful ivory *crosier* is also shown.

Hellenistic and Roman Quarter

This excavated area lies across the road from San Nicola. Sections of four parallel streets – *cardines* – running north and south, have been uncovered, together with the foundations of the houses lining them. The area seems to have developed towards the end of the second century B.C. and to have been occupied into the fifth century A.D. In plan the houses are either built around a peristyle or centred upon a large room or atrium. Some of the houses have good mosaic pavements, the best of which are preserved under cover.

Western section of walls

Continuing the circuit of the walls from the Temenos of an Unknown Divinity (*Map* 19): a path leads down off the platform on which stands the Temenos of the Chthonic Divinities – in fact several do so – and you should set your sights upon two standing columns of the deep golden ruin of the Temple of 'Vulcan' (*Map* 16), to be seen at the start across the valley and the railway in a generally northern direction, and make your own way there.

Or follow the S.S.115 westward outside the walls until, just before the river crossing, branching right by a track leading towards the railway viaduct, you may climb to the platform by passing through the ancient gateway of the temenos surrounding the temple.

Temple of 'Vulcan'
Map 16.

This was a small peripteral hexastyle with a cella divided into pronaos, naos and opisthodomos. It had thirteen columns along its sides. Its stylobate was built on a platform cut from the rock. The fragments of the cornice and the fluting of the remaining columns indicate an Ionic influence, which dates the temple in the latter three decades of the fifth century B.C. A smaller, archaic temple had occupied the site previously; pieces of painted terra-cotta decoration from this are in the museum.

The city walls in this westerly north–south stretch, are fragmentary, but their course is traceable.

Gate VI

A massive affair built to bridge the wide valley of a small stream flowing off the city shelf. It was a dipylon and had flanking towers, rather like Gate V.

Gate VII

This lies immediately north of the railway bridge. It was large with two gate-towers and extensive fortifications in depth, to which belonged the massive, so-called 'Ponte dei Morti' farther down the hill. Parts of the carriage-way of the road through this gate survive in the valley below the walls.

Gate VIII

Beyond this point the walls turned eastwards to avoid the more level ground of the plain lying at the foot of the acropolis ridge, then north again towards the position of Piazza Stazione. The gate is cut into the rock.

PRINCIPAL SIGHTS OF THE TOWN

This high place facing the African sea seems scarcely to belong to Europe. But inside the town of Agrigento, between its tall buildings, the people have made as it were a European refuge for themselves. From the era of the stumps of Doric columns to be seen in Santa Maria dei Greci (*Map* 2) to the surprising *fascisti* Post Office (*Map* 4) and the new flats climbing in blocks upon the Rupe Atenea, there has been continual habitation of the site, and something from most of the intervening periods and styles of building is somewhere to be seen.

Acropolis

Polybius is definite in stating that the hill to the east was Akragas' acropolis, and that Zeus and Athene were worshipped on its height. The city walls pass along the north of the ridge here; and on top, at the Rupe Atenea, the remains of some ancient buildings, and a *hypogeum* – besides numerous cisterns elsewhere – have been found. On the other hand, on the western hill – round which no trace of classical building can now be found – there are very extensive *cisterns*, unlikely to have been left outside the defended area of the city, a *temple*, now under Santa Maria dei Greci (*Map* 2), and another under the cathedral (perhaps that to Zeus) which is equally unlikely to have stood outside the town. The most sensible suggestion has been made that the eastern hill formed the original settlement and acropolis, while the western comprised the next area to be built upon when the population outgrew the first.

The parts of the ridge were then more sharply divided by a natural valley which has since slowly become filled in, and this may have been widened by quarrying. Late sources call the valley 'the Ship' and the 'Cleft of Empedocles' – he having gained in legend the qualities of a master magician.

Aelian records a story about 'the Ship' which, if the house where it took place was up here, would account for the oddness of the nickname: having noted that Plato, struck with the luxury of the inhabitants of Akragas, said that 'they built as if they would never die and eat as if they had not an hour to live', he tells that at a party the young bloods of the town got so reeling drunk that they thought they were at sea in a storm and began to throw the furniture out of the windows to lighten the ship. This so delighted the crowd that the house was ever after known as 'the Ship'.

Cathedral
At the crest of the town; Map 1. *Now closed.*

Founded by Bishop San Gerlando, the Norman who first occupied the see as reconstituted by Roger I, the church has been dedicated to him since 1365. The fabric largely belongs to the fourteenth century and much of the interior had been restored to this original form before a landslip occurred in 1966, severely damaging the church – you can see its cracks and bulges – and endangering anyone who enters it. The massive *tower* was started in the four-teenth century, with Gothic arched windows, and has never been completed. Inside, the great *arch* which divides the nave is a descendant of the triumphal arches of the early basilicas – though serene rather than triumphant in its effect. The open and painted ceiling belongs to 1518 (partly restored in the seventeenth century) and the fine, coffered ceiling to 1603. It is difficult to see what any money could do now to rescue this stately building, or the new-built *Museo Diocesano* by the foot of the steps to the west door, equally imperilled by the disaster. (The best of its contents are in the Museo Nazionale Archeológico (p. 196), for the time being.)

Church and Convent of Santo Spírito (La Badia Grande)
Map 5.

Founded towards the end of the thirteenth century by Marchisia Chiaramonte (née Prefóglio), this was a convent of Cistercian nuns, but it has now been acquired for the Antiquities Department as a monument to be preserved and for administrative offices. It has been much altered over the centuries, and badly damaged by bombing, but is now restored.

Basically a large, rectangular building on two storeys, backed, on the north, by the church, there remain the *refectory* and *chapter-house*, with corresponding rooms over them, and a small *chapel* on the ground floor. These spacious rooms are sparely decorated, their beauty being dependent upon their proportions and the effect of light and shade on the vaulting. The windows and doors of the façade, however, are richly and finely carved. The Chiaramonte family was a generous one, and enormously rich and powerful; they built so much in Sicily in their day that the whole late-medieval decorated style here is often called 'Chiaramonte'. Although there is still a trace of Frederick II's strong classicism, both in archi-tecture and the ornamentation of this convent, already this early work is, as it were, the prototype for the 'Chiaramonte' style.

The church has been even more altered than the convent, yet its very fine, thirteenth-century, *west doorway* survives. Inside, it is a delightful surprise to find oneself in a white church of beautifully simple proportions – alive and as if perpetually joyful with the stuccos of Serpotta. There is, too, a most pleasing *Madonna* of the Gagini school.

Church of Il Purgatório
Map 3.

In the main street, Via Atenea, this is late-seventeenth-century and contains some stuccos of the school of Serpotta.

Church of Santa Maria dei Greci
Map 2.

This is a thirteenth-century basilica, formerly a cathedral of the Greek rite. It has a fine entrance-door and painted roof-beams in the nave. There are also some faded frescoes on the northern wall. On the south of the church is part of the crepidoma and a fragment of a column, and in a passage below the northern aisle are the bases of six Doric columns upon the crepidoma of the temple platform. There is some of the original temple paving in the apse. Soundings made in the church and forecourt revealed that this peripteral hexastyle temple measured 34·70 metres by 15·10 metres and had hollow pillars – allowing for stairways – between the pronaos and naos of its cella. It dates from 490 to 460 B.C. and may have been dedicated to Athena. A piece from the temple's trabeation is preserved in the courtyard of the church.

Services formerly conducted in the cathedral are now held here.

Cisterns

Off the little Piazza del Purgatório opens the entrance to enormous and labyrinthine cisterns anciently cut into the hill. Their full extent is unexplored; but they were evidently excavated in conjunction with the temple building and the stone removed in blocks cut to the measurements of those used expressly for building temples. They are now flooded and cannot be visited.

Civic Museum
In the Piazza Município; Map 6. *May be open between* 09.00 *and* 12.00, *but may not.*

Before the new museum was built this was an adorable muddle of wonders and junk. Now only the junk – I am afraid it must be called that – remains, and since so few people want to see it the curators do not always bother to open it.

ENVIRONS

Excursioning in the vicinity of Agrigento must include **Heraclea Minoa,** for which see p. 173, where it is suggested that a special expedition might be made from there to Sant'Ángelo Muxaro, the significance of which is also there made plain.

To reach Sant'Ángelo without going to Heraclea, however, you would leave from Piazza Vittório Emanuele for Agrigento Basso (under the northern slope of the hill) and there take the S.S.118 to **Raffadali** (16 km.), turning right after the village centre to **Sant' Elisabetta** and **Sant'Angelo Muxaro** – a beautiful drive.

AGRIGENTO TO SYRACUSE

Route 1 S.S.115, 223 km.
Route 2 S.S.122, 117 bis, 124, via Caltanisetta, Enna, Piazza Armerina, Caltagirone and Palazzo Acréide. 257 km. (see pp. 290 and 296).
Rail (Route 1) Change at Licata. Slow journey, not advisable.
Bus (Route 1) Direct C.I.A.T. bus, also local services.
For Rail and Bus (Route 2) see pp. 290 and 296.

ROUTE 1

Accommodation en route At Licata; Gela; Vittória; Cómiso; Ragusa; Módica; Rosolini; Noto; also, off road and by the sea: Marina di Ragusa, Donnalucata, Pozzallo and Pachino-Portopalo.

Leave Agrigento by the S.S. 118 to the cross-roads beyond the old walls, then take the S.S. 115, left-hand turn (Route Exit F).

[25 km.] Just north of the road, **Palma di Montechiaro,** a town founded in 1637 upon the estates of the Tomasi family. Its grinding poverty depresses until the nice, upright and plain baroque of the *church* rises above a flight of steps and lightens the atmosphere.

This town would have little interest had it not been founded by an ancestor of the author of *The Leopard*, Don Giuseppe, Prince of Lampedusa, who inherited and described it.

[45 km.] **Licata**, on the mouth of the *Salso* river, which was the ancient, southern Himera. The town occupies the site of Phintias of Agrigento's colony which he named after himself.

There are some ancient reliefs in the *Municipio*.

Hotels
2nd Class   *Al Faro.*
3rd Class   *Fiume.*
4th Class   *Centrale;*
                Napoli

[80 km.] You reach Gela.

Gela

Population
Over 55,000.
Information
Azienda Autónoma, Corso Vittório Emanuele 222.
Hotels
2nd Class   *Autostello A.C.I.,* Via Scavone;
                Caposoprano;
                Mediterraneo;
                Motel Agip (on the S.S.117 bis to Caltagirone 2·5 km.) ;
                Venezia.
3rd Class   *Excelsior;*
                Itália;
                Sole.
4th Class   *Leone.*

This town now flourishes anew as once it did before it was ground between the upper and nether millstones of Syracuse and Akragas; no more, however, from the classic produce of corn, wine and olive oil, but on account of petroleum oil instead. After the desolation and degradation of the smaller towns one has passed, the sight of the sparkling refineries (the field is off-shore) is so refreshing that the eyes are opened to the strange but very real beauty of these enormous machines. Their setting, too, is becoming: a beautiful, rich plain girdled by hills and the long flat horizon of the African sea. People are apt to miss Gela on account of the more obviously colourful attractions of Piazza Armerina, but by doing so they make themselves the poorer.

Founded in 690 B.C. by the remarkable inter-state co-operation of Crete and Rhodes, its settlement broke the original monopoly over Sicilian colonization which Corinth and the Euboean cities had established, but these colonists were still Dorians, like the Corinthians. Of its two oikistoi (leaders of the expedition; semi-divine founders of the colonies), Antiphemus of Rhodes and Entimus of Crete, only the former became the object of a founder-cult, which suggests that the colony soon became predominantly a Rhodian one. Molino a Vento, the acropolis, would be the site of the first settlement, which quickly spread over the long ridge which is not yet again wholly occupied by the town. On this acropolis remains the single Doric column of a temple. Here, too, was a precinct of Demeter, the excavations of which yielded many terra-cotta figurines and fragments of excellent architectural terra-cotta decorations. Gela was famous for its pottery-ware, which it traded for imported Aegean ware. The city was defended – to small purpose – by a magnificent circuit of walls (see below).

That marvellous poet and dramatist, Aeschylus, died here in 456 B.C. The story is that he was brained by a tortoise-shell dropped by a passing eagle – a more possible circumstance than it might seem since eagles are both ambitious and clumsy with what they carry. Apollodorus the poet was born and bred here.

The history of these cities is uniformly saddening, a melancholic repeat-pattern. Gela's story is told in the History section on p. 50 and more fully in that of Syracuse (p. 212) and Akragas (p. 177), which of course was founded from flourishing Gela.

The rise of the tyrants at the end of the sixth century – Kleandros, his brothers Hermocrates and Gelon – ushered in a period of expansion, power and wealth. Gela needed a better port than its own to maintain the state's great prosperity and this Hermocrates blackmailed Syracuse to cede him, at Camarina; but it was Gelon who took what the Geloans really wanted: Syracuse itself (485 B.C.). He then drafted half the Geloans to Syracuse and a short decline set in at home until, on the death of Hieron I of Syracuse in 466 B.C., at the succession of the 'violent and murderous' third brother, Thrasybulus, many people returned and revivified the town. Decline set in with a vengeance when the Carthaginians destroyed the city in 405 B.C., taking advantage of Syracuse's continued weakness after the Athenian siege. Although Geloans were permitted afterwards to occupy the unfortified city, Timoleon found he must repeople it from Chios in 338 B.C., laying out a completely new town with new fortifications. The grain-lands and pasturage for horses, for which Gela was renowned, ensured the city a return of decent living, but Agathocles' self-interest overrode that of any townspeople; Gela was merely an incident in his war with Carthage, a place he took and ruined to be his temporary refuge, although he strengthened its fortifications. In 282 B.C., the Mamertines, Agathocles' rebel, companion mercenaries who had seized Messina, destroyed Gela for good and all. Phintias of Akragas housed the survivors at Licata and razed the foundations, and the site was deserted until Frederick II, most probably, refounded a town here which was known as Terranova until 1927.

The marvellous sandy beaches of Gela were where the American army landed on July 10th, 1943.

Walls

Gela's one real sight is the westernmost stretch of its classic walls. These are late-fourth-century B.C. and date from Timoleon's re-foundation. They stand among the Capo Soprano sand-dunes, in an Archaeological Zone to the west of the town, and have been wonderfully preserved by the drifting sand. They rise as high as 26 feet, run for over 400 yards, and are very thick indeed. The angle towers are tactically interesting. But most impressive is the beautiful workmanship of the masonry, and the stylishness of its spare decoration. The upper parts of sun-dried brick represent, first, their raising by Agathocles, because sand had buried the lower courses, and, second, a later heightening, most of which Phintias destroyed.

Museo Nazionale

Open 09.00–14.00 and 15.00–18.00 in summer; 09.00–16.00 in winter; 09.00–14.00 on Sundays and holidays. Entrance free.

The finest things of general interest are displayed; another collection and a store may be seen by students, etc., on application to the Director. A beautiful modern setting for the relics of – is it too much to say of Gela? – Greek Sicily's one really creative community. Here it is the terra-cottas which they made – descendants of their Rhodian tradition – which entrance you. The two great hoards of coins were collected, and lost, here rather than locally minted, but the earlier in particular makes one ask again why we no longer have artists willing even to *look* at such beautiful models as these, from which they could get some idea how best to fill a circular shape in a manner which excites and pleases – *why* are we always content with the fifth-rate when we can so easily look around and see how poorly that measures up to the first-rate?

Other things here either belong to the pre-Greek, Siculan town that the Greeks superseded on this site or to those of the hinterland which Gela was particularly interested in Hellenizing.

From Gela a diversion can be made to Piazza Armerina (p. 297), a journey of 45 km.

[112 km.] **Vittória**, yet again a princely foundation of 1607 in the centre of a wine-producing district. The foundress was a viceroy's daughter, Vittória della Colonna, and perhaps it was her taste that decreed that the two *piazze* of the town should be so elegant, although the neo-classic buildings among the baroque postdate her.

Hotels
2nd Class   *Itália.*
3rd Class   *Sicília.*
4th Class   *Firenze.*

Close to the mouth of the Cava di Randello, 13 km. south-west of Vittória, are the desolate remains of *Camarina*. It was founded in 599 B.C. and finally destroyed by the Romans in 258 B.C. There is little of interest to see now. Also off this road is Donnafugata (see next page).

[120 km.] **Cómiso.**

Hotels
3rd Class   *Ariston.*
4th Class   *Moderno.*

[137 km.] You reach Ragusa.

Ragusa

Population
Upwards of 60,000.
Information
E.P.T. office, Via Natalleli.
Hotels
2nd Class   *Jonio,* Via Risorgimento;
            Mediterraneo, Via Roma;
            San Giovanni, Via Traspontino 3.
3rd Class   *Nazionale,* Via San Giuseppe 14;
            Tivoli, Via Gabriele d'Annúnzio 60.
4th Class   *Belvedere,* Via A. Diaz 52;
            Ibleo, Giardino Ibleo.

This is a provincial capital. Excitingly situated on a ridge connecting two hills with deep gorges on either side, this oil and asphalt boom-town is a surprisingly civilized place after the *latifóndie* country.

The western end of the town was built after the 1693 earthquake, and is now again the modern town, while Ragusa Ibla, on the east, reached by the long flight of steps, is the old town. This was originally the Siculan town of Hybla Heraea. Ibla has charms and the baroque of the *Cathedral* and *San Giorgio* church is worth while looking at.

The *Museo Archeológico* is new and agreeable. You enter Ragusa across the Ponte Nuovo, on the farther side of which stands the Albergo Mediterraneo, whose ground-floor is below the level of the bridge. Steps lead downwards and there you will find the Museum. It is open on weekdays from 09.00 to 16.00; Sundays and holidays from 09.00 to 13.00. Closed on Mondays.

The collection it houses derives largely from the as yet rather inadequate diggings at Camarina (p. 206) and of those at the Greek cemetery of Rito on the southward slopes of Ibla, Scornavacche, a district of Chiaramonte Gulfi, and Castiglione – all of them Sikel towns, variously Hellenized, except Camarina, which was a Syracusan colony, sometime belonging to Gela. There are fine Greek wares from tombs, reconstructed graves and an interesting kiln similarly brought here. Some of the terra-cotta architectural details are specially nice – they make one sorry that this art has lapsed, from lack of demand.

South-west, 24 km. off from the town, lies *Marina di Ragusa*, a lido.

Hotels
3rd Class   *Bel Soggiorno;*
                Miramare.

Some 23 km. south-west of Ragusa, and most easily reached by rail, is **Donnafugata** – not to be mistaken for the country palace in *The Leopard*; Lampedusa borrowed only its beautiful name. The village nevertheless attaches itself to a *castle* which can be visited upon polite application. It contains a collection of paintings including *The Holy Family* by Lippo Lippi and a Corréggio sketch.

[152 km.] 3 km. to the left, **Módica** is sunk between hills and rises between the confluence of two torrents that have been channelled underground since a disastrous flood at the beginning of the century. The best part of the town is up the hill and away from the main road.

Some of the churches retain good details.

Hotels
2nd Class   *Motel Agip.*
3rd Class   *Minerva.*

South-west of Módica, 18 km., via **Scicli,** lies the lido of **Donnalucata.**

Hotel
2nd Class   *Riviera.*

[170 km.] Íspica.

A turning right, 11 km., to **Pozzallo** fishing village.

Hotel
3rd Class   *Villa Ada.*

[171 km.] A turning right at the edge of Íspica leads (19 km.) to **Pachino.**

The road leads on (4 km.) north-east to **Marzamemi,** a tiny port.

Also branching from Pachino is a road leading to **Portopalo** which stands on *Cape Pássero,* opposite the islet of that name.

Hotels
3rd Class   †*Le Caravelle.*
4th Class   *El Condor.*

[176 km.] Rosolini.

Hotel
4th Class   *Trieste.*

[191 km.] The road brings you to Noto.

Noto

Population
c. 28,000.
Hotels
4th Class   *Sole;*
                    Stella.

The town is entered after crossing over the *Asinaro* river, where Nicias' troops were butchered while drinking. When many towns in this part of Sicily were rebuilt considerably after the earthquake of 1693, the inhabitants of Noto abandoned their old and wrecked hill-town and started afresh on this site.

This is a prosperous corner of the island and the people of Noto were well off; they built their new town in style – and with imagination and taste. Nowhere can you see the baroque quite so delicately handled, plain and monumental where a great building is wanted, almost frivolous where used for a small *palazzo*. From the level main street, most of the town rises to a planned – almost a landscaped – pattern, while what is, on the whole, the poorer quarter was laid out with dignity below this miniature *corso*.

Visit the following – and by doing so you will see this adorable little town:

Church of San Francesco;
Convent of SS. Salvatore;
Church of Santa Chiara – elliptical in plan; an Antonello Gagini Madonna inside;
The Cathedral
The Bishop's Palace } – Piazza Município;
Palazzo Ducézio (Município)
Chiesa del Collégio;
Piazza Sédici Mággio – fountain from Noto Ántica;
Teatro Vittório Emanuele (1842);
San Doménico – library and museum within;
Palazzo Villadorata – Via Nicolaci;
Via Cavour;
Santissima Crocifisso – where two lions in the Romanesque manner have been preserved from the shattered Chiesa Madre of old Noto and which contains the very wonderful *Madonna della Neve* by Francesco Laurana (1417). This is the only signed work by him in Sicily, though signatures are a redundancy on any mature work by so highly individual an artist as he;
Museo Cívico – at 134 Corso Vittório Emanuele. Open daily 09.00–13.00; entrance free. Here are gathered prehistoric, antique and more modern things, many of them from Noto Ántica (below), others from sites in the neighbourhood, specially from *Hellorus*, a

Greek town founded by Syracuse in the seventh century B.C. near the mouth of the *Tellaro* river (some 6 km. away, and south of Noto Marina), where excavation has started and is to be continued. Upstairs there are very interesting architectural drawings for some of the buildings of the town. This small museum is a fine addition to this exquisite city.

Noto Ántica lies 15 km. away to the north-west. Take the S.S.287 towards Palazzo Acréide and turn left at 11 km.; passing the sanctuary of *Santa Maria delle Scale* (1718) and turning left again, you climb through this utterly ruined town, desolate though picturesque. At the far end is the *Éremo* (hermitage) *della Madonna della Providenza*, built in remembrance of the disaster. Here are displayed various salvaged details, not only from the old town and its churches but also from Hellenistic Greek monuments of the antique town on this site.

[210 km]. **Cassíbile.** Near here in an olive yard General Bedell-Smith and General Castellano signed the terms by which the Italian army surrendered to the Allies in 1943.

[223 km.] Syracuse.

ROUTE 2

Accommodation en route At Canicattì; Serradifalco; San Cataldo; Caltanisetta; Piazza Armerina; Caltagirone; Palazzo Acréide.

This route is described in sections on pp. 290–306. It is a longish drive over marvellously beautiful country-side, but quite possible to do in a day, even making a detour to glimpse Enna, seeing the 'Imperial Villa' and having a quick look at Akrai on the way. The roads in places are rather poor, particularly in the province of Enna; an early start would not be a bad thing.

SYRACUSE

Air
Buses run direct to Catánia airport (taking about 1¼ hours from the Alitalia terminal in Corso Matteotti – at the Piazza Pancali end – and from 92a Corso Gelone).

Sea
Connections with Naples, Genoa, Catánia; also infrequent services to Malta, Tripoli, Benghazi.

Rail
Connections to Catánia and Messina, Enna and Palermo, Agrigento via Catánia and Enna or via Ragusa. Local line to Caltagirone from where there are connecting buses to Piazza Armerina.

Bus
Services from near Post Office (*Map* **23**) to Catánia, Príolo, Noto, Ragusa, Gela and Agrigento; from round the corner in Via Trieste to Catánia, Noto and Pachino; from near Porta Marina (*Map* **28**) to Augusta and Lentini.

Information
E.P.T. office. Corso Gelone 92 (*Map* **17**).
Azienda Autónoma, Via Maestranza 33 (*Map* **30**).
Tourist Information office, Viale Paradiso (*Map* **13**).

Bathing
There are several beach establishments south of Syracuse and also to the north at Príolo (p. 253).

Hotels
1st Class	*Jolly*, Corso Gelone 45;
	Villa Politi (*Grand Hotel*), Via M. Politi 2. (Now being renovated.)
2nd Class	*Bellavista* Viale Acradina 20;
	†*Fontane Bianche*, Via Mazzarò 1;
	Grand Hotel, Viale Mazzini 12;
	Motel Agip, Viale Teracati 30;
	Panorama, Via Necropoli Grotticelle 33;
	Park, Via Filisto 22B.
3rd Class	*Aretusa*, Via F. Crispi 75;
	Neápolis, Via Carlo Forlanini 14;
	Riviera, Via Eucléida 7.
4th Class	*Centrale*, Corso Umberto 141;
	Circuito, Via Páolo Orsi 55;
	Gran Bretagna, Via Savóia 21;
	Milano, Corso Umberto 10;
	Miramare, Passeggio Aretusa 10.

Pension
2nd Class   *Bel Sit*, Via Oglio 5.

Restaurants
The *Villa Politi* (soon to reopen as Luxury Class) serves good food. Either side of the causeway to Ortygia Island, on the north side, are the allied restaurants of *Bandiera* (Riva Forte Gallo) and *Fratelli Bandiera* (Via G. Perno 4), the one, generally speaking, more outdoors than the other. If one is shut, as on one day a week it will be, the other is open. Not soignés, both are beloved by partisans of Syracuse. The *Minerva* (Piazza del Duomo) can be really good too; also *Trattoria Darsena* (Riva Garibaldi) for all sorts of fish, and shellfish straight from the sea.

A provincial capital, once the capital of the island and the greatest city of the West, Syracuse now has a population of over 90,000. It is a place which rouses people's passions. They divide between those who like it extremely and those who cannot abide it. To my mind old Syracuse is completely charming; its situation is remarkably beautiful, its climate unparalleled in Europe – Cicero claimed that no day passed without sunshine –, its 'touristic' interest varied and absorbing, and – above all – the life of the town, though provincial and even, as it were, marginal to contemporary living, strikes me as being vigorous and unusually agreeable.

Modern, recent, explosive growth to the city has become scattered. The very large Archaeological Zone splits those areas where the new town can expand. Perhaps the biggest of these is that lying over the north-east, rivalled by that to the north through which the Catánia (S.S.114) road passes. These are bewildering areas to anyone either newly arrived or who knew them of old. The main new business and shopping area, however, is clustered upon the spine of the Corso Gelone, running across the ancient quarter of Akradina. All this development on the mainland is drawing away the life from Ortygia, which begins seriously to crumble. This is tragic, for Ortygia is one of the gems of Europe.

'Syracuse' is of course an anglicized version of *Siracusa*, which is itself the italianized version of the ancient *Syracusae*. Once a great city of half a million inhabitants, recession brought it back on to the offshore island of Ortygia where it first began.

The sights of interest to a visitor are therefore almost all either scattered over the Archaeological Zone or concentrated upon Ortygia Island.

HISTORY

Many objects of Mycenaean provenance have been found in the neighbourhood of Syracuse and there is no doubt that this part of Sicily was known to Bronze Age Greeks. But contact would appear to have dwindled between the twelfth and eighth centuries B.C.

Modern scholarship tends to confirm Thucydides' dates for the founding of the western colonies, or at least to find no reason not to accept them. He states that Syracuse was founded the year after Naxos; we can take this to have been 733 B.C., when an expedition, led by the Corinthian, Archias, and composed of recruits from various Dorian cities, drove out the Sikels inhabiting Ortygia Island and established themselves there. Perhaps they did not realize what a superlative site they had chosen: they were farmers, primarily, and Syracuse, with its defensible island almost contiguous to a rich plain extending up valleys, while obviously desirable to them, may not have immediately revealed to them its industrial and mercantile potentialities. These are essentially urban qualities, and when one reflects that Corinth itself, though, like Syracuse, a port on the sea's highways, was a town very much like what Caltagirone is today, what settler could have been expected to envisage its future as the greatest city of the classical age?

The first settlers were allotted land, and as reinforcements poured into the colony, the fact of their land-holding raised them to be an aristocratic elite in whose hands an oligarchic power reposed. The Sikels were reduced to serfdom under Dorian Syracuse – the only colonial body to introduce the Peloponnesian practice of helotry into Sicily.

Syracuse was a boom town; during its first 150 years it had a turbulent time while it settled down and the rigidity of the initial oligarchic rule was modified. Akrai was founded in 663 B.C., far up the Anapo valley; Casmenae (Monte Casale) and Camarina were also founded, thus securing the whole south-east of the island. Further expansion was temporarily blocked by Gela, to the west, and Megara Hyblaea to the north. This was a period of peak prosperity for archaic Syracuse, before the great tussle for power had really developed between the Greeks of Magna Graecia, the Carthaginians, the Etruscans and, later, the Romans. (It was at this time that Sybaris – on the Italian mainland – earned its undying fame in the epithet 'sybaritic'.)

Paradoxically, the next period of expansion westwards came about through capitulation: having been ousted from power by a democratic revolution, the aristocratic party appealed to Gela for help, which placed the city in the power of Gelon, tyrant of Gela, an ambitious and able man. He had already allied himself with Theron, tyrant of Akragas, confirming the alliance by marriage – Theron to Gelon's niece, Gelon to Damarete, the first individually recognizable woman in Greek history, Theron's daughter. Gelon now duplicated the dictatorship of Gela and Syracuse. Theron had extended the territory of Akragas across to the north coast at Himera; their alliance dominated Greek Sicily and made possible the tremendous victory of Himera, reputedly on the same day of 480 B.C. on which the homeland Greeks defeated the Persians at Salamis, against the massive attack mounted by the Carthaginians. For three quarters of a century, Sicily was assured of its golden age.

The prizes of victory, above all, included vast numbers of slaves; these the tyrants employed in great civic works, and to build the galaxy of temples we can still see in Sicily today – reflections of the soaring prosperity of the time. And, in Syracuse, a golden ten-drachma piece was struck – most beautiful of coins ever made – showing Damarete's head, posing as that of the water-nymph Arethusa (p. 226) and surrounded by leaping dolphins.

At Syracuse, the Temple of Apollo and the Olympieion, and an archaic temple to Athena on Ortygia, had already been built; now Gelon began the Temple of Athena anew – that building which is now a cathedral. He did not live to see it completed, but, dying in 478 B.C., left his inheritance to his brother Hieron, his deputy at Gela. Hieron raised a monument to Gelon and Damarete near the Olympieion – a great structure with nine towers, now quite disappeared.

The city – Ortygia had long been joined to the mainland by a causeway – had already expanded over the neighbouring ground, and was to grow again, each suburb, as it was added to the perimeter, being walled round against outside attack.

Tyrants are often at pains to collect about them men whose brilliance, they hope, will reflect to their credit. Hieron, who was, says Diodorus, avaricious, violent, 'an utter stranger to sincerity and nobility of character', called the luminaries of his age to his court. Pindar stayed a year and extolled his host's successes in the chariot-racing at the Olympic and Delphic games. Aeschylus perhaps witnessed an eruption of Etna from Syracuse in 479–478 B.C. It is thought that he produced *Prometheus Bound* and *Prometheus Released* in the theatre there, which was specially designed to accommodate the needs of the new school of drama to which he belonged.

Hieron continued Gelon's policy of shifting populations about, the better to secure Syracuse's (or rather his own) hold upon eastern Sicily; and in going to the Greeks' aid in the great naval battle of Cumae against the Etruscans he was again following Gelon's lead. This battle of 474 B.C. was equally important as that of Himera. Etruscan sea-power was broken and the Etruscans never again seriously threatened Magna Graecia.

Hieron died in 466 B.C. and, in Syracuse, as at Akragas, there was a determined reaction towards democracy. The new leaders had some difficulty in ridding the city of the army of mercenaries on which the tyrants had relied for their power, and many of these were eventually settled in Messana (Messina).

A. G. Woodhead, in *The Greeks in the West*, points out that building went forward almost as much under the democracies of Sicily as under her tyrants. With the Carthaginians and the Etruscans successfully confined to their territories, prosperity in Magna Graecia reached its height.

Syracuse was not peaceful for all that. In 453–452 B.C., Elba was seized – it was rich in iron deposits – and Corsica invaded. About this time Rhegium, Leontinoi and Segesta all made alliances with Athens out of fear for Syracuse's ambition. So far as it had any, Syracuse's allegiance was to the Dorians of the Peloponnesus; Athens, jealous of Syracuse, was beginning its disastrous quarrel with Dorian Sparta.

While these sides were tentatively forming ranks, a remarkable Sikel called Ducetius rallied his normally pacific compatriots against Greek domination in the centre of Sicily. When he was defeated he not only sought sanctuary at the altar in the agora at Syracuse but was enabled to live at Corinth and then, possibly in fact (as Akragas maintained) with Syracusan help, to found a new city near Cefalù. This led to war between Syracuse and Akragas in which the latter was defeated.

By 443 B.C., the outbreak of war between Athens and Sparta now imminent, Athens reaffirmed her Sicilian treaties. The Greeks of the west did not, however, actively engage in the war until, in 427 B.C., fighting broke out between Syracuse and Leontinoi, which invoked its treaty with Athens. Syracuse supplied the Peloponnesus with grain, which Athens wished to cut off. She sent ships to aid her western allies, but Syracuse suddenly decided for peace in 425 B.C. and a treaty was concluded.

Tactical advantage in the struggle with Sparta, pride, greed and imperialistic aspirations, all combined to prompt the Athenians to attempt the conquest of Syracuse and, after, of all Sicily. In 422 B.C. they sent an ambassador to engineer the foundations of an anti-Syracusan alliance in Sicily, but it was seven more years before they were ready to attack.

The Great Expedition sailed in 415 B.C., under the joint command of the dazzling Alcibiades and elderly Nicias, who was to prove a fatally indecisive commander. Since few books make better reading than Thucydides' account of this war (translated by Rex Warner for Penguin Books, London, 1964), I shall only do what I can to help you transpose in imagination his text to the hills and bay which lie before you today.*

First luring the Syracusan army north towards Catánia, the Athenians entered the great harbour. This they crossed and landed near the Olympieion, where they built their camp. The attack might have been pressed home had not Alcibiades been put under political arrest and dispatched to Athens – he escaped *en route* and took asylum in Sparta. Nicias decided to await the spring; his surprise attack, when it came, gained him the eastern end of the Epipolae ridge. The citizens had built a wall which defended the suburbs of Neapolis and Tyche from attack, but had neglected to occupy Euryalus; and this omission allowed the Athenians to occupy all Epipolae and blockade the town by land. A pro-Athenian party in the city was in constant touch with the besiegers, and through them Nicias learned that there was much talk of surrender; this caused him to feel over-confident. Along the all-important Euryalus spur, a small relief army of Corinthians and Spartans under Gylippos was able to enter the city.

Gylippos, a Spartan, took command in the city; Nicias wrote home for reinforcements. Gylippos' men and his own skill put the Syracusans for the first time on equal terms with the Athenians. Athens managed, in 413 B.C., to send a second fleet, commanded by Demosthenes and Eurymedon; and Demosthenes planned a great attack upon Epipolae to clear it of Syracusans and drive them back into the town. This attack, made in moonlight, almost succeeded, but was suddenly turned into a rout of the Athenians. Demosthenes was now for returning home, but Nicias would not face the disgrace, and an eclipse of the moon on August 27th decided the Athenians to delay a month – an interpretation of an omen which should have discredited the practice ever after. For the Syracusans blocked the harbour mouth with a chain of boats and grapples, and the Athenians' attempt to break out was countered with a ferocious attack by the Syracusan fleet while the jubilant citizens watched from the town. More than half the Athenian fleet was destroyed.

Retreating southwards, the Athenian forces were overtaken and cut off piecemeal, the commanders, with hosts of others, captured.

Demosthenes and Nicias were put to death – an understandable

* Peter Green, *Armada from Athens* (see Bibliography), is almost as good to read, and far more scholarly and free of bias.

act on the Syracusans' part, though they have been much criticized for it, as also for the appalling sufferings they inflicted on the hordes of their prisoners by keeping them for months in the city's quarry pits, the *latomie* (p. 241). But where else, I wonder, could they possibly have accommodated so many prisoners?

The Athenians' defeat was total, but Syracuse too was weakened. An extreme democratic party arose – banishing the city's hero, Hermocrates, as a potential tyrant. They started a war with Carthage – an ill-fated war leading to a huge Carthaginian assault which desolated Selinus and Himera in 409–408 B.C. and led to the abandonment of Akragas in 406–405 B.C. Hermocrates returned with a band of followers in 407 B.C., but was killed in the agora with most of his companions.

One who escaped this slaughter was twenty-three-year-old Dionysius. This brilliant and ambitious man had himself elected supreme commander, as a first step to making himself tyrant over the state. Ruthless and cynical and self-interested, he was none the less efficient. His first efforts were bent upon the proper fortification of Syracuse, including Epipolae, a tremendous work which saved the city in 397 B.C. He concentrated on rearmament, and turned Ortygia into a palace fortress for himself and his 10,000 mercenary guards. He was the greatest despot of his time and, reigning as he did for thirty-eight years, he had the time to build the first Hellenic empire.

Having securely established his hold on eastern Sicily, Dionysius reopened the war with Carthage. After initial successes, Carthage beat him back to Syracuse itself, but there, encamped through the summer in the marshes, her army was attacked by the plague, an ally which helped Dionysius to rout his enemy for the time being. Later, he was severely defeated at Cronium, but continued his successful punitive campaigns to subdue Sicilian communities.

To quote Woodhead:

Aegean Greece looked on at these achievements with admiration and distaste. Dionysius' alliance was enjoyed by Sparta and coveted by the Athenians, who did not achieve it until 368. He entered impressively for the Olympic Games where in 388 an attack on him in a speech by Lysias so inflamed the crowd that the Syracusan tents were set upon. Dionysius' chariots were unplaced in the big race and no one would give a hearing to his poems ... the insult to his poetic gifts rankled particularly, for Dionysius fancied himself a tragic poet. But, though he possessed the lyre, pen and writing tablets of Aeschylus or Euripides (it is uncertain which), his offerings failed to please the Athenian judges at the Dionysiac festivals. In 368, the year of their alliance, the Athenians became opportunely convinced of the merits of his latest production, *The Ransoming of Hector*. Dionysius celebrated his victory with such enthusiasm that he caught a fever from which he died.

Dionysius was succeeded by his more moderate son, Dionysius II, who promptly made peace with Carthage and relaxed his tyranny over his dominions. His uncle and brother-in-law, Dion, a friend of Plato, invited the philosopher to Syracuse to make of Dionysius a practical example of his theory of kingship. Twice Plato came, and seemed to be making headway, when a rival faction at court turned the king against both him and his protector. Dion was exiled, and Plato returned to Greece. Dionysius now tightened his hold on the kingdom, playing his father's part without his ability,* and Dion presently determined to rid Syracuse of its despot.

Landing, with a welcome, at Megara Hyblaea, he captured the mainland quarters of the city. Dionysius' mercenaries assaulted the city and massacred the people in Akradina, immediately across the causeway; Dion drove the mercenaries back and forced Dionysius to retire with them to Locri. His son surrendered Ortygia. This citadel

---

* Plato had failed entirely. Mary Renault, *Fire From Heaven* (Longmans, London, 1970), has Aristotle think this about his task as tutor to Alexander of Macedon:

.. generations had seen each decent form of government decay into its own perversion: aristocracy into oligarchy, democracy into demagogy, kingship into tyranny. With mathematical progression, according to the number who shared the evil, the deadweight against reform increased. To change a tyranny had lately proved impossible. To change an oligarchy called for power and ruthlessness, destructive to the soul. To change a demagogy, one must become a demagogue and destroy one's mind as well. But to reform a monarchy, one need only mould one man. The chance to be a king-shaper, the prize every philosopher prayed for, had fallen to him.

Plato's exact case with Dionysius II. The tyranny that had lately proved impossible to change was that of Syracuse, and Aristotle, Plato's pupil, tried again, with better material to work upon.

of tyranny Dion refused to destroy, for circumstances had forced him to become a tyrant *malgré lui*. He was assassinated in 354 B.C.

There followed a swift decline under a succession of petty tyrants. When Dionysius II returned and reoccupied Ortygia in 346 B.C. the city was decayed through neglect. The citizens, now in fear of a new Carthaginian attack, appealed to Corinth for help. In response, Corinth produced the amazing Timoleon, though supported only by nine ships and 1,000 mercenaries. With this tiny force he rid the city of Dionysius, together with all the other tyrants of Sicily, excepting only the benevolent Andromachus of Tauromenia (Taormina) who had facilitated his landing.

Timoleon organized moderate democracies in all the cities and banded them together in some sort of effective confederation. With desolate cities and, worse, desolate fields to restore, he initiated a campaign to fetch more settlers from Greece. Syracuse accommodated 60,000 Greek settlers. Akragas and Gela were refounded.

Timoleon died a simple citizen of Syracuse in 336 B.C. leaving history the impression that he was something the world does not see enough of, a benevolent tyrant whose position is owed to an earned and personal popularity and to the justice with which he uses his power.

Without Timoleon the Sicilian Greeks, and the Syracusans in particular, behaved as though he had never been. The oligarchic government that succeeded him brought an intriguing opposition into being; wars were made upon Akragas and Rhegium – which last was so ably saved by a Syracusan exile, Agathocles, that he was invited home to overthrow the government; but in this he was only partially successful. The situation developed into a civil war and the oligarchs were restored to Syracuse with the help of Corinth. In 317 B.C., however, Agathocles again drove the oligarchs from the city and this time successfully retained his power. At first 'supreme commander', in 304 B.C. he styled himself king, and for twenty-eight years he reigned as the most vicious tyrant that even Syracuse had been obliged to suffer.

Carthage was alarmed by his rising power and when he attacked Akragas they went to its help. This war continued, with repeated sieges of Syracuse, until Agathocles was in control of all the opposing Greek cities except Akragas.

Agathocles died in 289 B.C. Petty and parochial tyrants arose again everywhere. Carthage saw a new opportunity to gain all Sicily. Akragas went once more to war with Syracuse, and the Carthaginians, profiting by the absence on campaign of the Syracusan army, sailed into Syracuse harbour in 278 B.C. This brought the two Sicilian cities together and they appealed to Pyrrhus of Epirus – then in southern Italy – for help. He quickly swept the Carthaginians back into their western corner; but he tired of a long siege of Lilybaeum (Marsala), and quit Sicily in 275 B.C. The fruitlessness of 'Pyrrhic victories' seems to have originated in Pyrrhus' own lack of interest in following them up. On his withdrawal, the Carthaginians recaptured all their lost territory and Sicily was much as it had been before his coming. Messana encroached upon Syracusan territory, but the Syracusans were successful in pushing them back. The general in this campaign was called Hieron; the grateful people made him their king – Hieron II.

Hieron II proved a great blessing to Syracuse. He reigned for fifty years, from 265 to 215 B.C., and was in all ways a moderate man. He made good laws, particularly in the sphere of taxation, allowed a constitution and secured a fruitful peace for the kingdom during difficult times for the rest of Sicily.

Not wishing to be the vassal of Carthage, Messana invited the Romans across the Straits to maintain their independence, and the Romans, in accepting, engaged themselves in the first Punic War. Hieron now found himself the strange bedfellow of Carthage. He held off the consul Appius Claudius during the first year, but during the next lost his north-eastern cities and found the Romans outside Syracuse itself. A treaty was made between them by which Syracuse lost some outlying territory, but secured its independence. Thus the war, which was ruinous to most of Sicily, benefited Syracuse. By 241 B.C., when Carthage and Rome disengaged, Rome was master of all Sicily except the Syracusan kingdom. This Rome did not molest, and, as Woodhead points out, 'the Syracusans could thus have no adversaries and no ambitions' – an enviable state to be in.

Hieron II now embarked upon his monumental works in the city, enlarging the theatre, building the vast Altar of Zeus Eleftherios and apparently making Neapolis over anew. His death led once more to trouble as he was succeeded by his grandson, Hieronymus, who was a minor. Rome and Carthage were again at each other's throats and almost all the Magna Graecian cities sided with Hannibal. The consul Marcellus marched upon Leontinoi and sacked the town; too late, Syracuse sent help, thus bringing Marcellus upon the city. After a siege – much protracted by the effectiveness of defensive devices engineered by the great mathematician and natural philosopher Archimedes, a native of the city – and a long struggle with the city's Carthaginian allies, the Romans entered the city in the spring of 211 B.C. The heart of Syracuse was sacked, though Cicero commended Marcellus for his restraint when confronted by the enormous wealth and splendour of Ortygia and Akhradina. Archimedes met his death, it was reported, by accident, Marcellus having ordered that the great man was to be spared. A year later the Romans had pacified the island once more. The towns of Messana, Tauromenium, Netum, were 'independent allies'; Segesta, Panormus and some others earned less conspicuous privileges; and all the rest was administered as a Roman province from the beautiful Ortygian palace of Syracuse. Though just and pacific, and, for their age, wise administrators, the Romans were slow to realize the extent to which they needed not only Sicilian supplies but Sicilian co-operation in obtaining them. The country-side fell largely into the hands of absentee landlords, a situation which caused the ruinous slave revolts of 135–132 and 104–100 B.C.

With a strong garrison, and the governor in residence, Syracuse was probably little affected by the sorrows of the country-side. It certainly suffered under Verres' two years' looting between 73 and 71 B.C. But it was over the Syracuse of that time that Cicero waxed so very enthusiastic, calling it the most beautiful city in the world. Indeed, Republican Rome could have been no match for it.

In 44 B.C. Augustus granted the Sicilians Roman citizenship. Yet the island remained so very Greek that a generation later a Sicilian writer actually boasted that he had been able to learn perfect Latin from the Romans living in Sicily.

Save for the north-east corner, Sicily did not suffer much, materially, from the Roman civil wars, although when the island was seized by Pompey's son, Sextus, there was a serious seven years' loss of export trade. Pompey and Sextus both looted in Syracuse itself. As was the case with the whole of the Italian peninsula, the real prosperity of Roman Sicily came with the long Imperial Pax Romana. Syracuse was now provincial, but important, and at the centre of the thriving Mediterranean trade-routes. St Paul spent three days here on his way, under arrest, to Rome.

The comfortable placidity which seems to have been Syracuse's lot for a time was violently broken when Sicily was raided by a band of Franks between A.D. 276 and 282. These barbarians were only passers-by, but they sacked the city and slaughtered many of the inhabitants. When the Empire was divided under Constantine, Sicily was apportioned to the West. In the mid fifth century the Vandals made repeated raids upon it, presently occupying it, but, in A.D. 476, the island fell into the hands of the Ostrogoths of Italy and it was recaptured for the Empire of the East by Belisarius in A.D. 535. The great city could not recover, however, as an outpost of any empire. It still cannot, because it is not by nature the capital of a province on the Italian frontier, but an international market, a Mediterranean city. However, things were comparatively better in Syracuse during the next three generations or so.

The Emperor Constans (p. 55) was here for a few years from A.D. 663 to 668. After the years of Arabo-Byzantine struggle in the eighth and ninth centuries, Syracuse became the main Byzantine base, as Palermo was the Arabs', from A.D. 831. Syracuse did not fall until A.D. 878, after a long and desperate siege of which we have a survivor's account in the monk Theodosius' letter to a certain Archdeacon Leo. The defenders, he says, had an adequate supply of water, but were forced to eat 'human flesh and herbs, leather and the skins of oxen'. A part of the wall fell on the defenders, but they fought on some days more. When the resistance broke, the citizens were massacred and the city sacked. Theodosius hid in the cathedral while Arabs searched it for loot – and carried off plate weighing 5,000 pounds of silver. The city was fired; and the whole Arab booty was later computed to be worth a million pieces of gold. Sixteen hundred years after its foundation the proud city of Syracuse reached this calamitous nadir.

The Arabs were tolerant of Christians, and the archbishopric of Syracuse seems to have existed, uninterrupted, throughout their domination. In the eleventh century, the island was divided into a number of principalities, Syracuse forming one of these.

After Count Roger de Hauteville (p. 57) had established Norman rule in Sicily in the eleventh century, Syracuse recovered a good deal of her importance. The Normans' trade with the East and Africa, and their intermittent invasions of North Africa, animated its port. The cathedral was embellished with a new front and other churches restored or enlarged. Frederick II built the Castello Maniace not only to be a fortress but a splendid palace also.

Yet Syracuse never really thrived again on anything like its ancient scale – not even to the extent it had under the Byzantines. Its many palaces mostly belong to the odd period when it was the seat of the Cámera Reginale, the administrative centre of a royal domain which was the Spanish queen's dowry – over a period lasting from the fourteenth to the sixteenth centuries.

Calamity befell again in 1693 when the great earthquake of that year ruined much of the town – a quarter of the inhabitants dying in the ruins of their houses; this was, for once, a natural, as against a humanly contrived disaster, and even worse than the bombardment that the town received in 1943.

PRINCIPAL SIGHTS ON ORTYGIA ISLAND

We give first those sights which will help you to orientate yourself, then continue with the others, grouped under Ancient Sights, Museums, Churches and Palaces. The Chart of Excursions (opposite p. 27) indicates the most important sights.

Piazza Archimede

The real centre of the city, the turning-point of the evening *passéggio* up and down the Corso Matteotti, and, with its café tables, the chief sitting-about place of the town. The fountain in the centre is a nice twentieth-century extravaganza called an 'Arethusa'. On the southwest side is the *Palazzo Lanza* with its restrained façade of the fifteenth century and double-arched windows; and on the west the *Banca d'Itália* which, through the arch, preserves a fifteenth-century stair that spells out Catalonia in an unmistakable way.

Piazza del Duomo

One of the most beautiful squares in Sicily. Besides the Cathedral (*Map* 33), and the Museum (*Map* 34), the buildings listed below also front on to the Piazza:

Municipio (*Map* 31), on the corner of Via Minerva. Built in 1628, as the cathedral seminary, by Giovanni Verméxio. The niches were to contain statues of the kings of Spain. This building is at last being restored and added to. Either side the entrance, the first rooms contain massive architectonic fragments and a few showcases. The rest of the building is to house the municipal offices once again.

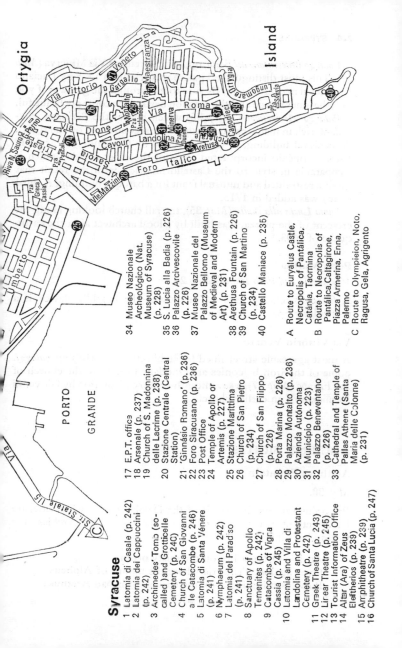

Palazzo Beneventano del Bosco, opposite the end of Via Minerva (*Map* **32**). This most distinguished palace was rebuilt in 1775 by Luciano Ali, a local master-mason. Be sure to go through the gateway if you can; the inner façade and the pavilion beyond the court are beautiful.

Palazzo Arcivescovile (*Map* **36**) which houses the *Biblioteca Alagoniana*, rich in manuscripts (through the second court on the right). A medieval building, it was converted by Giovanni Verméxio in 1618. Verméxio incorporated some of the older façade, which is comparable in style to the Castello Maniace, with the result that this is a restrained and unusual front for a baroque building. A third storey was added in 1715.

Santa Lucia alla Badia (*Map* **35**), the tall church looking along the crescent of the piazza, was built by a local architect after the earthquake of 1693.

Porta Marina

Via Savóia and Foro Itálico; Map **28**.

A fifteenth-century gate of the town – the heraldic device is a particularly Spanish feature.

Via Vittório Véneto

A most agreeable street lined by architecturally satisfying *palazzi*. Some of the iron balconies are especially fine. Note the church of *San Filippo* (*Map* **27**), a seventeenth-century adaptation by Giovanni Verméxio of an earlier church.

ANCIENT SIGHTS

Arethusa Fountain

Map **38**.

Pausanius reports the words of the Delphic oracle when uttering its directions for the founding of the colony to Archias, the Corinthian oikistos:

> An isle Ortygia lies on the misty ocean
> Over against Trinacria where the mouth of Alpheus
> Bubbles mingling with the springs of broad Arethusa.

These place-names belong to an apocryphal translation, but the gist of the verse is probably authentic. So fine and profuse a spring as Arethusa, so admirably sited upon a defensible, offshore islet, could scarcely help but have its divinity – the nymph Arethusa. Syracuse's ancient greatness enhanced her fame; classical authors often refer to the fountain – even Nelson, having watered his fleet at it, wrote: 'surely ... we must have victory', and sailed off to win the battle of the Nile. There are some patriotic Dorian 'myths' concerning her: Arethusa, they write, was changed by Artemis into a fountain to escape the advances of Alpheus, the god of the river across the bay of Syracuse. This river was itself said to rise in the Peloponnesus and flow underground before reappearing in Sicily; a cup – this story is quoted by Strabo as an example of the incredible things attributed to Arethusa – thrown into the river at Olympia, came to the surface of Arethusa's pool, which could also turn red from the blood of the sacrifices at Olympia. These tales at least demonstrate the strong sentimental attachment which the Syracusans felt for Greece.

Once the spring gushed from a natural grotto and the water had to be dammed to prevent it all flowing into the near-by sea. The pool was full of fish. Now the place has been altered out of recognition, planted with papyrus, a tip for tin-cans and wrapping-paper, although it is still full of grey bream. But it grows mysterious again under its nightly floodlighting.

Temple of Apollo or Artemis
Piazza Pancali; Map **24**.

These ruins, lying partly below the level of the modern town and encircled by the flow of traffic, are rather forlorn except at night when they are illuminated. They have had a chequered history, the temple having been converted to a Byzantine church, then to a mosque and finally incorporated into a Spanish barracks. The remains, although partly reconstructed, are worth looking at closely, however.

The temple was probably the earliest of its size to be built on Sicily – in the first half of the sixth century B.C. A Doric peripteral hexastyle with seventeen side columns; the six frontal columns were repeated by a second row also standing before the pronaos, which was entered between two more. The cella is a long one, the pronaos short; and the long naos – or, more strictly speaking, in this case the sekos – leads to a short adytum. The interior of the cella was divided into aisles by two rows of columns upon which second, shorter rows were mounted to uphold the roof. Learned controversy rages over the shape of the metopes because the columns of the peristasis are placed unusually close together and have shallow flutings. The cornice was decorated with painted terra-cotta – a common practice in those early times – pieces of which are in the museum.

On the stylobate is a dedicatory inscription to Apollo made by Cleomenes (or Cleomedes – the text is defaced), who may have been a tyrant of the city. Cicero, however, calls this a temple of Artemis, which is less confusing than might appear since Apollo and Artemis – Zeus' children by Leto – were hatched from the same egg and not uncommonly worshipped in association, as at sacred Delos among the Cycladic islands.

The plan of this temple closely resembles that of the Olympieion (p. 250), which it possibly antedates by only a very few years.

MUSEUMS

Museo Nazionale Archeológico (National Museum of Syracuse)
Piazza del Duomo; Map **34**.

Open In summer daily 09.00–13.00 and 15.30–18.00; Sundays and holidays, morning hours only. Closed Mondays; in winter 09.30–16.00 daily, Sundays and holidays 09.30–13.00. Entrance fee except Sundays.

This is an important collection for students either of prehistory or Greek periods, and it contains much that is of universal interest and appeal, though, as yet, little of outstanding aesthetic importance. Do not let this statement discourage you, however.

Here is what Peter Quennell writes in *Spring in Sicily* (Weidenfeld and Nicolson, London, 1952) about the museum's three chief sculptures – I quote him because I wholly concur with his views:

... the mutilated fragments of only two distinguished statues. Each is the torso of a young man, one archaic, the other of the early fifth century; and, whereas there is an exquisite formalism

about the earlier statue – the lines of the body flattened and
elongated, an ideal rhythm superimposed upon the artist's
knowledge of the actual fleshy structure – in the second the
archaic convention is losing its rigidity, though its influence can
still be felt, checking any hint of exuberance, giving an air of
dignified reserve to this gravely steadfast athlete … The work
is 'classical' in the noblest sense of the word; a lively appreciation of the charm of the living flesh co-exists with a resolute
aversion from emotionalism for its own sake … How coolly
and chastely sensuous, if one compares these two male statues,
produced in the spring of Greek art, with a product of its tired
and sultry autumn, the renowned and atrocious Aphrodite,
dug up at the beginning of the last century by an archaeologist
named Landolina! Maupassant … saw the Aphrodite when he
visited Syracuse and voiced his admiration of it … The marble,
he declared, was really alive. 'On le voudrait palper avec la
certitude qu'il cédera sous la main, comme de la chair … C'est un
corps de femme qui exprime toute la poésie réelle de la caresse.'
Certainly the marble looks as if it would yield to the touch;
there is a surprising verisimilitude in the deep-carved dimples
of those over-generous haunches; but poetry is an attribute
that we can no longer claim for them … a stout hetaera who
emerges from the bath and, with a practised gesture of
immodest modesty, attempts to gather up her fallen robes …

UPSTAIRS

The museum is ordered chronologically, beginning with the first
room, where Paleolithic and Mesolithic finds are housed; then
Neolithic; sub-Neolithic and early Bronze Age; the full Bronze
Age and early Iron Age, and native Sicilian cultures at the time of
the arrival of the Greeks, showing the interesting beginnings of
Greek influence upon them. The next rooms concentrate upon finds
from certain small sites and do not keep to a strict chronological
order; note the fourth-century B.C. bronze armour – so small!
Then come finds of the ninth to fifth centuries B.C. from certain
sites; then finds from Syracusan and south-east Sicilian sites to the
Hellenistic period, particularly the Gelan finds. Finally there are
displays of early Christian and Byzantine antiquities together with
finds belonging to Mithraic and other Oriental cult-centres contemporary with the rise of Christianity.

The collection is thus arranged in a scholarly way, but unless it is understood by the visitor he will easily think it is a perplexing jumble. Though the better examples of all sorts are on view, much that might not be so interesting out of its context is shown, and the less studious are probably best advised to try and wander around the rooms in their sequence and simply let their eyes light upon whatever attracts them – there should be plenty to do so in so rich a treasury.

GROUND-FLOOR

The ground-floor of the museum has more to offer inexpert tastes, being given over largely to sculpture and architectural exhibits. Here are the torsos of the kouroi, the older one (sixth-century B.C.) with the inscription on its leg saying that it belongs to Sombrotidas, son of Mandrokles, a doctor; and that later one (early-fifth-century B.C.) from Leontinoi which was perhaps carved in Greece. I have let Quennell have his say, but he does not mention the immense vitality and confidence of these early Greek sculptures – the quality about them which enraptures me the most.

Off in a small room is the unspeakable Venus 'Landolina' of Syracuse, and a good Herakles of the school of Lysippos, *c.* 300 B.C. Opposite, another room holds some splendid archaic sculpture: the headless Goddess (name unknown), seated and suckling twins, comes from Megara Hyblaea, mid-sixth-century B.C. – a unique and, in its way, uniquely wonderful sculpture, so formal and so very tender. In the room devoted to Christian and Byzantine art is the fourth-century A.D. sarcophagus (from the San Giovanni catacombs) of Valerius and Adélphia with carved sides depicting Old and New Testament scenes. Everything illustrative of this transitional period between the art we think of as 'pagan' and that we associate with Christianity is fascinating; and here we have a first-class job of the time.

A new museum is planned – there is a model of it in the foyer of the building – and while it is nice that this tremendous collection will be less cramped and dingily housed than now, it is sad that it will be away from Ortygia, on the mainland.

Museo Nazionale del Palazzo Bellomo (Museum of Medieval and Modern Art)
Via Capodieci ; Map **37**.

Open 09.30–16.00 on weekdays; Sundays and holidays 09.30–13.00. Entrance fee on weekdays.

The lower part of the front of this Swabian palace belongs to the original thirteenth-century building; the upper part with the double- and triple-arched windows to the Siculo-Catalan fifteenth century. Inside, there is a Catalan outdoor *stairway*, a *portico* and a *loggia* on the first floor, all fifteenth-century. Thence you can pass on into the fourteenth-century *courtyard* which really belonged to another house, the Palazzo Parísio. So little is left of the domestic architecture of Frederick II's time that one looks eagerly at what little remains here.

The Palazzo houses a small and choice collection of works of art, of which the treasure is an *Annunciation* by Antonello da Messina. Though it is tragically damaged, the essentials of its startling composition (it was probably the centre panel of a triptych) and enough of the figure of Mary – steadfast, and graceful in all senses, her drapery cascading with humility – yet survives to make this painting eternally memorable.

This gallery is currently being enlarged by the addition of the adjoining Palazzo Parísio.

CHURCHES

Cathedral and Temple of Pallas Athene (Santa Maria delle Colonne)
Piazza del Duomo; Map **33**.

It hardly matters which way you approach this extraordinary building, whether along the Via Minerva – where you see the medievally walled-up, northern side of the peristasis of a Doric temple, its entablature crowned with decorative Norman battlements above the triglyphs and metopes, and the outer sides of twelve fluted columns standing upon their stylobate – or from the piazza where you first see the exceedingly beautiful baroque front of 1728–54, designed by Andrea Palma, with statues of great verve and presence by Ignazio Marabitti.

The temple was started at the beginning of the fifth century B.C. upon the site of a temenos to Athene, which had been established there since the foundation of the colony in the eighth century B.C. The site had previously been occupied by Sikels. Fragments of the painted terra-cotta frieze from a sixth-century construction in the temenos, and two altars, are in the museum. This building was apparently demolished to make way for the temple which Gelon himself almost certainly started to build in thanksgiving to the Warrior Maiden for the Greeks' victory at Himera.

This was a peripteral hexastyle with fourteen columns along the sides. It had a long, narrow cella entered through a pronaos between two columns, and an opisthodomos in antis also entered between the two columns whose interior faces can be seen either side of the present west door.

The riches of this temple were fabled in the ancient world, and we owe most of our knowledge of its contents to Cicero's speech for the prosecution against the ex-praetor Verres, who despoiled the temple. The walls were painted with scenes of Agathocles' victories over the Carthaginians and portraits of the 'kings' of Sicily – so far as is known, among the earliest examples of portraiture in European art, for Cicero makes it plain that they were indeed portraits. Of the doors to the temple, Cicero said: 'more splendid doors, doors more exquisitely wrought in ivory and gold, have never existed in any temple at all'. On the roof – at the apex of the pediment, probably – stood a huge statue of the goddess carrying a gilded shield which flashed as a beacon in the sun and guided sailors into port from far out at sea.

The temple was converted into a church at an early date, though just when is not known. In A.D. 640 Bishop Zosimus transferred the cathedral of Syracuse from San Giovanni, on the mainland, to this church, but it had probably already been converted by then. Gregorovius confirms that it was already a church by the time Constans II moved his seat of government to Syracuse. Zosimus at any rate extended the size of the church, filling in the inter-columniations of the peristasis and cutting the existing eight arches in the sides of the cella walls. The side aisles thus made were barrel-vaulted and the cella walls raised to make a clerestory below a timbered roof over the nave. It is thought that the western end was walled up at this time, but it may have had a narthex of which all trace disappeared in the subsequent Norman rebuilding of this front. Excavation and structural exploration have disclosed a half-domed apse in the end of the northern aisle, so probably the usual three were then built into the temple – as they were in the pronaos and peristasis of the Parthenon.

In the eleventh century, further alterations were made, including the building of a west front which collapsed in the earthquake of 1693, after which the present one was built. The church had already been damaged by earthquake in 1543 and patched up, but after 1693 a thorough restoration was undertaken in the baroque style, although a lot of this was dismantled early in this century, the better to reveal what lay beneath. One is very grateful that archaeological fervour went no further (as at the Temple of 'Concord' at Agrigento), since the interior of this church is quite exceptionally beautiful; taste, practical considerations and happy accident, one presumes, having between them done little to disturb the beauty of its Doric proportions.

All its long history can be seen in the interior of this very sacred building – sacred, now, for nearly 2,500 years: the *Doric pillars*, *Byzantine arches* and *apse* (end of northern aisle). The *font* in the Baptistery (westernmost chapel on the south) is made of a Greek block and bears a Greek inscription, but is of Norman cutting and rests on twelfth-century bronze lions. Remnants of twelfth-century mosaics are on the wall.

The next chapel south (that of Santa Lucia) has beautiful bronze *gates* between Doric columns, made in 1605 by Pietro Spagnuolo, and contains the very good silver image of Santa Lucia – patroness of the town – by Pietro Rizzo, made in 1599. The silver casket was probably the work of the Gaginis, and belongs to 1610; the silver-leaf *altarpiece* is by Desio Furnò (1781).

The large *Chapel of the Holy Sacrament* (southern aisle), closed with admirable early-nineteenth-century iron gates, was almost certainly designed by the excellent Giovanni Verméxio about 1650. The eighteenth-century tabernacle itself was designed by Vanvitelli, architect of the palace of Caserta.

From the eastern end of the southern aisle there opens the *Chapel of the Crucifix* in which, on the northern wall, is a painting of St Zosimus which is attributed to Antonello da Messina, and, on the southern wall, another of St Marcian generally attributed to da Messina's school. Both have excellence and charm, but neither, to me, proclaims the hand of the master.

Out of the Chapel of the Crucifix, a door leads into the *Sacristy of the Chapel*, where there are two sixteenth-century *paintings*. Beyond is the Treasury, which is closed to the public. The *Sacristy of the Church* is reached through that of the Chapel, left. Here are fine carved stalls of 1489 and thirteen panels from a polyptych belonging to the school of Antonello da Messina.

A monolithic block from the temple entablature is employed in the structure of the altar in the *Presbytery*.

In the Byzantine apse at the end of the northern aisle stands a *Madonna della Neve* (of the Snow), a good and moving Antonello Gagini of 1512. Another and more pedestrian Antonello Gagini stands in the northern aisle, of *Santa Lucia* (1526). The *Madonna and Child* near by is by Doménico and another unnamed Gagini.

The Doric pillars in this aisle show how the earthquakes shook them despite the walls and roofs helping to strengthen them – and which they, in their monumental strength, helped so much to uphold.

Church of San Martino
Via San Martino; Map **39**.

A very early basilican church, rebuilt in the fourteenth century. It is an unassuming church in which one senses both its great antiquity and a deep, parochial placidity. Few churches offer this quality of ancient repose, particularly in harassed and emotional Sicily.

The church has a beautiful Gothic *doorway* and *rose-window*; and inside there is a pleasing *triptych* of the Madonna and Child with SS. Marcian and Lucia.

Church of San Pietro
Via San Pietro; Map **26**.

This is one of the very old churches of Italy. The tradition is that Bishop St Germanus built four churches in Ortygia in the second half of the fourth century, immediately following the conversion of Constantine and the official establishment of Christianity as the religion of Rome. Architecturally there is no reason to suppose this church was not, in fact, the one St Germanus is known to have dedicated to St Peter, or to doubt its dating.

The church has suffered various modernizations, much of which has recently been cleared away to reveal as nearly as possible its earlier condition, while enabling us to establish that it was originally built as a basilica of late Roman type with three aisles divided by tall, narrow arches leading westwards to three apses. The real arches were reflected by blind ones cut upon the side walls. The Byzantines of the seventh and eighth centuries drastically remodelled the church, elongating it and transferring its altars to the east, where a central apse (later dismantled) was built.

In the fourteenth century, the arches were remodelled to delicate Spanish-Gothic proportions, and the very fine north door was added with the chapel on the south.

PALACES

Castello Maniace
Piazza Frederico II Imperatore Romano; Map **40**.

Built by Frederick II, *c.* 1239, as a fortress-palace, this is now a barracks. It may be visited with permission obtainable, between 09.00 and 12.00 on weekdays, from the Commando del Presídio Militare, which is on the Lungomare Ortygia near by. However, some have succeeded in visiting the castle simply by walking through the gates.

It is a square castle, built round a courtyard, with round angle towers. Much of the original structure remains, though it was formerly one third higher. The vaulted chambers of the ground-floor, one with a fine chimney-piece, remind one of the Castel' del Monte in Apúlia. The noble Gothic portal added to the front is flanked by two original niches in which Frederick placed a pair of Hellenistic bronze rams, one of which is now in the National Museum in Palermo (p. 118).

Palazzo Gargallo
Via Gargallo.

A fifteenth-century palace with a delightful *portico* and a nice Catalan outside *stair*.

The incidence of really good, very old buildings of this kind gives Ortygia its special feel of having always been a cherished and mildly prosperous place.

Palazzo Montalto
Via Montalto; Map **29**.

Built, as the inscription on the front says, in 1397, in a rather free and fanciful interpretation of the Chiaramonte style. While there is a vacant lot next door one may see its arcaded rear. This noble building is derelict, however – and anywhere else in Europe people would be glad to pay a high price for such a dwelling.

Palazzo Lantieri
Via Roma; at the Piazza Archimede end.

This delightful little house is exceptional for its decorated front, an extravaganza in stucco. Late-Renaissance in date.

Palazzo Migliáccio
Passeggio Aretusa.

Part of the erstwhile Jolly Hôtel des Étrangers whose name is still over its door. At the back in Via Picherale the black lava chevrons set in the white marble of the terrace balcony give a notable hint of what the city's palaces were like in the fifteenth century; very Catalan in feeling.

PRINCIPAL SIGHTS ON MAINLAND

AKRADINA

The first mainland quarter of the ancient city and that part which is closest to Ortygia, to which it was joined by bridges and a causeway, now with one bridge only. Towards the west end of the Corso Umberto are gardens called the *Foro Siracusano* (*Map* **22**) with a modern war memorial (*fascisti* – 1936). In the gardens are a few remnants of the old *agora*.

Farther along on the right of the Noto road (Via Elorina) is the '*Ginnásio Romano*' (*Map* **21**). Probably built in the first century A.D., it is no gymnasium but a small Roman theatre. So far as it can be reconstructed, it was a rectangular enclosure surrounded by a portico opening inwards, and originally entered by the east; in the eastern half stood an altar before the entrance to a small temple raised on a podium, of which a part of the north side remains. The rear of this temple acted as the architectural background of the stage set against it. The orchestra is now usually flooded, as the water-level has been raised hereabouts, and the lower tiers of the cavea surround a pool. Some statuary was found here.

On the northern side of the Via dell'Arsenale are the excavated remains of a *Byzantine bath-house*. It would be a bit too coincidental if this were, as has – inevitably – been suggested, the very bath where Constans II was assassinated with a soap-dish. It is not on Ortygia, nor of an imperial size.

The neighbouring excavated site is that of the ancient *Arsenale* (Map **18**); the foundations of a hoist by which ships were brought from the – then closer – Porto Píccolo into dry dock can be seen there.

On the shores of Akradina, at the south of what is now the Porto Píccolo, stood the shipyards of old Syracuse. A good port was necessary to the real success of a colony, not only for its trade and communications, but as a secure place in which to build its fleets. Syracuse was pre-eminently well situated in this respect.

Whereas the original colonists' ships may have been some 40 feet in length, Moschion – a Hellenistic describer of wonders – tells of the huge ship which Hieron II ordered Archimedes to build for him here.

Wood 'enough for sixty triremes' was felled on Etna; other woods came from elsewhere, including mainland Italy; rope from Spain, hemp and pitch from the Rhône. It took 300 shipwrights, with assistants, a year to build. Archimedes invented the 'helix' to launch it – giving us the screw and the Archimedean drill. The hull was lead-plated and the bronze nails plugged with lead and pitch. Propelled by twenty banks of oars, it carried three bronze-tipped masts, the foremost having eventually been found in Bruttium and transported here. It carried eight towers and a number of fighting machines: catapults, arrow-dischargers, slung grapples and beams which swung outwards to tip boulders on to attacking vessels – all to Archimedes' special designs. A palisade of iron protected the sides, manned by 120 soldiers. There were as many again upon the towers and masts, etc.

It sounds a cumbersome vessel, but along the sides were ranged telamon figures, twelve cubits high, which 'supported the weight placed above them and the triglyphs, all fixed at convenient distances from one another. The whole ship was adorned with suitable pictures.' This was marvellous enough, yet the living quarters (couches for thirty-two are enumerated) comprised apartments with mosaic floors depicting 'all' the scenes of the *Iliad* 'marvellously well'; a kitchen; a marble bath-house; a temple to Aphrodite – the sailors' deity – of cedarwood, ivory and marble, magnificently furnished; a lounging room with boxwood walls, a bookcase and a clock; with a gymnasium and shaded decks where there were bowers of ivy and vine among gardens of other plants set in tubs. There was stabling for twenty horses, many 'rooms' for the marines, a mill, ovens, a huge fresh-water cistern and a fish tank. Archimedes designed a pump to clear the holds, worked by pulleys.

Governed under Syracusan law by a tribunal of the captain, pilot and officer of the watch, this wonderful ship put to sea laden with 60,000 measures of grain – for, ultimately, she was a merchantman – and 10,000 jars of fish, 20,000 talents' weight of wool and as much other miscellaneous cargo, besides her provisioning. She sailed with an escort of galleys, led by a light one acting as scout.

During her building Hieron visited the yards daily and he named her *The Syracusan*. But then he found that 'some harbours in Sicily were not large enough to admit this ship and that other harbours were dangerous', so he changed her name to *The Alexandrian* and sent her as a present to King Ptolemy of Egypt.

It can be difficult to gauge the scale of ancient things, to sense the reality of wealth then, judge the range and standards of technology or get the feel of the realizable demands which people then made of living: Moschion's description of *The Syracusan* helps with this, and the result is no end surprising. Hieron would not sail without entertainers and an orchestra, which leaves the *Q.E.II*, with her swimming-pool and cinema, only two up in luxury.

At No. 11 in slummy Via degli Orti di San Giorgio a figure of the Virgin – of a mass-produced type – wept for five days during 1953 and a large circular church of *S. Madonnina delle Lacrime* (*Map 19*) has been built there now to house it, as a sanctuary.

ARCHAEOLOGICAL ZONE

Entrance is from the Viale Augusta. Buses 3 and 4 from Piazza Archimede. There is a Tourist Information Office and nearby restaurants.

Open 09.00–15 minutes before dusk in summer; in winter 09.00–13.00 and 14.00–dusk. There is an entrance fee for the Latomie lying in this zone or park.

Altar (or Ara) of Zeus Eleftherios
Map 14.

Lying west of the amphitheatre, this enormous altar – it is 650 feet long and 79 feet wide – was raised in the latter part of Hieron II's reign, between 241 and 215 B.C. to honour Zeus the Giver (or Bringer) of Freedom. The annual festival celebrated here was in honour of Timoleon's 'liberation' of Syracuse and Diodorus says 450 oxen were sacrificed during it.

Only the base now remains, most of its material having gone to build the Spanish walls of Ortygia. Originally, a ramp, up which the sacrifices were driven, rose to the top at either end, and there were two entrances by stairs in the western face at either end. These had porches within the bulk of the altar and were flanked by telamons; of these the feet of one remain in position in the northern entrance, while the 'Atlas' figure in the museum is supposed to belong to one of the others. The sacrificial fires were lit along a ledge rather lower than the platform's top. Below this ledge was a cornice with lion-head water-spouts.

The area to the west of the temple was found to contain many votive offerings. Here a rock-cut street ran parallel with the altar, from the agora to the theatre; in its side were cut niches in which some of the votive offerings had been placed. In the Augustan period, however, this area was redesigned on a grand scale, being made into a piazza with a rectangular tank – stuccoed and with statues upon plinths at its corners – in the centre, and the open part planted with five rows of trees, while the south, west and north sides were surrounded by a pillared portico. This monumental glamorization was very typical of the Romans' attitude to local cults; by seeming thus pompously to honour them, they took much of the traditional heart out of them – and Eleftherios, one can see, would be an aspect of Zeus inimical to the Emperor Augustus whose only god – whatever lip service he might pay to Apollo – was Capitoline Jove, for whom one might substitute Gaius Julius Caesar Augustus.

Amphitheatre
Map 15.

Entered by the garden to its north containing tombs from local cemeteries and that of Megara Hyblaea. Built in the second half of the second century A.D., this is an Imperial Roman building of excellent workmanship. Its ellipse measures 459 feet by 390 feet. The slope of the hill was used as far as possible in the construction of this arena, much of it being excavated in the rock and only the higher tiers and the rest of the curve being built up. It is these parts that have been the most damaged, particularly by stone-robbing for the walls of Ortygia.

The main entrance for spectators was by the south. The arena is surrounded by a parapet, many of whose blocks are inscribed with the names of the owners of the seats immediately behind them. Under the front-rank seats runs a corridor with doorways giving on to the arena through which the gladiators, victims, animals – the performers – entered it. In the centre is a tank with a wide channel connecting to the south entrance, and a narrower one to the west. Being too small a basin in itself for aquatic displays, this puzzles scholars, but its purpose may have had to do with the drainage as well as the flooding of the arena.

The Viale Páolo Orsi, named after the famous archaeologist who uncovered so much here and all over eastern Sicily, enormously extending our knowledge of the island's past, cuts across a vast open piazza which lay south of the Amphitheatre and was used as a stabling area for the beasts used in the displays. There is an antique horse-trough to its north. Perhaps also it was a park for chariots, coaches and litters.

The footings of a *triumphal arch*, belonging to the time of Augustus, bestraddle the old road which is parallel to the Viale Páolo Orsi on the north. This road is Hellenistic and was remade in Roman times.

The Amphitheatre is a considerable monument; and so large an amphitheatre – second in size, though by very little, to Verona – testifies to the importance and size of Roman Syracuse.

Archimedes' Tomb (so-called)
In the Grotticelle cemetery – above the Latomia di Santa Vénere; Map **3**.

A Roman and Byzantine necropolis; there is here a tomb with a Doric pediment which is certainly not Archimedes' tomb, though this Roman columbarium of the turn of the first millennia B.C. and A.D. may earnestly be shown you as such.

Cicero, however, described how he searched for and found the real tomb (no longer in existence) near the gate of Akradina, among briars, and with only a column standing, a sphere and a cylinder rurmounting it. He sent for men with scythes to clear away the underbrush and found the inscription on the base, though already, he says, the latter parts of the verses were almost effaced. The search, rewarded, was a nice tribute from one great man to another.

Latomie

There are a number of these ancient quarries, from which the stone to build the early town was cut, along a line below the bluff of Epipolae, which would seem to mark the greatest extent to which the first Syracusans thought their town might spread. They have a strange charm, being deep cuttings with vertical sides, in many places undercut into caverns upheld by massive, square-cut pillars of natural rock – sometimes collapsed – and filled now with trees and sheltered citrus groves. Most can be visited for a small entrance fee during the hours when the other sights are open.

Some of the *latomie* – the word derives from Thucydides' Greek term – are listed below:

Latomia del Paradiso (*Map* 7) – east of the Greek Theatre; a large and more open quarry than some. Its chief 'sight' is the artificial *cave* called (originally, it is said, by the painter Caravággio – because of the shape of its opening) the *Ear of Dionysius*. It has accidental acoustical properties beloved of the guides and all modern myth-makers. Actually, the purpose of this carefully cut, high-vaulted and curving passage containing a single niche and one overhead opening is unknown. The 'grottoes' of the Cumaean Sibyl seem its nearest counterpart, but the true use of these, too, is doubtful. Also here is the traditional *cave of the rope-makers* (*Grotta dei Cordari*), where scored rope-marks can be seen on the limestone pillars, on which, too, lichens and luxuriant maidenhair ferns grow. Nearby is a Roman *piscina*, a reservoir into which one of the three aqueducts crossing Epipolae ran. A channel from the reservoir to the amphi-theatre suggests its use for flushing the arena.

Latomia di Santa Vénere – east of that of Paradiso and connected to it (*Map* 5). Contains a pleasingly wild sort of garden, and its walls have in places been niched for use in the cult of Heroes.

In addition, scattered around the rest of the town are other Latomie.

Latomia di Casale (*Map* 1). A rich beautiful garden.

Latomia di Villa Landolina (*Map* 10) – Viale Teócrite. This small latomia contains the *villa* of its name and also the *Protestant Cemetery*, where August von Platen, the romantic poet, was buried in 1835 (permission to visit the villa is obtainable at the Amministrazione Interlandi – Pizzuti, Piazza del Duomo No. 1).

Latomia dei Cappuccini (*Map* 2; near the Villa Politi hotel) – if not all the quarries were used as the Athenians' prisons, this one, it is thought, certainly was. Large and enclosed, the monks' gardens are beautiful – and there is an odd little rock-cut stage.

Nymphaeum (or Mouseion)
Map 6.

In the rock face behind where the porticoes above the theatre stood, niches are cut, the largest, central one being the Nymphaeum. Around it are the weathered remains of a rock-cut frieze and architectural decoration; water from a Greek aqueduct plays into the pool here. This was not a sanctuary of the Muses as its alternative name suggests, but a Nymphaeum built by Hieron II. Some second-century B.C. statues from here are in the museum.

Of the other niches, some are Byzantine graves and others memorials of the Hellenistic ancestor-cult of the Heroes – not the semi-divine heroes of myth, but forbears of the heroic days of the colonies' foundation, and doubtless of the less heroic days of Hellenic squabblings thereafter. These cavities held paintings or bas-reliefs (often of a mounted warrior) representing the pious descendant's heroic ancestor. A rather pathetic cult, in fact, and an early evidence of that nostalgic archaism so often apparent in Sicily.

Sanctuary of Apollo Temenites
Map 8.

The existence of this sanctuary was known from literary sources – Cicero mentions the very large bronze statue of the god which stood in it, and which Tiberius was later to carry off to Rome – but it has only recently been discovered.

The remains of a rectangular enclosure, crossed by the foundations of a later wall, was found to contain a number of altars, the earliest of which was associated with late-seventh-century B.C. 'proto-Corinthian' ware, while several others date as late as the Hellenistic period. With no temple, the sanctuary evidently retained that archaic nature as a sacred precinct, standing well outside the early city, with which it had begun.

Street of the Tombs
Leading from west of the terrace above the Theatre across the main road.

The deep-cut lane is lined with Hellenistic votive niches and Byzantine rock tombs. Near the top of its winding course are reliefs, cut in the rock, of the mounted Dióscuri and Triptolemus in a snake-drawn car. Ruts in the lane were made by carts plying to the windmills which, in Spanish times and later, stood along the top of the theatre.

The top of the lane crosses the rock-cut *Galermi aqueduct* bringing water from the thirteen miles' distant Bottigliera spring.

Theatre (the so-called **Greek Theatre**)
Map 11.

The Syracusans were keen theatre-goers and seem to have welcomed visits from the playwrights of Greece. Close by, to the south-west, lies the 'Linear' Theatre (below), which was probably much earlier than this rather more than semicircular one which, as it is now, dates from Hieron II's reign (*c.* 230 B.C.). However, it is probable that this Hellenistic theatre is basically an enlargement of an earlier one, or even of several. Such enlargements would entail a cutting back of the hillside, out of which the theatre is largely hollowed, at an ever lower angle, thus obliterating the old cavea. Evidence of the theatre's history is therefore difficult to obtain, while Roman alterations to it – both to bring its stage up to date and to accommodate games before the amphitheatre was built – have further damaged any traces of its original plan.

It remains, though, one of the most splendid of Greek theatres left to us. It used to command a wide and placid view of the harbour to Plemmyrion – which the Romans blocked with the high and elaborate, permanent architectural background they liked for their stage-sets and which the raging suburbs of modern Syracuse have now again obliterated.

The *cavea* consists of nine wedges of forty-two rows of seats, the remains of the fifty-nine original rows; the upper tiers, which were constructed and not cut in the rock, have now fallen away or been pillaged. The theatre could seat some 15,000 people and is 453 feet in diameter.

Close to the top, the ranks of seats are interrupted by an ambulatory or *diazoma* which facilitated the coming and going of the huge audience. Along the sections of the barrier between this and the higher seats are cut inscriptions in great letters which apparently name each wedge of seats: in the centre, Zeus Olympios with King Hieron (damaged) and his wife, Queen Philistis, on either side; and Queen Nereis, daughter of Pyrrhus and wife of Gelon, Hieron's son, who was obviously also named on the last section.

The deep, straight trenches in the floor of the orchestra are the best evidence for the existence of an earlier theatre on the site; if so, its plan would have been trapezoidal.

Above the theatre are the scant remains of two porticoes of similar date which were apparently built at least partly as shelters for the audience in case of rain.

Performances were given in the early mornings of May and June – a time and season when the view is particularly fine. The dramatic festivals were biennial, being held on years of even date.

One is so conscious of the outlook from Greek theatres that one easily forgets that, in fact, there was a built-up stage (or proscenium) behind the orchestra with a building behind it to serve as a background – usually that of a palace in the tragedies, and often the agora in comedies. Though this was low in classical times, it would effectively block the view of spectators from the best seats, while, by the time this theatre was built, it was already certainly two, if not three, storeys high and joined to the sides of the cavea by wings. A detail of the decoration of this, a caryatid, is in the museum.

The orchestra area and that of the stage behind has been much and often altered and the excavated remains of all this is incomprehensible to the layman. Briefly, the major alterations were Roman; they brought the stage forward and this blocked the original public entrances to the lower seats and the orchestra, which had been from either side, so they cut tunnels in, instead; they also re-cut the lower twelve seat rows and faced them with marble, an operation which enlarged the orchestra – making it more suitable for games; and they removed the seventeenth row and cut out the centre of rows four, five and six in a way that suggests that they made a gubernatorial box there.

Among the confusion around the stage are drainage channels and scene-shifting ones, and means of flooding the orchestra for aquatic fights, etc.

Theatre (the so-called Linear Theatre)
Map **12**.

Its odd name refers to the form of this small theatre, simply shaped as a wide, straight flight of seventeen stepped seat-rows cut on the hillside. The seats, arranged in three sections divided by stairs, could have held a thousand people.

It is thought this may be the earliest theatre in Syracuse – possibly that in which Aeschylus saw two of his own plays performed, though Hieron I may have built another on the site of the great Hellenistic one round about that time. The opening of a new theatre designed to accommodate the needs of the, then, new type of drama which Aeschlyus wrote, would after all make a most fitting occasion to invite the great, and currently the most successful, dramatist to the city.

OTHER SIGHTS

Catacombs of Vigna Cássia
Map **9**.

Among the earliest catacombs (from mid third century A.D.) to be seen in Syracuse, these are connected with those of the earliest type of Santa Maria di Gesù, which are now closed to the public.

The earliest catacombs were the hidden graves of martyrs and those who wanted to lie near them after death. As places of pilgrimage they declined when the relics of the martyrs could later be removed to churches.

These galleries of subterranean tombs are simpler than the later ones. The paintings in Catacomb E have disappeared, but there are copies in the museum.

Church of San Giovanni alle Catacombe
Map **4**.

Open 09.00–12.00 and 15.00–17.30. There is a small entrance charge.

The earliest cathedral of the city built over the crypt or catacomb-tomb of St Marcian, first bishop of Syracuse, who was martyred (*c*. A.D. 254) under Valerian and Gallienus.

The ruined church, save for the impressive seventh-century *apse*, has more than once been rebuilt. It was destroyed by the Arabs in A.D. 827, rebuilt by the Normans and altered in the fourteenth century, then felled by earthquake in 1693 and, on a smaller scale, rebuilt once more. The porticoed *façade* belongs to this last rebuilding and is a pastiche made up of rescued fragments from the fourteenth-century fabric. The *rose-window* in the western end, however, withstood the tremors. The church was deprived of its cathedral status in 1640, but retains that of a basilica.

A ring at the bell at the labelled door to the right of the church will summon a monk to let you into the most interesting *crypt* and *catacombs*.

St Marcian was buried in an ordinary Roman – as distinct from a Christian – hypogeum, part of which was presently extended and converted into a chapel, and the rest filled in. Considerably later, the pious began to build catacombs adjoining this crypt.

The *chapel* is entered from inside the ruined basilica. It is planned in the form of a Greek cross in the inner angles of which are four Norman capitals, later re-worked, to bear the Evangelists' symbols. In the south-east corner chamber or chapel is the open tomb itself. A modern altar in the eastern arm marks the spot where, very problematically one would think, St Paul is said to have preached. Quite as doubtful is the claim that St Marcian was flogged at the pillar standing in the north-east chapel – pillars of the kind are incorporated elsewhere, horizontally as well as vertically, in the fabric of the place – which was not a chapel or prison, but a tomb, at the time of the bishop's martyrdom. Also shown is what purports to be his episcopal chair. In the arms of the cross are some traces of fourth- and fifth-century frescoes, with later ones also.

The catacombs, entered separately, are mostly late, and while none so far found antedate Constantine and the Edict of Milan (A.D. 313), they continue up to and during the sixth century A.D. The unusual lateness of date at which this form of entombment was still customary in Syracuse is due to there having here been no destruction of catacombs by Alaric the Hun, who did not reach the city.

Thousands of niches – or loculi – in the sides of the many, dank gallery-walls are grouped around the tomb crypt of St Marcian. They have mostly been robbed long ago, and what was left of interest has been taken for the museum, the most spectacular item being the mid-fourth-century A.D. *sarcophagus* of Count Valerius and his wife Adélphia (p. 230). Alaric may not have come here, but the Vandals under Gaiseric in A.D. 440, Totilla in A.D. 549, and the Arabs in 827 all did – and damaged these graves.

An interesting feature of this catacomb complex is the main gallery, which was once part of a Greek aqueduct, though later widened by the Christians.

Church of Santa Lucia

Piazza Santa Lucia (a good way to reach it from Ortygia is by taking a boat across Porto Piccolo from near the Post Office, then walk); Map 16.

The church is built over the traditional site of Santa Lucia's martyrdom – and in this case there are small grounds for thinking tradition mistaken. The *apses* and the *entrance*, with the lower part of the *bell-tower*, are twelfth-century, though restored in the seventeenth and eighteenth centuries – good solid work and satisfying proportions. The *rose-window* is fourteenth-century.

Santa Lucia, patroness of Syracuse as well as of her quarter of Palermo, probably lived from A.D. 281 to 305, the known year of her death, inflicted against a column (preserved in the presbytery) during Diocletian's persecutions.

Here, too, she was buried, under what is now the octagonal *Sepolcro* building beside the church, which is by the excellent Giovanni Verméxio. The body was, however, carried off to Constantinople during the Byzantine emperors' days of relic mania (1038), and from there grabbed by Venice during the sack and spoliation of Constantinople by the pseudo-Crusaders of 1204. Venice did not even build her a church; she lies in San Geremia.

Here, though, there is Carávaggio's painting of her burial hung in the apse. It was painted in 1609. Caravággio looks very well in the vigorous setting of Sicily. In this fine painting he is, as so often, perverse; the grave-diggers get the most attention, the saint the least.

The underground *burial chapel* is shown if you apply in the church, together with the *catacombs*. These enormous labyrinths have not been fully explored as yet but are of early date, being mostly second- and third-century, though they were later embellished – in Byzantine and even Norman times – and in places frescoes can be faintly seen. It is interesting that many of these galleries are earlier than the death of Santa Lucia.

Environs

EURYALUS CASTLE

Hourly buses 8 or 10 from Piazza Pancali and Corso Gelone to Belvedere (get off at outskirts of village); 8 km. north-west from the town (leaving by route Exit A and turning off the S.S.114).

Recent studies of this major defence-work of old Syracuse, in its time a major feat of engineering, have shown that little of what is now to be seen belongs to Dionysius' first castle, although it probably largely follows the plan he or his engineers laid down between 402 and 397 B.C. Far more that we see belongs to a remodelling under Hieron II and is most likely to have been the work of Archimedes, who was Hieron's chief of defence-works and acted as such again during the Roman siege. Agathocles may also have had a hand in redesigning the castle. Heavy ballistae had come into use by then and the outer works at least appear to be designed for their use, the outer ditch being just in their range from the towers of the keep.

Parts of the latest system of outworks are still incomplete; they were presumably finally abandoned in A.D. 212 when the castle unexpectedly surrendered to Marcellus without a blow. Subsequently there was some Byzantine modification to the castle, traces of which remain.

The importance of a stout defensive work on this site was realized during the Athenian siege, as was that of defending the entire Epipolae; and, by so doing, the Syracusans secured the approach to the city, over Epipolae, of the main road into the interior which passed just north of the castle's spur, through a gate whose defence-works are linked with that of the castle.

To the west, outside the town, there was a main entrance, which is by the present custodian's hut. There is a *ditch* here, uncompleted, whose distance from the towers of the castle is that of a missile launched by a heavy ballista. The two inner ditches, neither of them completed, were separated by an unfinished outwork. Over the south of the second ditch there was a later drawbridge, the *piers* of which remain and one of which blocks the entrance to one of a system of underground passages, connecting with the unfinished ditches, that seem to have been built in accordance with Philo of Byzantium's suggestion that three outer ditches were generally desirable and should be furnished with underground passages by which the defenders could remove at night the blocking material that the besiegers threw into them by day. The entrance to the fort itself from the drawbridge was under a covered way, built over lower chambers and passing the bastion which advances from the main keep. The strong western wall of this, which is now the most imposing part of the ruin, was further strengthened by five square towers that were originally about 50 feet high. This *wall* has been remodelled as can be seen by the differing masonry and blocked-up arches. The lion-head spouts, now in the museum, were found below this wall, and belong to Dionysius' building. On the southern side of the court are some Byzantine *chambers* resembling stabling. Beyond is a further court with a strong *postern* on the south, and a stout southern wall leading to a fort at its eastern end, and to a junction with the city wall. In the north-east side of this court was an entrance upon Epipolae, and at the northernmost point was a strong fort over the junction of the castle and the Epipolae wall – very thick here where it leads to the gate. The *gate* originally had three arched entrances, the centre one of which was later blocked up. These were set across the top of a re-entrant in the wall and behind screening walls. The left-hand flanking wall as you entered the gate was built up higher and more powerfully than the right-hand so that the defenders could bear more heavily upon the attacker's shield-arm side – indeed this wall was built into a fort, the inner wall of which has now gone, but a part of the transverse forward defence-wall of which lies below the re-entrant. A long underground ditch running outside the walls connected this fort with the inner ditch of the castle.

A pleasant walk can be made from Euryalus Castle along Dionysius' *northern wall of Epipolae*. The walls are broken, but still much of their line can be seen, here and there interrupted with towers and postern gates.

On the clifftop above Contrada Targia is the probable site of the Labdalum fort which the Athenians built after they had captured Epipolae.

You rejoin the main coast-road at Scala Greca. Just to the west of this suburb are the ruins of a *gate* which was possibly the *Hexapylon* ('the gate with six openings') which Dionysius built. It led into the Tyche quarter. The once marvellous view from here, like so very many others here in Syracuse, has vanished behind apartment blocks. I think it right to revile 'progress' which, as here and at Palermo, advances in inexorable ignorance at the expense of all real and meaningful, valuable poetry.

OLYMPIEION AND SOURCE OF THE CIANE RIVER

The Olympieion is on the right bank of the Ciane River, some 15 *minutes by road from the town (Route Exit C, turning off the S.S.113). The Fonte Ciane lies about* 3 *km. north of the Olympieion, which stands on the little river's right bank. Bus* 14 *infrequently goes close by there, but the classic way is to go by boat across the harbour and up the river as far as it is navigable. C.I.T. (Via Dione) can organize a boat for up to five people, or you can hire a boat on the Marina yourself. You need a picnic as the trip takes about five hours if it is to be comfortably leisurely.*

Two columns on a broken stylobate, standing in a glorious position, are all that is left of the Olympieion and its temenos. The temple was built in the first half of the sixth century B.C. just after that of Apollo in the city, and follows a similar Doric plan – a peripteral hexastyle with seventeen columns at the sides and a second row of columns behind the first, on the east. These led into the pronaos, with a narrow sekos inside and an adytum at the west end of the cella. The close-set columns of this early large temple were of single blocks, unlike the later ones.

Diodorus Siculus tells how Hippocrates of Gela, when he brought his victorious army here in 491 B.C., found the priest of Zeus with others removing golden votive offerings and the robe of the statue, into which a lot of gold had been worked, and how he chid them as despoilers of temples, sent them home and forbore to steal the gold for his good name's sake. Such precious details make the place and the times very alive.

Below the eminence of *Polichne*, on which the temple stands, lay the pestilential Lysimelia marshes – now drained – in which the many armies invading ancient Syracuse were virtually forced to camp, usually providentially for the Syracusans. South-east lies Plemmyrion point, now called *Penísola delle Maddalene*, which Nicias fortified, but lost to Gylippus, so the tables were turned upon the Athenians.

The Fonte Ciane, a small pool formed by a spring, is the source of the Ciane River.

At the sides of the stream and the pool, tall papyrus grows wild – the only place north of Equatorial Africa where it does. It may have been introduced here by the Arabs; or, it is said, it was a gift to Hieron II from Ptolemy Philadelphus.

'Ciane' meant 'blue' to the Greeks and before it became so vilely polluted as now, the pool at the source was blue under the sky. A most ancient water-cult existed here – not unnaturally – yet, though Cicero reports a popular annual festival at the spring, the only evidence we have of there ever having been a shrine here is one archaic stone head, now in the museum.

The myths about Ciane are confused: she was a nymph of Persephone's whom Hades had carried off, striking the ground here to open it so that his chariot could pass into the Nether Regions; Ciane's tears filled the pool, or she was turned into a pool because she wept so copiously; or she tried to prevent Hades from abducting Persephone. We have enough here to tell us that Ciane is Persephone over again, and the cult therefore was a chthonic one associated with water.

The modern Greeks are partial to festivals at chapels in the country, and some of these are by copious springs where the dedicatory saint of the chapel is heir to the nymphs. On these occasions the peasants collect, overnight or very early in the morning, bringing on donkeys a feast and a great deal of wine; and small bands of musicians materialize – itinerants and village groups. All the time, there is eating in family parties, bright rugs spread on the ground, voices singing and fiddles playing, and a sharing of food and a drinking of toasts; and dancing in long lines moving in a slow circle. Each family's fire shows in the darkness while spirits rise gloriously high. The walk home clears fuddled heads; or a sleep under the trees, then a fresh bout of feasting ... I think the ancients did almost exactly the same.

NECROPOLIS OF PANTÁLICA

34 km. north-west of Syracuse (Route Exit A) lies Sortino village, and 9 km. to its south is this fine prehistoric site. Or one can approach this gorge site from Ferla to its west, 52 km., but an easier road (Route Exit B). The office of the Soprintendenza alle Antichità in Syracuse is most helpful to intending visitors.

The steep-sided plateau of Pantálica is almost encircled by the valleys of the Anapo and Bottiglieria. It has recently been identified with Hybla, the capital of the Sikel king who allowed the Megarian colonists to occupy Megara Hyblaea. Previously this town was considered almost to be legendary.

Of the city, only the foundations of one building remain, but the numerous tombs cut in the cliffsides testify to its earlier size and the duration of its existence – thirteenth to eighth centuries B.C. It would seem to have been an early victim of Syracusan expansion and its end coincides with the foundation of Akrai. The tombs each housed one family's dead, and they seem to have been grouped together in what may have been clans of some sort.

Some of the caves show that they were turned into dwellings at the time of the barbarian invasions of Sicily – a fact which suddenly and pathetically illuminates that particular Dark Age of Europe.

Above, on the cliff edge, stand two very small *Byzantine chapels*, one to San Micidiário, the other to San Nicolícchio.

SYRACUSE TO CATÁNIA

Route (Route Exit A.) The S.S.114, a splendid highway allowing fast driving, excellently signposted; 60 km.
Rail Reasonably fast.
Bus A good service.
Accommodation en route At Príolo; Augusta; Agnone Bagni.

[5 km.] **Scala Greca**, where the road begins to drop to the littoral plain.

[14 km.] At **Príolo** a turning on the right continues for 5 km. to reach *Penísola Magnísi*, which can be seen to seaward. This low islet is connected to the mainland by an isthmus of sand and salterns.

Hotels (at Príolo)
4th Class   *Conca d'Oro;*
             Royal.

The Magnisi Peninsula was the ancient *Thapsos*, especially interesting as the type-site of the 'Thapsos culture' which connects a line of known sites of a more or less allied Bronze Age culture from the Lípari Islands to the Plemmyrion point south of Syracuse harbour. If the people who settled here *c.* 1400 B.C. did not come from the east, they were in contact with a Mycenaean culture and traded with it, as also with Malta; some of their traditions are derived from a Mycenaean-type culture. About 1270 B.C. the coastal villages were abandoned for safer inland sites such as Pantálica – and, presumably, ultimately, Sant'Ángelo Muxaro, for here and at the latter place there are tholos tombs. (To find these, take a track to the left as soon as you are across the narrow isthmus; the most interesting are along the rocky shore west of the lighthouse.) The rather unfortunate Megarians who eventually established themselves at Megara Hyblaea attempted for a while to live here, in the late eighth century B.C. They were led by a certain Lamis who died here and, poignantly, suggestively, only one grave of the period has been found here: even problematical archaeological confirmation of such remote literary knowledge is for some reason curiously wonderful – Cicero finding Archimedes' tomb, we perhaps finding that of the oikistos Lamis, these too faint spoors left by Daedalus' wanderings which, in sober fact, suggest a likelier trail from Cumae to Lípari, Milazzo or Thapsos than to any site on the south Sicilian coast. The Athenian fleet moored to the north of this promontory before slipping into the harbour of Syracuse, and Marcellus also took advantage of its shelter during the Roman siege of that city.

Also at Príolo, the old Catánia road (114) diverges leftwards, but Lentini is now more conveniently reached from farther on (see below).

The coastal area, with its views across to Augusta, becomes

lined now with great, and in a way beautiful oil installations. The oil-strikes and the building of refineries – Esso's, here, is the third largest in Europe – gave rise to high hopes for a new beginning in Sicily; but the real benefits of all this seem to be felt more on the mainland than in this Cinderella among islands.

[21 km.] The S.S.193 leads, right (11 km.), to Augusta. Before this is reached, however, you pass (about 2 km. from the S.S.114) a turning right signposted to the ruins of (*Scavi di*) *Megara Hyblaea*. Do not be discouraged by its unlikely neighbours, which include a cement factory, for the lane becomes a rustic one. It crosses the northern edge of a section of the archaic wall that has been excavated (the necropolis lying below it to your right and the base of a third-century B.C. tower just inside). Some 370 metres later you cross the line of the Hellenistic walls and finally end by the small Antiquarium.

Megara Hyblaea was, traditionally, founded three years later than Syracuse. The Megarian expedition that established it found that the Syracusans and Leontinoians had already pre-empted all the good and available land hereabouts, but they tried at first to settle at Brúcoli – a small town north of Augusta. There they proved a nuisance to the Leontinoians, who tried to absorb them rather than drive them out. The Megarians were too independent to allow this and moved to Thapsos peninsula, and then to this site below Hyblaea, whose Sikel king granted them the land. The existence of the colony was always a precarious one, being dependent first upon Sikel good-will and, secondly, on Syracusan tolerance. This last did not hold and in 482 B.C. Gelon destroyed the city.

Most of the ruined foundations to be seen today belong to a third-century B.C. revival which was halted by the Romans' descent upon Leontinoi and Syracuse. They include the foundations of a temple on the point, of another beside the agora, and those of some houses. Two other, archaic temples have been found nearer the older walls. The *Antiquarium* – the resident guardians on the site let one in – contains some pleasant as well as some informative things, but the treasures so far discovered here are in the museum at Syracuse. Excavations, however, continue.

Augusta

Population
Over 29,000.
Hotels
2nd Class   *Kursaal Augusteo* ;
                †*Villággio Valtur.*
3rd Class   †*Europa Club* (Monte Tauro district, beyond the town) ;
                Megara ;
                †*Villa Marina.*
4th Class   *Centrale.*

Augusta is a small town curiously like Ortygia in foundation and situation, but never an important place in antiquity – it was probably the site of *Xiphonia*. It is a naval base though now more important as an oil and commercial port. The town occupies what is actually an islet connected to the mainland by a bridge, with ports on either side, that on the west, Porto Megarese, having two forts of 1595 for its defence. The modern town was founded by Frederick II in 1232, and totally destroyed by the earthquake of 1693.

By taking a right-hand fork on leaving Augusta one can return to the main road, joining it at Asnone Bagni Lentini. Before, however, you reach the main road, a turning right off this road leads to *Brúcoli*, the most modest of the sites occupied by the hopeful Megarians.

[27 km.] Keeping to the S.S.114, a left turn leads in 18 km. to **Lentini**, the ancient *Leontinoi,* founded in 729 B.C., as a daughter city to Naxos (for its ancient history, see that of Syracuse). Despite the earthquake of 1693 there remain some bits of a thirteenth-century *castle* and, to its south, something of the Greek city's main *gateway*. In what was formerly the *cathedral* are some fifth-century A.D. tombs with proto-Byzantine frescoes. If you approach Lentini along this road you descend into a valley through **Carlentini** village and as you do so you will see the wooded hill upon which the Greek city stood. It is now an *Archaeological Zone* into which you scramble much as you please. Traces of walls surround the hill ; the pincer-type *south gate* is interesting (though the more so if you have already seen the explanation of it in the Museum). Little really systematic excavation has yet been undertaken here. The *Museum*

(Piazza del Liceo, next to the school buildings; open weekdays 09.30–13.00 and 15.00–17.00, Sundays and holidays, mornings only; entrance free) is a small and agreeable one, but the best finds so far made have already gone to Syracuse and Catánia.

From Lentini the main road can be rejoined at Ponte Primosole (47 km. direct from Syracuse). On the drive northwards the road crosses country where on every side can be seen the heart-lifting work of the Cassa per il Mezzogiorno, the Government trust fund for capitalization of public and – on certain conditions – private improvement schemes. The whole of the Simeto valley and plain, which the road now approaches, has been transformed in recent years from an unproductive swamp to rich and settled farmland. Quarries in the hills, where mechanical stone-cutters slice the soft rock into blocks, provide all the new terracing that you see now planted with young citrus trees. The desolation that this stretch of Sicily was a dozen or more years ago had its wild charm, but anyone who knew it then must rejoice to see what petroleum and the Cassa has made of it in so short a while.

[35 km.] Agnone Bagni.

Hotel
4th Class   †*Triángolo.*

[47 km.] Ponte Primosole. On the northern bank of the Simetus river stood *Symaethus,* the necropolis of which has been found. The Simeto-Dittáino valley – the Plain of Catánia, as it is now called – was known as the Laestrygonian Fields by the Greeks, who identified this area with the land of the Laestrygones, a race of cannibals whom Ulysses encounters in the tenth book of the *Odyssey.*

[60 km.] Catánia.

CATÁNIA

Air
From Rome, Milan, Naples, Malta, Réggio di Calábria, Palermo. Airport at Fontanarossa (5 km. south of the town).
Sea
Connections to Naples, Syracuse, Venice, Genoa, Trieste, Malta, Tripoli, Benghazi. Hydrofoil to Réggio di Calábria.
Rail
Stazione Centrale (*Map* **8**) — connections to Taormina, Messina, Syracuse, Enna, Agrigento, Palermo ; local line to Caltagirone from where there are connecting buses to Piazza Armerina, as also to and from Dittaino on Catánia–Enna line.
Bus
Services to Gela, Taormina, Messina, Etna, Syracuse, Enna, Piazza Armerina, Ragusa, Palermo.
Information
E.P.T. office, Largo Paisello 5 (*Map* **5**).
Tourist Information Office, Stazione Centrale (*Map* **8**).
Bathing
Bathing can be had in the Catánia area at La Plaja, Acireale (p. 270), Riviera dei Ciclopi near Acitrezza (p. 270).
Hotels

Luxury	*Excelsior*, Piazza G. Verga.
1st Class	*Central Palace*, Via Etnea 218 ;
	Jolly Trinácria, Piazza Trento 13.
2nd Class	*Bristol*, Via S.M. del Rosário 9 ;
	Costa, Via Etnea 551.
3rd Class	*Itália*, Via Etnea 310 ;
	Mediterraneo, Via Dr. Consoli 27 ;
	Moderno, Via Alessi 9 ;
	Motel Agip (S.S. 114 on northern edge of town) ;
	Motel Plája (S.S.114 3·5 km. south of town).
4th Class	*Centrale Europa*, Via Vittório Emanuele 167 ;
	El Torero (S.S.114 Vaccarizzo district) ;
	Pea Yacht, Via G. Oberdan 119 ;
	Peloro, Via Paternò 12 ;
	Primavera, Via Vittório Emanuele 5 ;
	Sangiorgi, Via A. di Sangiuliano 237 ;
	Savona, Via Vittório Emanuele 210.

Pensions

2nd Class	*Residenza*, Via Umberto 285 ;
	Royal, Via A. di Sangiuliano 337 ;
	San Doménico, Via Cifali 76B ;
	Sicilia, Via Gagliani 10 ;
	Sudland, Via Etnea 270 ;
	Torino, Via P. Toselli 43 ;
	Villa Dina, Via Caronda 129.
3rd Class	*Centrale*, Via Pacini 17 ;
	Continental, Piazza Trento 6 ;
	Corona, Via Crocíferi 81 ;
	Ferrara, Vía Umberto 66 ;
	Internazionale, Via A. di Sangiuliano 293 ;
	Laudani, Via Coviello 16 ;
	Rapisardi, Via Padova 7 ;
	Sangiuliano, Via A. di Sangiuliano 108.

A go-ahead place, Catánia stands to Palermo in much the same relationship as Milan to Rome – though very much less industrialized than Milan. It is a provincial capital with a population of over 360,000. The next most important city in Sicily after Palermo, Catánia is growing steadily. It has so often been the victim of Etna's eruptions that there is little to show for its long history, but it always rises anew from its disasters. The hinterland upon the slopes of the volcano is most fertile and densely populated, and the lively town – if not in itself very interesting – is a comfortable place to stay while visiting this part of Sicily.

The axis of the modern city is the Via Etnea, which runs north – south to the Piazza del Duomo, once the centre of the old town, most of which now lies to its north-west and south-east.

HISTORY

The Greek colony of *Catana* was founded in 729 B.C. by Chalcidians from Naxos. The laws given it by its tyrant Charondas (seventh century B.C.) were generally adopted as a model over all Magna Graecia; Xenophanes, the philosopher, adopted Catanian citizenship during the following century. Hieron of Syracuse exiled the inhabitants left alive after his capture of the city to Leontinoi, whence they returned in 461 B.C. to drive out his new colonists. Catana was the ally of Athens against Syracuse from 415 B.C., but Dionysius made the Catanians pay dearly for this by selling them into slavery in 403 B.C. Having fallen to Hamilco, it welcomed Timoleon and Pyrrhus, then fell again to the Romans in 263 B.C. (see history of Syracuse). Roman Catana became a privileged place on account of the help it gave Augustus against Pompey's faction during the civil wars.

An earthquake in A.D. 1169 wrecked the city, then a rebellious place, Henry VI and Frederick II both having occasion to sack it later on. Frederick built the very fine Castello Ursino to overawe the town.

An eruption of Etna – the worst recorded – overwhelmed almost the whole town in 1669, and most of what was then rebuilt was shattered in the earthquake of 1693. The subsequent rebuilding makes of the old quarters of modern Catánia a most complete and agreeable baroque ensemble.

Catánia was badly bombed and shelled in 1943 before the British landings on the coast of the plain, but the city was spared a battle for its streets by the eventual German withdrawal to the north.

PRINCIPAL SIGHTS

After reference to streets and *piazze* to help orientate you, sights are described in alphabetical order.

Piazza del Duomo

A large and attractive piazza with the Cathedral on its east.

The *Município* (*Map* **14**) stands on the north side; it was built in 1741 – a delightful example of eighteenth-century fenestration.

Porta Uzeda (*Map* **21**), in the south-east corner, is an eighteenth-century archway (leading to a public garden and the port).

The church of *Sant'Ágata* (*Map* **15**), with a bold façade by Vaccarini, is just east of the square, in Via Vittório Emanuele. Eighteenth-century.

The Elephant Fountain, in the centre of the piazza, represents Catánia's arms and was constructed by Vaccarini in 1736 out of an antique lava elephant carrying an Egyptian obelisk, probably once an ornament or turning-post in the Roman circus.

The *Palace* on the south side of the piazza is by di Benedetto, early-eighteenth-century; and the *fountain* beside it is nineteenth-century. Behind this is a meat-market, the fish-market being a little to its south.

Via Crocíferi

On either side of this rising street there is a succession of quite delightfully exuberant, eighteenth-century houses and church fronts. It is one of the prettiest streets – architecturally – in Europe. The church of *San Benedetto,* on the left (*Map* **10**), has a particularly good façade on to the street.

Catánia

Via Garibaldi
Leading west out of Piazza del Duomo.

A street of baroque palaces and fine houses, with here and there a church, and interrupted by the very pretty arcaded Piazza Mazzini. The columns of the arcades were brought from the site of a Roman basilica which is now occupied by *Sant'Agostino* in the Via Vittório Emanuele.

Amphitheatre
Piazza Stesicoro; Map **7**.

This remnant belongs to what was formerly the next largest amphitheatre after the Colosseum at Rome. Most of the stone from it was plundered in early times, beginning under Theodoric the Ostrogoth. It dates back perhaps as early as the second century B.C.

Bellini's House
Piazza San Francesco; Map **16**.

This contains a small museum of the composer, Vincenzo Bellini, who was born here in 1801.

Castello Ursino and Museo Cívico
Piazza Frederico di Svevia; Map **22**.

Open Weekdays 09.00–13.00 and 16.00–18.00. Entrance free.

Built for Frederick II, after 1232, by Riccardo da Lentini, the keep alone survived the flow of lava in 1669. This has hardened as a platform around it. Part, too, of the structure was damaged, and restored in mid nineteenth century. It is a fine example of a Swabian castle and, since it houses the Museo Cívico, one of the few in Sicily which it is easy to enter. There are some very beautiful vaulted rooms inside.

The museum includes an archaeological collection left to the city by the Prince of Biscari. There are some good Roman sculptures; an Attic *head of an ephebus* from Leontinoi that is coolly beautiful; and the marvellous *Camarina Krater*, on which is a scene of Perseus beheading the Gorgon, both of the early fifth century B.C. There are also many pleasant things from old churches, and armour, etc. The fifteenth-century *tarot cards* are interesting and pretty. Among the paintings is a fine *Madonna* by Antonello de Saliba of 1497; an *Adoration of the Magi* by Simon de Wobrecht, dated 1585; and a Mattias Stomer of *Tobias Healing His Father*.

Cathedral
Piazza del Duomo; Map **19**.

St Agatha, it is claimed, was martyred at Catánia in A.D. 253 and is patroness of the city. The cathedral is dedicated to her; it was founded by Count Roger in 1092, but had to be rebuilt after the eruption and earthquake of 1169 and 1693, the Norman *apses* of black lava almost alone withstanding both shocks. These can be seen by going into the courtyard of the seminary behind the cathedral, in Via Vittório Emanuele.

The *west front* is by Vaccarini and was built in 1736; its columns came from the Roman theatre. The *north doorway* is a survival from 1577.

Catanian baroque is different from any other in Sicily, being rather more fantastical. This has a homely effect in many instances, though here it achieves a lightness combined with considerable dignity.

Inside, there are still the ghosts of its Norman proportions, though there is little of special interest to see. Even the two Norman chapels of the *Cappella della Vergine* (south transept) and the *Cappella del Crocifisso*, off the north transept, are scarcely recognizable as of such an early date. The *tomb* of the Viceroy Fernandez d'Acuña (1494) is a beauty, however; it is in the chapel of Sant'Ágata to the right of the choir, where the tombs high up contain the ashes of Frederick II of Aragon (d. 1337), King Louis and Frederick III (d. 1355 and 1377 respectively) together with other members of the House of Aragon. The composer Bellini is buried in the southern aisle by the second pier on entering.

Below the cathedral are the remains of *Roman baths* known as the *Terme Achelliane*; a sacristan will let you see what has so far been uncovered.

Church of Santo Cárcere
Via dei Cappuccini; Map **6**.

This is built over the traditional site of St Agatha's prison. The thirteenth-century *doorway* – and a very good one it is – was taken from the cathedral.

Church of Santa Maria di Gesù
Via Androne; Map **3**.

Here the *Paternò chapel* – alongside the main front, on the left – escaped the disasters of the seventeenth century. Its *doorway* of 1519 is by Antonello Gagini. There is a group of the *Madonna with Angels* in the second chapel in the northern aisle by the same sculptor. The master is, here, on form. The *Madonna with SS. Catherine and Agatha* by Angelo di Chirico is dated 1525.

Church of Santa Maria della Rotonda
Via Rotonda; Map **11**.

This ancient church is worth while seeing. It was built into the ruins of a Roman bath by the Byzantines. Several of the houses near by also incorporate bits of the baths. The key is with the custodian of the Roman Theatre (p. 264). Interesting rather than beautiful with its alterations and vestiges, such as a mosaic and bits of frescoes, of the stages the building has been through.

Church of San Nicolò
Piazza Dante; Map **10**.

Atop its hill, facing the charmingly planned, eighteenth-century *Piazza Dante*, the tall front of this, the largest church in Sicily, is an odd sight, being very much unfinished. One is reminded of the Olympieions of Akragas and Selinus, which must have been built in a similar spirit of thanksgiving for deliverance. It was built between 1693 and 1735.

The interior is quite splendid; lack of funds to ornament it as grandiosely as it was doubtless hoped have left unhindered its admirable proportions.

A curiosity is the meridian line let into the floor of the transept. The *choir-stalls* by Nicolò Bagnasco are notable: also the enormous, though elegant, *organ* of 2,916 pipes.

One can climb to the dome for the sake of the view – with the co-operation of the sacristan.

Adjacent is the *convent*. Its rich and most Catanian front should not be overlooked. It is used as a school and nobody seems to mind if you walk in and up its grandest of grand stairways or look around the two courtyards. In the first is a pretty garden; in the second, the arcading has a pure and unusual grace for the period. For this, too, had almost wholly to be rebuilt after 1693; and it was the largest convent in Europe barring only the colossus of Mafra in Portugal, accepting only monks of impeccable nobility. Though a Benedictine convent, the rule was so relaxed as to make its luxury and its easy ways a scandal. (For a savage picture of this epoch in Catánia read Frederico de Roberto, *The Viceroys*, trans. Archibald Colquhoun (MacGibbon and Kee, London, 1962).)

The parts of the convent that are not used as schools house the *Municipal Library* – a very rich one – and an *Astrophysical Observatory*.

Palazzo Biscari
Via Biscari; Map **20**.

This handsomely decorated palace is east of the Piazza del Duomo. Take a look into the courtyard if you can. This section of the street is in any case very fine and unspoiled, Sicilian-noble in manner.

Palazzo delle Scienze
Corso d'Itália; Map **2**.

Here are shown the University of Catánia's geological and vulcanological collections.

Teatro Greco and Odeon
Just north of the Via Vittório Emanuele; Map **17**.

Open Daily from 09.00–13.00 and again from 14.00 to dusk.

These are two rather dismal skeletons of black lava. The erstwhile marble facing has almost completely gone.

Neither building is Greek, but Roman; although the real Greek Theatre probably did occupy this site. The cavea of the theatre was 318 feet across, its seats banked in nine wedges.

The theatre is being cleared of the overgrowth of medieval and later buildings which obscured its form. The Odeon was used for performances of music and recitations. Alcibiades exhorted the Catanians to support Athens against Syracuse in that Greek Theatre which, it is thought, formed the basis on which the Romans constructed theirs.

Università
Via Etnea; Map **13**.

The courtyard is by Vaccarini – a nice one. The church of the *Collegiata* (*Map* **9**) beside the Università was a royal Bourbon chapel, built in 1768.

EXCURSION UP MOUNT ETNA

As everybody knows, this very active volcano is the largest in Europe. It is 10,725 feet high and its cone measures about 25 miles, or 40 kilometres, in diameter.

Though the summit is not permanently covered by snow, warm clothes are needed even in high summer, and also stout shoes, if you are going up it.

The volcano has erupted over 130 times in the historical era. It probably originated as a submarine volcano and rose in what was once a large gulf. Its unlikeness to the conformation of the rest of Sicily is very noticeable. Myths were gathered about it in ancient times – it was the forge of Vulcan or of the Cyclops; the mountain under which Enceladus the Titan was restively imprisoned. For the Empedocles legend see p. 170.

Pindar and Aeschylus both described the great eruption of 475 B.C. Another in 396 B.C. was said to have interposed a fortunate stream of lava between Hamilco and Syracuse. In the eruptions of 1169 and 1329 the lava reached the sea near Acireale, and again in 1381 at Catánia. In the terrible eruption of 1669, a cleft in the volcano was opened from the summit down to Nicolosi and a vast flow of lava overwhelmed a large part of Catánia. During this eruption the *Monti Rossi* were formed. There have not been any very serious eruptions this century, although several have been quite severe; that of 1911 interrupted the railway near Castiglione, and in 1923 the stations of Castiglione and Cerro, with Cerro village and a part of Catánia, were destroyed. If the lava flows slowly there is ample time to remove before its advance, but sometimes, as in

1925, it flows dangerously fast. The worst disasters are caused by explosive splittings such as that with which Vesuvius blasted Pompeii and neighbouring towns. In 1928 a lava stream engulfed the village of Máscali and interrupted the railways. The longest recorded eruption continued from 1950 to 1951, since when the volcano has continued to be lively.

The attraction of the ascent lies in the tremendous views and the wonderfully fertile *pedemontana* (lower slopes) cultivated to 1,650 feet and the forests that grow as high as 6,900 feet, rather than in the repulsive desert zone above where ash and lava too thinly cover the fires below. With its clefts and subsidiary volcanoes, *fumarole* and vapour jets, this is nature in its uttermost indifference, at its most inimical to life. The contrast between this and the *pedemontana*, which supports a population of up to 1,200 people per square mile, is most extraordinary. In summer, when the snow melts, cold ash is laid over it where it lies in clefts of the mountain's north face. This preserves it throughout the hot season. Nowadays, there is little call for expensively transported snow in summer, but this was formerly a flourishing trade, the monopoly of the bishops of Catánia, who, to their great profit, exported it over considerable distances. Graceful presents of snow to such dignitaries as the Grand Master of the Knights of Malta at Valletta, or the Pope himself at Rome, usually led to most satisfactory orders for more.

If you want to climb the mountain the hard way, you should consult the Italian Alpine Club at Via Musumeci 122, Catánia, where guides can be booked – at not less than a day's notice. Mules and porters can also be hired through the Comitato Sículo del Consórzio Guide e Portatori del C.A.I. at Nicolosi, or at Catánia, as above.

The less ambitious will be glad of the cable railway which now carries one to the observatory, from which the summit can be reached in an hour's smart walking. Keep to the well-marked path to the left and persevere to the very lip of the crater, beyond where the crater evens out at the top of the path. In winter the cableway stops at its halfway point, where there is the *Píccolo Rifúgio*, and the walk up is then longer by another hour.

The cableway begins at the *Rifúgio G. Sapienza*, where the Strada dell'Etna ends, and you may drive or take a bus to this point. One way and another, you should give up a day to this excursion. The drive alone takes one and a half hours – the bus rather longer –

and you will need quite three hours to the top; so one had better calculate the trip as taking eight to nine hours in all.*

[3 km.] You are scarcely free of Catánia (Route Exit A) before the road to Nicolosi (Strada dell'Etna) runs by the *Barriera del Bosco*, a lava ridge of 1669.

[5 km.] You pass **Sant'Ágata li Battiati**.

Hotels
3rd Class   *Balanzone;*
              La Villetta.
Pensions
2nd Class   *Nord-Ouest.*
3rd Class   *Due Palme.*

[8 km.] At **Gravina** there are evidences of the 1381 eruption; the craters called the *Pomiciari di Santa Maria*, and the cleft above, opened at the time.

[10 km.] **Mascalucia** is the centre for the production of the 'de Bosco' wines. You are already 1,380 feet high here.

[13 km.] **Massannunziata**. The road avoids lava of 1669 on which grow pistachio trees. The crater on the left is prehistoric. The Monti Rossi rise behind it.

[16 km.] **Nicolosi** (2,290 feet). The active Monti Rossi can be climbed from here (an hour and a half) if you do not want to go farther.

Hotels
2nd Class   *Biancaneve.*
4th Class   *Belvedere;*
              Monti Rossi.

The Strada dell'Etna climbs on, to cross lava of 1886 and 1910, reaching (32 km.) a turning left leading in 1 km. to the hotel about which the *Serra la Nave* winter-sports fields are centred.

Hotel
3rd Class *Grande Albergo Etna,* with tennis-courts. (Open January to March, and mid-June to mid-September only.)

* The sizeable eruption of 1971 put the cable railway out of action and at the time of going to press one cannot say when it will be repaired, or whether our directions from its terminus will meet the case thereafter. It is not clear to us whether the Observatory and the other buildings on the heights survived, were damaged or destroyed.

[34 km.] *Casa Cantoniera* (6,175 feet and now a section of the Institute of Vulcanology). The terrace here commands a most marvellous view – at the right seasons and/or times of day. There is a bar-trattoria for the weary at the *G. Sapienza* (4th Class).

Rifúgio G. Sapienza stands a little higher up. It is an Alpine Club hostel open to all, all the year round. From here the cableway slings you up to the *Observatory* (9,653 feet). There is another hostel here. Anyone interested in the work, either of the Observatory or the Institute of Vulcanology (Catánia University), should apply beforehand to the directors for permission to visit here. From the Observatory you must walk if you have not arranged for mules. Follow the left-hand path. (See footnote on p. 267.)

The reeking crater is indescribable. Its walls are coloured with sublimated chlorides and sulphates. Its depth constantly varies with the thrust from below of the molten matter it holds. From here it is not far to walk to the *Fumarola*, an outbursting of hot vapour.

Ideally, you should be here before dawn, when the lava in the crater can be seen to be glowing redly with its heat, and when, as the sun rises, all Sicily and Calábria is spread below you in vivid relief. The shadow of Etna creeps slowly across the land, diminishing as it moves. Malta can sometimes be seen to the south, but it needs the clearest of days if it is not to be lost in the sparkling haze upon the sea. The sides of the volcano are pitted by hundreds of lesser craters.

A path descending by the south-east goes close by the *Torre del Filósofo*, probably a Roman monument to Hadrian's climb up the mountain and not Empedocles' observatory. Beyond is the *cisternazza*, a chasm formed in 1792; and the *Valle del Bove*, a vast chasm 12 miles in circumference, three sides of which are sheer drops of up to 3,000 feet. A further hour's walk brings you back to the road.

On the whole, the descent is the pleasantest part of the excursion, for the views are always before you – and though your faith in the stability of this world may have been shaken, you are returning to normality and the daily illusion of security.

Descents in various directions are possible if you have mountaineering experience – best to talk them over with the Alpine Club before attempting them. The less adventurous come down the way they went up.

EXCURSION ROUND ETNA

This classic excursion can be made by train (144 km.), taking the main (Messina) line from Catánia – the stopping, *diretto* trains – to Gíarre-Riposto, where you cross stations for the Circumetnea line; a connecting train awaits you. The whole journey takes about $4\frac{1}{2}$ hours.

It is pleasanter, of course, to drive. For one thing you can take the higher road between Catánia and Linguaglossa that is so very preferable to the S.S.114. That road is described on p. 273; that between Randazzo and Linguaglossa on p. 308 and the section between Adrano and Catánia on p. 307. These leave the stretch Randazzo–Bronte–Adrano undescribed. This is the loneliest and perhaps the scenically most grand, but Bronte (p. 309) apart, it is otherwise an uneventful 34 km. By this route, the whole round is 135 km.

CATÁNIA TO TAORMINA

Route 1 (Route Exit B.) S.S.114, a good road. 52 km. (The Autostrada under construction will shorten the distance, running farther inland. It will be immesurably faster too.)
Route 2 (Route Exit A.) Vla Trecastagni, Linguaglossa, Castiglione di Sicília, joining the S.S.185 at Francavilla di Sicília and the S.S.114 4 km. before Taormina ; goes through beautiful country of the *pedemontana* of Mount Etna.* 87 km.
Rail (Route 1) Quite good service to Giardini, connecting by bus with Taormina.
Bus Direct connections along Route 1 ; local services on Route 2.

ROUTE 1

Accommodation en route At Cannizzaro ; Acitrezza ; Acireale ; Giarre ; Máscali ; Fiumefreddo di Sicília ; Giardini ; Mazzarò.

[7 km.] **Cannizzaro.**

Hotels
3rd Class   *Motel Maremonti ;*
             Venere Jonica.

[9 km.] **Acicastello.** The fine *castle* was built in 1076; it belonged to Roger di Lauria, the admiral who rebelled against Frederick II of

* This road was breached by the lava flows of 1971 in the neighbourhood of Milò and Fornazzo. It will probably soon be mended.

Aragon in 1297. The king had to build a wooden fort alongside it before he could reduce it.

[11 km.] The road passes rocks standing a little distance from the shore. These are variously called *Faraglione* or *Isole dei Ciclopi* – 'Cyclops' Islands'. Since the ancients knew that Ulysses' voyage took him through these waters it was natural enough they should seek to identify the places mentioned in the *Odyssey* with actual places on the Tyrrhenian coasts. We do not know how much the colonial Greeks were following traditions that were already old to them when they did this. If the divine, though non-Olympian, personages whom Ulysses encountered can be regarded as local western deities, then it is possible that there was quite a strong tradition to go upon. Some such traditional identification seems to lurk behind the association between Etna and Polyphemus the Cyclops. He is not at all a Vulcan/Hephaestus-like figure, but a shepherd; yet probably the *pedemontana* afforded magnificent grazing in primitive times. However this may be, the tradition is a very old one that claims these were the rocks which Polyphemus hurled after Ulysses' ship when he and his men had blinded and tricked the giant into letting them escape from his cave.

The incidence of place-names hereabouts that are prefixed by 'Aci' recalls another local association with Polyphemus. Acis was a shepherd whom Galatea loved and Polyphemus killed in jealousy or rivalry. At his death the River Aci sprang from the earth. Galatea is usually represented as a marine deity, but in this case she seems to have belonged to the chthonic realm of fresh water. Of course, the sudden, mysterious emergence of a plentiful spring is not an impossible occurrence upon the sides of a volcano.

[12 km.] **Acitrezza.**

Hotels
1st Class   *I Faraglioni*
2nd Class   *Eden Riviera.*

[17 km.] **Acireale.**

Information
Azienda Autónoma, Corso Umberto 173.
Hotels
2nd Class   †*Aloha d'Oro ;*
                   Maugeri.
3rd Class   *Pattis.*

Seven streams of lava form the platform upon which the town stands, 500 feet above the sea. It was rebuilt after the earthquake of 1693.

The *Palazzo Communale* was built in 1659 and contains a little museum and a good library.

The *Municipal Gallery* contains a *Madonna and Child* attributed to Rubens and a collection of excellent drawings by Luca Giordano, Guido Reni, Salvator Rosa, and a bust of Julius Caesar.

[31 km.] Giarre.

Hotels
3rd Class   *Sicília.*
4th Class   *Terminus.*
  There is also a Youth Hostel.

[35 km.] Máscali.

Pension
3rd Class   †*Sette Nani.*

[39 km.] Fiumefreddo di Sicília.

Hotel
4th Class   *Delle Grázie.*

[45 km.] *Capo Schisò* is formed by an ancient lava-flow and its headland was the site of *Naxos*, the first Greek colony to be established in Sicily – by Cumaeans and Euboeans, rather doubtfully in alliance with Naxians – as early as 757 B.C.

This was the first landfall of a ship crossing from Cape Spartivento on the Calabrian shore, a fact that may have had an influence in the siting of the colony, which was not otherwise particularly desirable from the colonists' usual point of view and may, indeed, have been from the first designed only as a stepping-stone to further, more practical, colonization. Naxos' daughter cities – Catana, Leontinoi – were certainly founded in the expectation of their prospering much more than their parent.

Naxos never grew to be anything but a small town and it was one, morcover, that could never defend itself at all well. Its altar of Apollo the Leader, however, which the oikistos Thucles established, was venerated by all Sicilian Greeks. The ambassadors from the island cities to religious celebrations like the Olympic and

Delphic festivals always came to Naxos to sacrifice upon it before crossing to Greece.

Parts of the *walls* have been recently uncovered and their circuit fully traced. The major portion of these as yet excavated lie south-west of the cape itself and alongside the little river of *Santa Vénera*. They belong to the sixth century B.C. and round a corner, in which is a postern that leads to a temenos situated in the angle. This could be the sacred enclosure of Naxos' noted temple of Aphrodite – the foundations of a small temple lie here, but no proof of this yet exists.

A *Parco Archeológico* has been established over the headland and excavations continue within it. At the end of the parade on the northern, bay side of the headland an *Antiquarium* has been opened. Its contents will grow more interesting as finds increase. It is, like the Parco, open from 10.00 to 12.00 and again from 15.00 to dusk; the entrance to the ruins is at the end of the Strada Communale Schisò and, if you cannot find the custodian, ask at the house near the entrance.

It would appear from excavation that the city revived after Dionysius of Syracuse's destruction of it in 403 B.C. although those descendants of old inhabitants who returned in 358 B.C. from various places of exile started anew at Tauromenium (Taormina). A street has been found which belongs to a revised lay-out. It is of the fourth century B.C. and grave deposits found continue into the Hellenistic period. For more of its history, see that of Syracuse (p. 212).

The modern settlement of **Schisò** (or **Naxos**) clusters between the bay, the S.S.114 and the headland.

Hotels

2nd Class	†*Arathena Rocks*;
	†*Assines*;
	†*Nike.*
3rd Class	†*Báia di Naxos*;
	Costa Azzurra;
	Panoramic.

Pensions

2nd Class	†*Sábbie d'Oro.*
3rd Class	*Del Sole*;
	Il Pescatore;
	La Riva;
	La Sirena.

There is also a youth hostel.

Restaurant

Rocce Naxos; on the parade. Here you can eat gorgeous sea-food, perfectly cooked, and absolutely without any restaurateur-ish pretensions.

[47 km.] **Giardini** is the railway station and a seaside resort for Taormina. From here Garibaldi sailed on August 19th, 1860, against the Bourbon army in Calábria.

Hotels

2nd Class	†*Touring;*
	†*Tritone.*

Pensions

3rd Class	*Jonio;*
	Vinci Tálio.

[49 km.] A turning left 3 km. to Taormina (p. 275).

[50 km.] **Mazzarò,** the principal seaside resort for Taormina. Though, strictly speaking, Mazzarò is outside this section it obviously belongs here. A cable-car connects the town above with its beaches here (08.00–20.00, every 10 minutes; 20.00–23.00, every 15 minutes; 150 l. single, 250 l. return).

Hotels

Luxury	†*Mazzarò Sea Palace.*
1st Class	†*Atlantis Bay;*
	†*Villa Sant'Andrea.*
2nd Class	*Báia Azzurra;*
	Isola Bella;
	†*Lido Méditerranée;*
	Stockholm.
3rd Class	*Ionic Hotel Mazzarò.*

Pensions

1st Class	*Villa Amenta.*
2nd Class	*Villa Espéria.*
3rd Class	†*Elisabetta;*
	Maison Jolie;
	Raneri;
	Tuna Irmi;
	Villa delle Rose;
	Villa Irmi;
	Villino Gallodoro.

[52 km.] Taormina.

ROUTE 2

Accommodation en route San Giovanni la Punta; Trecastagni (and Viagrande, Pedara); Zafferana Etnea; Milò; Linguaglossa; Francavilla di Sicília.

Take the road for Trescastagni, from the north end of Via Etnea (Route Exit A).

[9 km.] **San Giovanni la Punta.**

Pension

2nd Class	*Villa Paradiso dell'Etna.*

[15 km.] **Trecastagni** – the name means 'three chestnut trees' – has a fine church, the *Chiesa Madre*, which is most probably the work of Antonello Gagini; its beautiful lines would do that master credit. It is the purest Renaissance building in Sicily. Seeing Gagini's work as an architect one realizes upon what firm foundations he based his strength as a sculptor.

Hotel
3rd Class   *Trecastagni.*
(Also, 3rd Class, *Madonna degli Ulivi* at near-by Viagrande, and, 2nd Class, *Bonaccorsi* at Pedara.)

(While (1971) this road is interrupted by a fresh lava flow, it will be as well to fork right at Fleri (20 km.) to Santa Vénerina la Bádia, left to San Álfio, whence it should be possible to regain this route beyond Milò. This is about 10 km. longer, some of it very attractive. The road is not broken until after Zafferana Etnea, however, so there are alternative roads to Santa Vénerina later on.)

[24 km.] A vague, inhabited area – a summer station – called **Zafferana Etnea**. A road on the left climbs 11 km. up Etna and will eventually cross to join the Nicolosi–Cantoniera road (p. 267).

Hotels
3rd Class   *Airone;*
              Del Bosco, 5 km. up the Etna road (a centre for religious
                  instruction, in a marvellous situation; very comfortable;
                  plain but good fare – institutional atmosphere);
              Motel Euro Etna.
Pensions
2nd Class   *Villa Margherita;*
              Villa Salemi.
3rd Class   *Russo;*
              Villa dei Pini Solitari.

[27 km.] **Milò**. From here one gets a good view of the astonishing *Valle del Bove* above.

Hotels
3rd Class   *Dei Ciclamini.*
4th Class   *Belvedere.*
Pension
3rd Class   *O.D.A.*

[50 km.] **Linguaglossa.**

Hotel
4th Class   *Centrale.*

[55 km.] **Castiglione di Sicília,** a much-damaged – by the Germans, this time – but ancient town which still manages to look much as it must have when it was a stronghold of Roger di Láuria.

[60 km.] **Francavilla di Sicília,** where by a medieval *bridge* crossing the Alcantara river there is the domed ruin of a *Byzantine chapel*.

Hotel
4th Class   *Centrale.*

[79 km.] Rejoin the S.S.114 at Capo Schisò.

[87 km.] Taormina.

TAORMINA

Air
Bus connections to Fontanarossa Airport outside Catánia.
Rail
Bus connections to station at Giardini for Messina and Catánia.
Bus
Services to Messina, Enna, Catánia.
Information
E.P.T. office, Corso Umberto (*Map* **11**).
Azienda Autónoma, Piazza Santa Caterina (Palazzo Corváia; *Map* **4**).
Tourist Information Office. Stazione Giardini (*Map* **21**).
Bathing
Bathing can be had at Mazzarò (reached by cable-car; p. 273), Spisone, Giardini (p. 272), also Naxos (p. 272).
Hotels (see also Hotels and Pensions at Mazzarò on p. 273)

Luxury	*San Doménico Palace,* Piazza San Doménico 5.
1st Class	*Bristol Park,* Via Bagnoli Croce 92 ;
	Excelsior Palace, Via Toselli 6 ;
	Jolly Hotel Diódoro, Via Bagnoli Croce 75 ;
	Méditerranée, Via Circonvallazione 61 ;
	Miramare, Via Guardiola Vécchia 27 ;
	Timeo, Via Teatro Greco 59 ;
	Vello d'Oro, Via Fazzello.
2nd Class	*Bel Soggiorno,* Via Luigi Pirandello 60 ;
	Continental, Via Dionísio Primo ;
	Corallo, Via Madonna delle Grazie 6A ;
	Grande Albergo Monte Tauro, Via Madonna delle Grazie ;
	Imperial Palace, Via Circonvallazione 11 ;
	Metropol, Corso Umberto 154 ;
	Sirius, Via Guardiola Vécchia ;
	Sole Castello, Via Rotabile Castelmola ;
	Villa Belvedere, Via Bagnoli Croce 79.
3rd Class	*Ariston,* Via Bagnoli Croce ;
	Firenze, Via Luigi Pirandello 31 ;
	Garden, Via Costantino Patrício 1 ;
	Isabella, Corso Umberto 58 ;
	Panorama di Sicília (at Castel Mola) ;
	President Hotel Splendid, Via Dietro Cappuccini 10 ;

    Residence, Salita Dente 4 ;
    Villa Carlotta, Via L. Pirandello 81 ;
    Villa Nettuno, Via L. Pirandello 33 ;
    Villa Schuler, Via Bastione 16 ;
    Villa Sonia (at Castel Mola) ;
    Vittória, Corso Umberto 81.

4th Class   *Badia Vécchia,* Via Fazzello 32 ;
    Basile, Via Fazzello 6 ;
    Casa Costa, Via Damiano Rosso 27 ;
    Casa Sarina, Via Timeo 4 ;
    Césare Ottaviano, Via Césare Ottaviano 26 ;
    Condor, Via Dietro Cappuccini 25 ;
    Euro, Via Giardinazzo 5 ;
    Plaza, Piazza Santa Caterina 3 ;
    Riviera, Via Nazionale 182 ;
    Salus, Via Cuseni 8 ;
    Taormina, Via Circonvallazione 28 ;
    Villa Gaia, Via Fazzello ;
    Villa Piccina, Via Roma 10.

Pensions
1st Class   *Internazionale,* Corso Umberto 19 ;
    Villa Paradiso, Via Roma 6 ;
    Villa San Giorgio, Via San Pancrazio 46 ;
    Villa San Michele, Via Damiano Rosso ;
    Villa San Pancrazio, Via Luigi Pirandello 22.

2nd Class   *Adele,* Via Apollo Arcageta 16 ;
    La Campanella, Via Circonvallazione 3 ;
    Palazzo Véchcio, Salita Ciampoli 9 ;
    Villa Kristina, Rotabile Castelmola ;
    Villa Le Terraze, Corso Umberto 172.

3rd Class   *Berna Helvétia,* Via Bagnoli Croce 63 ;
    Casa Emmi, Via Zecca 31 ;
    Castelmola, Via Rotabile Castelmola 19 ;
    Colúmbia, Via Iallia Bassia 13 ;
    Corona, Via Roma 7 ;
    Cuscona, Corso Umberto 238 ;
    De La Paix, Via Dietro Cappuccini 23 ;
    Elios, Via Bagnoli Croce 98 ;
    Etna, Via del Ginnásio 20 ;
    Falanga, Via Zecca 5 ;
    Fortuna, Via Damiano Rosso 33 ;
    Holiday, Via Giardinazzo 24 ;
    Impero, Via Luigi Pirandello 20 ;
    La Prora, Via Luigi Pirandello 111 ;
    Luna, Corso Umberto 99 ;
    Milano, Vico B. San Pancrázio 16 ;
    Moderno, Via Nazionale 36 ;
    Santo Stéfano, Via Sesto Pompeo 16 ;
    Svizzera, Via Luigi Pirandello 26 ;
    Trinácria, Corso Umberto 99 ;
    Villa Astória, Via L. Pirandello ;
    Villa Eden, Via San Pancrázio 50 ;
    Villa Lina, Via Luigi Pirandello 26A ;
    Villa Margherita, Via Dietro Cappuccini ;
    Villa Marina, Via Sirina 3 ;
    Villa Sirena, Via Luigi Pirandello 36 ;
    Villa Valverde, Via F. Strazzeri 12.

Restaurants
António, in the town ; small and simple, best if you can order in advance (tel. 45.70).
Il Pescatore, Isola Bella beach ; fairly grand and unusually good, specializing in sea-food of course.

A remarkably well-preserved medieval town with a population of over 8,000, Taormina is Sicily's most famous holiday resort, and one of the few southern wintering-places still to attract numerous visitors. It has a good winter climate; spring is delightful here, and it is now a popular, crowded summer-holiday place.

It is a small town these days – not at all what it was in Hellenistic and Roman times – and more medieval than anything else in appearance. Its views are glorious, especially those towards Etna. Besides its well-known antique theatre there are many good buildings from the later Middle Ages which are ornamented with lava and various stones of different colours in a peculiarly local manner.

The fantastic growth of hotels (where both the water and electricity supplies have already been seriously overburdened) has eclipsed the once agreeable life led by residents, native and foreign – as, too, it has completely made away with the internal charm of this hill-town, once all gardens and lanes and its grand little main street. But honour where honour is due: until recently all this massive urban development was netted down by a mesh of wires, cables, supported by a forest of poles, and now all has gone underground and you can see the view and the sun again.

HISTORY

After Dionysius I of Syracuse destroyed Naxos he established this town of Tauromenium in 403 B.C., and in 358 B.C. it received another colony of exiled Naxiots during the reign of Andromachus, its tyrant and the father of the autocratic historian Timaeus.

It was founded in time to be buffeted about during the bad times of Greek decadence. Its harbour was the landing place of Timoleon, who was welcomed here to Sicily by Andromachus. Timoleon left his host upon his throne, the only Sicilian tyrant whom he did not overthrow. Pyrrhus also landed here – but see the history of Syracuse (p. 212) for this period of Tauromenium's history. The city's complaisance towards Rome earned it specially favourable treatment until it misjudged the way things were going and sided with

Sextus Pompeius against Octavianus in the civil wars. Octavian removed the population in 35 B.C., but, as Augustus, later re-established the city, which then flourished.

In A.D. 902 it was first destroyed and then rebuilt by the Arabs. Count Roger took it in 1078. The Sicilian Council which decided whom to proclaim king upon the death of Martin II, the last of the line of Peter I of Aragon, met here. It chose Ferdinand of Castile, husband of Isabella of Aragon, whose marriage had already united the thrones of Spain. Isabella's dowry was thus increased by Sicily which, henceforth, was to be governed as a part of Spain.

When Marshal Kesselring moved his headquarters into the comfort of Taormina's hotels he did the town the disservice of bringing down Allied bombs upon it.

PRINCIPAL SIGHTS

Cathedral
Corso Umberto Primo; Map **19**.

This simple, battlemented church belongs to the thirteenth century. It occupies the site of an earlier basilica and was restored in the fifteenth and sixteenth centuries. To these dates belong the side doorways, and the late *rose-window* in the west front. The main *west door* is of 1636.

Inside there is a triptych of *The Visitation* by António Giuffrè (mid-fifteenth-century) and a polyptych by Antonello de Saliba (1504).

The *fountain* in the little piazza outside is of 1635.

Church of Sant'Agostino
Piazza Nove Aprile; Map **14**.

Built in 1448, it has a Gothic doorway and now houses the *Library*.

Church of Sant'António
Piazza Sant'António; Map **16**.

This fifteenth-century church, with its good doorway, was damaged by bombs in July 1943.

Church of San Pancrázio
Outside the Porta Messina; Map 1.

This is built upon the ruins of a Greek temple, the *cella* of which it is still possible to trace.

Convent of Badia Vécchia
Via Dionísio Primo; Map 10.

All that remains of this is a magnificent *tower*, battlemented and pierced by superbly shaped and decorated windows. It is fifteenth-century. A museum is to be opened in this building shortly.

Former Convent of San Doménico
Map 20.

Now a hotel – what remains of the convent is principally the late-sixteenth-century *cloister*. The church was destroyed during an Allied air-raid in July 1943 when the convent was Kesselring's headquarters. (Sir Winston Churchill held a carousal of a family holiday here in the mid 'fifties which has gone into local legend. Reverence for the man's deeds too often causes his memorialists to be reticent about the fantasy side of his existence: one would like to know what is fact and what fiction among these heroic legends.)

Greek Theatre
Via Teutro Greco; Map 9.

Open 09.00–13.00 and 16.30–dusk.

This was the next-largest Hellenistic theatre in Sicily after that of Syracuse. With nine wedges of seats excavated from the rock of the hill, it was 358 feet in diameter and the orchestra 115 feet across. Contrary to the usual state of these antique theatres, the cavea has been the part to suffer with time while the scena has survived in a remarkably good state.

The ruin is largely Roman, the original Greek theatre, built perhaps as early as the third century B.C., having been made over in the second century A.D., and the scena itself rebuilt in the third century A.D.

Of all Greek theatres, this one faces the most spectacular view

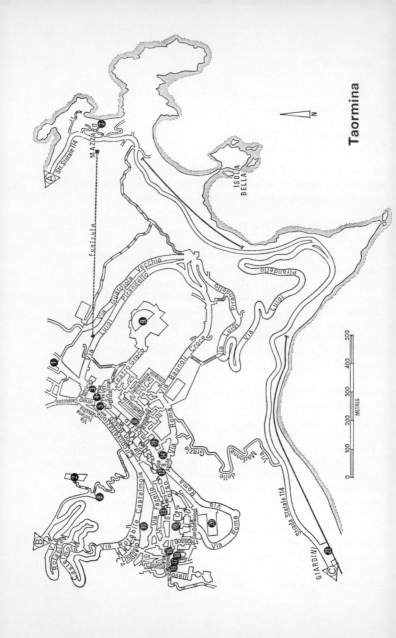

imaginable: the sleepy, sometimes snow-sprinkled shape of Etna rising as a diagonal between sky and land, the beaches and headlands below, the richly covered slopes coming almost up to the gaps in the scena.

Around the top of the cavea ran a portico; the forty-five standing columns belonging to it were re-erected in 1860, as were the columns of the scena also. Notice the outside of the brick walls of the scena which are much in their original state; the interior was faced with marble.

This theatre was famous for its excellent acoustics, and they are still very good, as you can easily test.

The little *Museum* attached to the custodian's house (which you can see as you enter) contains some pleasing things and interesting tablets recording Tauromenium's finances from 150 B.C. to the Empire, and also lists of generals from the second and first centuries B.C. Open on request if the custodian happens to be there.

Naumáchia
Via Naumáchia; Map 8.

This is a rather romantic name for what was an enormous cistern, possibly connected with the supply of water to the baths. It is not open to the public at present, though 400 yards of its arcaded retaining wall can be seen from the street.

1 Church of San Pancrázio (p. 279)
2 Castello (p. 283)
3 Porta Messina
4 Palazzo Corváia (Azienda Autónoma) (p. 282)
5 Odeon or Teatrino Romano (p. 282)
6 Madonna della Rocca Sanctuary (p. 283)
7 Lido Mazzarò (p. 273)
8 Naumáchia (p. 281)
9 Greek Theatre (p. 279)
10 Convent of Badia Vécchia (p. 279)
11 E.P.T. Office
12 Torre dell' Orologio (p. 282)
13 Palazzo Ciámpoli (p. 282)
14 Library (formerly Church of Sant' Agostino) (p. 278)

15 Porta Catánia or Porta del Tocco (p. 282)
16 Church of Sant' António (p. 278)
17 Post Office
18 Palazzo del Duca di Santo Stéfano (p. 282)
19 Cathedral (p. 278)
20 Former Convent of San Doménico (Hotel) (p. 279)
21 Stazione Giardini and Tourist Information Office (p. 272)

A Route to Lido Spisone, SS. Pietro e Páolo, Messina
B Route to Castel Mola
C Route to Naxos, Catánia, Enna

Odeon or **Teatrino Romano**
Off Via Circonvallazione; Map **5**.

These vestiges, which incorporate those of a Hellenistic temple which the Odeon superseded, are pretty dismal as a 'sight'.

Palazzo Ciámpoli
In an alley north of the Corso Umberto Primo; Map **13**.

Built in 1412 (and now a hotel), it is a good example of its period, with a fine doorway.

Palazzo Corváia
Piazza Santa Caterina; Map **4**.

Late-fourteenth-century and recently restored. This severe, battlemented building is most characteristic of the Taorminian style, with its ornamentation of black lava and white pumice inlaid in the limestone of which it is built. The *courtyard* is very pretty with its outside stair and the panels of Adam and Eve in relief. Inside is the *great hall* (or *Sala del Parlamentário*) where the council of A.D. 1410 met. There are two other *salons*. The graffiti on the walls of the entrance-rooms are interesting.

Palazzo del Duca di Santo Stéfano
Just south of Porta Catánia; Map **18**.

This beautiful fifteenth-century palace is newly restored.

Porta Catánia or **Porta del Tocco**
Piazza Sant' António; Map **15**.

Built in 1440.

Torre dell'Orológio
Map **12**.

This is perhaps as early as the twelfth century, though it was restored in 1679.

The *archway* through this leads into the western section of the town called the *Borgo Medioevale*. The Corso Umberto is lined with pretty palaces mostly belonging to the fifteenth century.

ENVIRONS

Castello
Map 2.

This can be reached from the Castel Mola road, or by the path from the Via Circonvallazione, which passes the *Madonna della Rocca sanctuary*.

The ruined *keep* of this medieval castle offers nothing save the magnificent view which is all that it now commands.

Castel Mola
A village three miles farther inland from Taormina, which is the only place from which it can be reached. (Route Exit B.)

Another *medieval castle* dominates this place, with an even better view than that from the *castello* of Taormina. In the Caffè San Giórgio is a famous collection of autographs.

Via Fontana Vécchia
Off the Via Circonvallazione.

On this road, a half mile outside the town, is the house where D. H. Lawrence lived in 1920 and 1921; and where, since, Aubrey Menon also has lived. A tablet records Lawrence's stay.

Naxos (p. 271) is within easy reach of Taormina.

The wonderful Norman church of *SS. Pietro e Páolo* at San Francesco di Páolo (p. 284) is less easily reached unless you have a car, but most worth while making the effort to see.

TAORMINA TO MESSINA

Route (Route Exit A.) Drive down by the coast to join the S.S.114, an awful, traffic-clogged road awaiting the relief of the motorway. 48 km. from the junction.
Rail Bus connection to Giardini station for good railway service by the Messina–Catánia line.
Bus Direct C.I.A.T. bus, but also local services.
Accommodation en route At Letoianni, Forza d'Agrò, Roccalumera, Alì Terme.

[5 km.] Letoianni.

Here in the parish church there is a medieval *gonfalon*. (Gonfalons were standards, the predecessors of banners, regimental flags, etc.)

There is also a *painting* by Antonello de Saliba – a painter whose work it is always worth stopping a few minutes to see.

Hotel
3rd Class   †*Park Hotel Lido Silemi.*
Pensions
3rd Class   *Da Peppe ;*
Emanuele ;
Sant'Antonino.

[10 km.] Forza d'Agrò lies 4 km. inland up a side-road.

This small medieval town is pleasant to visit. The church of *SS. Trinità* contains a painting of *Three Angels visiting Abraham* by Antonio Giuffrè (*c.* 1500), which is particularly fine. In this church there is also another *gonfalon* in the shape of a Gothic shrine.

Hotel
3rd Class   *Souvenir.*

[13 km.] A turning left (narrow, backing off a sharp right-hand bend in the S.S.114 and leading unpromisingly under a railway arch ; hard to spot) leads to the hamlet of **San Francesco di Páolo**, on the north bank of the *Agro* river. Here the road degenerates into a track and in dry weather it is best at once to take to the tracks up the shingly river-bed – do so as soon as you have passed under the motorway viaduct – and after some 6 km. you will see the almost tower-like structure of the monastery church of *SS. Pietro e Páolo* rising on the north bank. Drive as it were for the landing-stage below it and you will find you can quite easily drive up to it.

SS. Pietro e Páolo is the most important Norman building in eastern Sicily, built, as the inscription in Greek over the west porch records, by Master Gerard the Frank in 1171–72 for the Basilian order of monks. The Basilians are an Orthodox order although their remaining houses in Italy are in communion with Rome. The Arabs banished them, but the Normans allowed their return ; the buildings they then erected incline – the effect, perhaps, of their richly textured, decorated exteriors – most to emphasize the Byzantine elements in the Siculo-Norman synthesis of styles.

There is always someone around the houses into which the

tumble-down monastery buildings have been converted who will open the church for you.

Tall, narrow, with twin domes set on high drums, the exterior is banded and decorated with mingled brick, buff-coloured limestone and dark lava, made graceful with an interlacing of blind arches. The wide *west porch* is very notable.

Inside, the plan reveals its unusually subtle design: in essence, that of a three-aisled basilica, but one in which, by shortening the nave to the span of three pairs of arches and opening a cupola between the second pair, the traditional Byzantine, Greek-cross plan is contained. But instead of opening the three apses in the east end directly off the square containing this Greek cross – as at SS. Trinità di Délia, for instance – a sanctuary crossing, with another dome in its centre, both suggests transept arms and re-emphasizes the basilical form. Here you see most clearly illustrated the suggested affinity between 'Arab' stalactitic decoration and Norman use of squinches of allied forms, piled to close and transform, while raising a quadrangular-shaped opening to the semicircular or circular base of half-domed apse or fully domed cupola. This is remarkable in the southern apse and the dome over the sanctuary, which actually rises from a rectangle to an octagonal drum. Most beautiful, this bare, spare and intellectual interior – to my mind it is one of the finer medieval sights in the island; and even the little expedition it takes to see carries you into that little-visited, very different and rural Sicily which is still the most significant aspect of the island's life. Further exploration up the river-bed, too, is rewarding on this score.

[18 km.] Roccalumera.

Hotel
4th Class   *Aurora.*

[24 km.] Alì Terme and a turning left 6 km. to **Alì** village where the mid-fourteenth-century *Chiesa Madre* shows a remarkable and fine bent for archaicism.

Hotel (at Alì Terme)
4th Class   *Terme Marino Giuseppe.*
Pension
3rd Class   *Terme Granata Cassibile.*

[38 km.] Itala Marina and a turning left 3 km. to **Itala.** Here the *Chiesa Madre* has two painted *crucifixes* of the fourteenth century, well worth looking at, and the *Church of San Pietro* offers a very fine though slightly less splendid example of a Basilian church of Norman date than SS. Pietro e Páolo (above). It was in fact built by Count Roger in 1093 as a thank-offering for a victory over Arab forces and is therefore considerably earlier than its neighbour on the Agrò, for which it is in many ways the model. Again, the very rich exterior and the internal grandeur of proportions. We haven't much left to us that the first Roger built and this adds a special, associative flavour to one's appreciation of this beautiful church.

[39 km.] **Mili Marina** and a turning left to **Mili San Pietro** village where, below the right-hand bend from which the village is first sighted, stands the *Church of Santa Maria*, a third Basilian monastery church and an even earlier foundation of Count Roger's, belonging to 1082. Here Roger's natural son Jordanus was buried in 1092, perhaps in its small and interesting *crypt*. The key to this rather ruinous church is with the parish priest (next door to the church), but if it does not open the door you can scramble in through the south side from the farmyard of what was formerly the monastery. The exterior is ornamented with attached intersecting arches and three domes, one before each apse and, from the interior, not the marked features which they are on the outside. Inside there is but one nave aisle divided from the sanctuary by a broad arch flanked by two smaller ones. The *central dome* is the only one of the three to make its presence felt inside, as the central apse is the only deep one, the side ones being indicated by niches. Everything about the architecture of Sicily at this period suggests something else, either from which it derives or to which it gives rise. Here are mixed suggestions: of the five-domed chapels of Byzantium; of the *mihrab* of Muslim prayer-halls (the niches); while the arched screen pre-visions the Latin cruciform churches to come.

[42 km.] **Tremestieri.**

Restaurant
La Tavernetta: modest but as good as good home-cooking hereabouts.

[48 km.] Messina (p. 79).

Routes in Centre of Island

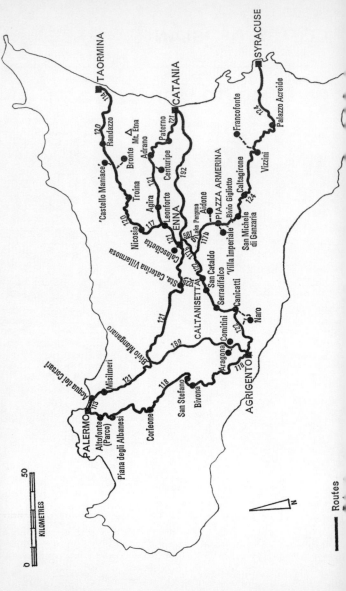

KILOMETRES

0   50

—— Routes

N

CENTRE OF ISLAND

PALERMO TO AGRIGENTO

Route 1 (Route Exit J.) By the main road, a good one; 131 km. Take the S.S.113 7 km. to Acqua dei Corsari; branch right on the S.S.121 52 km. to Bívio Manganaro, where you go right again by the S.S.189, 80 km. to Agrigento. (No hotels en route.)
Route 2 (Route Exit G.) Via Piana degli Albanesi, joining the S.S. 118 after 41 km. and continuing via Corleone, at 58 km., to S. Stéfano, at 96 km. This is the prettier road, though neither good nor fast. 171 km. As a glance at the map will tell you, there are ways of combining these two routes.
Rail Several trains daily.
Bus One bus a day.

ROUTE 1

[14 km.] **Misilmeri** – *Menzil el-Emir*, or 'the Emir's village'. Stop for a drink of *passito*, a very good local white wine of high alcoholic content.

[59 km.] **Bívio Manganaro.**

[118 km.] 3 km. after **Comitini** a road leads right for 2 km. to **Aragona**, and from there a short walk, if you are guided, takes you to the *Macalube,* tiny volcanic boils from two to three feet high in which a salty mud bubbles.

[131 km.] Agrigento (p. 176).

ROUTE 2

Accommodation en route At Bivona.

[12 km.] **Altofonte** or **Parco** (p. 147).

[24 km.] **Piana degli Albanesi.**
   A colony of northern Greeks settled here in the fifteenth century. Many still adhere to the Orthodox, though Uniate, rite. The people use their own Greek dialect at home, and they keep up their connections with Greece (the change of the town's name to 'Albanians'

was political). Formerly you would have seen much evidence of Sicilians' pride in the traditional costumes worn here by women, but these valuable heirlooms now appear only for weddings and great occasions. They resemble those worn on feast-days at Megara, an 'Albanian' settlement in Greece. At Easter and Epiphany there are ceremonies of a Byzantine flavour.

[58 km.] **Corleone.**

[96 km.] **San Stéfano.**

[105 km.] **Bivona.**

Hotel
3rd Class   *Ducale.*

[171 km.] Agrigento (p. 176).

AGRIGENTO TO ENNA

Route (Route Exit C.) S.S.122 and S.S.117 bis. 106 km. to the Quadrívio di Misericórdia cross-roads in Enna near the station, which is at the bottom of the hill on which the town stands.
Rail Several trains daily to Enna station where buses meet trains to run you up to the town.
Bus No direct connections.
Accommodation en route At Canicatti, Serradifalco, Caltanisetta.

[22 km.] A turning to the right leading in 11 km. to **Naro**, a picturesque, battlemented town.

Inside the *Chiesa Matrice*, a church of 1612, there is rich stucco work, a *Madonna* of 1534 by Vincenzo Gagini and a 1424 *font* decorated with reliefs by a little-known master called Nardo di Crespanzano.

The fine *Castello dei Chiaramonte* of the thirteenth and fourteenth centuries does not belie its owners' splendid reputation.

You can rejoin the S.S.122 at Canicattì by taking a road northwards out of the town.

[35 km.] **Canicattì.**

Hotels
3rd Class   *Belvedere.*
4th Class   *Lodato.*

[47 km.] Serradifalco.

Hotel
4th Class   *Itália.*

[60 km.] San Cataldo.

[68 km.] You reach Caltanisetta.

Caltanisetta

Population
Over 64,000.
Information
E.P.T. Office, Corso Vittório Emanuele 109.
Hotels
2nd Class   *Di Prima,* Nuovo Scalo Ferroviario;
             Europa, Via B. Gaetani 5;
             Grand Hotel Concórdia 'Villa Mazzone', Via F. Crispi 25.
3rd Class   *Aurora,* Corso Vittório Emanuele 56;
             Moderno, Via Mangione 2.
Pensions
3rd Class   *Bristol,* Via Barone di Fíglia 6;
             Flávia, Via M. Tumminelli 14.

The centre of the sulphur trade, a provincial capital and largely a modern town where even the baroque buildings have not much to be said for them.

The *Cathedral* (1570–1622) in the centre of the town was damaged in 1943. The painted *ceiling* which was Borremans' masterpiece, if that can be said of his work, suffered considerably.

The church of *Santa Maria degli Ángeli,* near the Castello, is a small and quite charming fourteenth-century church.

The *Castello di Pietrarossa,* a romantic ruin on a fantastic crag, was a residence of Frederick III of Aragon.

Museo Cívico
Via Nicoló Colajanni 3.

Open 09.00–13.00, closed Sundays and holidays.

This new museum contains a good collection of indigenous Sicilian articles, both native and hellenized, brought from various local sites. The treasure is the small terra-cotta, sixth-century B.C. model of a shrine, a little temple in antis with its pediment decorated with two heads and three shield-like bosses and surmounted by a horse and rider. This came from Sabucina and represents a Sikel's view of a Greek prototype. There are fine imported Greek vases too. And a lot more material, mostly from the Sabucina excavations, yet to be displayed.

Bádia di Santo Spírito

This lies on the edge of the town as you leave for Enna by the S.S.122, 2·7 km. along which there is a left-hand fork (the S.S.122 bis going to Santa Caterina Villarmosa) and along this, very soon on the left, this monastery church stands. Key from the farmhouse next door. It was founded by Count Roger and his wife Adelasia, though not consecrated until 1153. It has three little apses decorated with rows of attached arches. Inside, it has one nave only and the side apses are reduced to niches. The central apse is frescoed (sixteenth-century) and another, fifteenth-century fresco is in the lunette over the exterior of the side door. The font is very much of the twelfth century.

[89 km.] Branch left on to the S.S.117 bis.

[106 km.] Enna – a dramatic approach by this road; and you can climb to it by any of the roads leading to the left up the hill.

ENNA

Rail
Services to Palermo, Catánia, Agrigento. The station is at the bottom of the hill, but trains are met by local buses.
Bus
From the bus station in Piazza Vittório Emanuele buses run to Palermo, Caltanisetta, Caltagirone and Catánia; and locally to Calascibetta, Lake Pergusa and Piazza Armerina.
Information
E.P.T. Office, Piazza Garibaldi 1, off on the left on the way up to the Duomo (2nd after Piazza Umberto).
Hotels
2nd Class   *Autostello Aci* (near the station, below the town);
             Belvedere, Piazza Francesco Crispi 5;
             Grande Albergo Sicília, Piazza Colaianni;
             Park Hotel La Giara (near Lake Pergusa).
3rd Class   *Pergola* (near Lake Pergusa).
4th Class   *Enna*, Via Sant'Ágata 43.

HISTORY

Enna stands on a plateau rising precipitously from this already high part of the island and clings, too, to its southern slopes. Such a position, 3,110 feet high, must always have attracted anyone looking for a defensible position in which to live, and indeed, unless it was taken by treachery, its sieges have been long and arduous ones.

As *Henna* it was for long a Siculan stronghold. Here was the centre of the Sicilian cult of Demeter and Persephone. The town overlooks the plain in which lies the Lake of Pergusa (see p. 69).

Henna was much hellenized from Gela, showing this influence as early as the seventh century B.C. While Syracuse pursued a conciliatory policy towards the Siculans, Henna remained independent, and Gelon built a temple to Demeter here in 480 B.C. as an earnest of his goodwill. But Dionysius I of Syracuse took the city by treachery in 397 B.C. Called by the Romans *Castrum Ennae*, in 135 (or 134) B.C. the first Slave Revolt broke out here under Eunus, and it was not until 131 (or 132) B.C. after a two-years' siege, that the Romans retook the town.

The Arabs were able to capture the city, in A.D. 859, from the Byzantines, only by crawling in through a sewer, one by one.

Kasr Janni, as they called it, was not reduced by Count Roger – using a characteristic mixture of force and 'diplomacy' – until 1087. He renamed it *Castrogiovanni*, which it remained until 1927 when it became, as the capital of a province, Enna. Enna was bombed in 1943, though not very seriously.

PRINCIPAL SIGHTS

The main sights are signposted from Piazza Vittório Emanuele where the buses come into.

Castello di Lombardia

The Lombards were one of the few Italian curses which Sicily was spared, so how this great castle got its name is a mystery.

It was built by Frederick II to be like a fist gripping the centre of his island kingdom. It had twenty towers where now only six are standing. You may climb the tallest, the *Torre Pisana*, and, if the wind is not too cold, look long at the extraordinary view of the plain where the rape of Persephone (p. 69) occurred. Etna seems its great height from here, and the Lake of Pergusa, when grey in the shades of approaching night, used very well to seem a likely doorway to the underworld realm of gloomy Dis – but see below.

In the ruin of the castle's chapel, an *open-air theatre* has been made where opera is given for a season in summer.

Frederick II of Aragon converted this castle into a palace where he often resided. He summoned the Sicilian parliament and assumed the title of King of Trinácria here.

Temple of Demeter

The *Rocca di Cérere* juts out to the north-east from the castle rock and you can walk out to it from the promenade which encircles the castle.

Some scraps of antique masonry show that there was a fifth-century B.C. building here, probably belonging to the temple to, or temenos of Demeter, which Gelon built in 480 B.C.

Cathedral

Built in the early fourteenth century, it was badly damaged by fire in 1446. Subsequent restoration was carried out largely during the sixteenth century.

The *front* is in such a very odd baroque style that it is thought to have been an attempt to preserve the lines at least of its Gothic original – Sicilian archaism again. Both the *transepts* and the *apses,* which are polygonal, are from the original construction. The *south doorway* is partly original.

Inside, the antique base of the stoop on the left may have come from the temple of Demeter – only a fragment, and only a slender possibility.

I like the *ceiling* of the nave, and the carved *choir-stalls,* the first certainly the work of Filippo Paladino, the last possibly so.

But the black alabaster *pillars* of the nave are the most interesting things in the church. They belong to the sixteenth-century restoration; their strange bases and varied capitals represent a provincial idea of the principles and taste of the Renaissance – with the fashion for the grotesque much in evidence. For all their curiosity they have a certain stunted grandeur.

Museo Alessi
Next to the Cathedral, beside the apse.

Here are displayed the contents of the unusually rich cathedral treasury. There are also numerous coins and quantities of weapons dating from the battle for Enna during the Slave Revolt (134 B.C.).

Piazza Francesco Crispi

The arresting fountain in the square represents the *Rape of Persephone*, and is a copy of the group by Bernini in the Villa Borghese at Rome.

Torre di Federico II

Approached from Via IV Novembre, this is a Swabian look-out tower. Its octagonal plan recalls Frederick II's Castel del Monte in Apúlia.

ENVIRONS

Calascibetta

To reach Calascibetta, travel north-west from the Quadrívio di Misericórdia cross-roads 3 km. in the direction of the S.S.290. This town looks very inviting across the valley between the two outstanding hills (buses run from Enna station). It is as far removed from the twentieth century and as Saracenic as it looks from a distance. It is poor and strange. The occasional sight of a peasant in something approaching a national costume intensifies the feeling of Calascibetta's remoteness.

In the *Cappuccini* church there is a good *Epiphany* by Filippo Paladino. King Peter II died here in 1342.

See under Enna for its hotel.

Lake Pergusa

This is about 12 km. away to the south-east of Enna, reached by the S.S.192 and S.S.117 bis, then the branch road, left, to Varco Ramata. It is a brackish mere covering 450 acres, a dead-water lake with no apparent outlet.

Of all myths, that of the triangle of chthonic deities, Demeter, her daughter Persephone and Hades, is the purest archetype; and therefore as meaningful and influential upon us as any emotional or spiritual experience undergone by ourselves personally. The existence of this allegorical story is more important than any ruined temple to the trio, and indeed more so than that of this mysterious lake. But that modern Sicilians could have built a motor race-track around the verges of Lake Pergusa, and having done so thought it so appealing as to build summer villas and restaurants, with a 'Tourist Village' around *that*, defies belief. I have no words eloquent enough to express my sense of outrage or the depth of my contempt for this tribe of neo-primitives, unworthy as they are to share even a descriptive label with their creative forefathers.

If you still want to stay here, see under Enna.

See Guido, *Sicily: an archaeological guide*, for prehistoric sites in the neighbourhood of Enna.

PALERMO TO ENNA

Route (Route Exit J.) S.S.113 to Acqua dei Corsari (7 km.), branch right on to S.S.121 for Enna. 157 km. Quite a good. though in places a winding road.
Rail Several through-trains ; buses meet trains to take you up the hill to the town.
Bus Connection exists but it is slow and not advisable.
Accommodation en route Nil.

[15 km.] **Misilmeri** (p. 289).

[124 km.] **Santa Caterina Villarmosa**. Just past this village the 122 bis leads on the right to the Bádia di Santo Spírito (p. 292).

[157 km.] Enna.

ENNA TO SYRACUSE

Route From the Quadrívio di Misericórdia cross-roads take the S.S.192 in the direction of Catánia for 2·5 km., then turn right on to the S.S.117 bis ; after 1 km., take the left turning on to the S.S.561 towards Lake Pergusa. You return to the S.S.117 bis 12 km. after this turn and continue via Piazza Armerina to Bívio Gigliotto, then on by the S.S.124 via Caltagirone and Palazzo Acréide to Syracuse. 175 km.
Rail By rail to Dittaino from where buses organized by the Railways run to Piazza Armerina, and on to Caltagirone to connect with a local railway service to Syracuse ; it is usually quicker, however, to go back to Dittaino and continue by rail to Catánia and on to Syracuse.
Bus Buses go from Enna to Piazza Armerina and Caltagirone.

[34 km.] Follow left turning for 7 km. to **Aidone**, a pleasantly medieval-looking place where, 6 km. north-east of the town, is the site of *Morgantina*. This prehistoric site was colonized in the sixth century B.C., very interestingly by Chalcidians from Catana who

settled alongside an enduring Sikel township. The site goes back to
the Castelluccian early Bronze Age and was one of those that the
Thapsos people (p. 253) retreated inland to (Mycenaean XIII ware
has turned up here). Current excavations progress very interestingly,
but largely lay bare the Hellenistic city which belongs to a re-
colonization under Timoleon or Agathocles, the earlier having
probably been destroyed by Ducetius, the Sikel leader.

Excavation has disclosed a very large and unusual *agora* upon
two levels connected on three sides by flights of steps. On the
lower level is the base of the rostrum mounted by the speakers
during debates. This great meeting-place was later overbuilt in
parts and there are the remains of houses rising on terraces towards
the acropolis. A third-century B.C. theatre, a fourth-century sanctuary to Demeter and Persephone, many houses and other buildings
can now be seen. A *museum* is to be opened on the site.

[38 km.] You reach Piazza Armerina.

PIAZZA ARMERINA

Population
Over 25,000.
Rail
Railway buses from the station run to Dittaino for connections to Enna, Palermo,
Agrigento, Catánia, Syracuse, Messina; also to Caltagirone to connect with local
line to Syracuse.
Bus
Direct buses from Catánia, Enna, Caltagirone, Gela.
Hotels
1st Class   *Jolly.*
2nd Class   *Selene;*
            Villa Assunta.
4th Class   *Gangi.*
Restaurant
Zio Totò, a noisy room when busy, but good country-fare.

A spectacular hill-town, this is quite a lively and important centre
as well as being the base for visiting the famous Villa Imperiale.
There are several pleasant baroque churches, a little *Museo Cívico*
in which to while away a half-hour, and a fourteenth-century *castle*
with square towers, built after Frederick of Aragon convened here
the council of 1296 which decided to combat the cession of the
island to Charles d'Anjou.

Sights in the town

The *Cathedral* atop the town is largely of 1627, with a façade of
1719, but it houses a Provençal painted *crucifix* of 1485 that is

really beautiful, and a good Byzantine icon of *Our Lady of Victory* which Pope Nicholas II gave to Count Roger. This is carried in procession on the Feast of the Assumption (August 15th). In the *treasury* is an equestrian statue of Count Roger and a fine reliquary of about 1400 by Simone d'Aversa.

Not far from the station is the plain little church of *San Giovanni di Rodi* (St John of Rhodes), a thirteenth-century chapel belonging to the Hospitallers of St John of Jerusalem, then based upon Rhodes.

North of the town is *Sant'Andrea*, a Norman church built in 1096 by the Count of Butera, a relative of Count Roger. Turn west from the station, down the Via Guccio to find it; there is a custodian on the site. This beautiful priory is to be restored and already an interesting cycle of frescoes found in it has been taken to the National Gallery of Art at Palermo.

'Villa Imperiale'

Open Summer, 09.00–2 hours before dusk; winter, 09.00–13.00 and 14.00–dusk. Sundays, mornings only. Closed on public holidays.

This lies about 6 km. south-west of the town on the pretty road to Barrafranca and is situated in the *contrada* of Casale after which the Villa is sometimes called. Follow the signposts, *Scavi Archeológica Casale* – they are everywhere about. 4 km. out of the town there is a left-hand turn to the villa itself. It is possible to negotiate a reasonable price for a taxi to take you there and back and wait for you during your visit.

By the time that you reach this most important sight, so very intriguing in itself, you will have understood why anyone should go to the trouble of building so splendidly in so remote a place – though there was a Roman town at Soffiana, a hill-town over the Nocciara torrent three miles to the south; its name – so appropriate for a retreat – was Philosophiana; and the road between Catánia and Agrigento then passed close by the town.

For various reasons it has been surmised that this hunting-lodge could have belonged to the Emperor Maximianus Heraclius, co-emperor with Diocletian. Hence the name 'Villa Imperiale'. However, Stewart Perowne has recently noticed that the two mosaic pavements illustrating circus games which it contains (one in the *Salone del Circo*, which is identifiable beyond dispute with the Circus Maximus at Rome built by Maximianus, and the other the scene of children racing in the right-hand room off the atrium to the 'family's' suite of rooms – 9 and 22 on the plan) both show the spina, the long traffic-island around which races were run, as being decorated with that obelisk which now stands in front of the Basilica of St John Lateran. This was the first and tallest of the Egyptian obelisks imported into Rome, brought especially for erection on this site in the circus by Constantius II, the youngest son of Constantine the Great, in A.D. 357. There are good stylistic grounds for dating the building and its mosaics about A.D. 300. Maximianus died in A.D. 310. These two circus mosaics must however now be put at some sixty years later, and there is no obvious reason to suppose them to be exceptional. Yet the most telling reason to suppose the house was an imperial property is the *Adventus Imperator* mosaic in the main entrance (1 on the map) which shows men hailing anyone entering the building in a manner befitting only an emperor of the period. Everything else about the house would aptly become a very grand, lordly supplier of wild beasts for the circus games – a noble contractor; perhaps one who was also an official – but a man whose business embraced all the Empire from Africa to Armenia (i.e. from west to east.) The explanation of the Adventus Imperator mosaic then might be either that Constantius – for it could hardly be a later emperor still – visited the villa, or that it was built by an animal importer as a gift, with a suitable estate to hunt over, for that emperor. Neither explanation is inherently unlikely. At all events we must now think of the date of building as being around A.D. 360. This raises the further small puzzle of its being so obviously a pagan's house. The early Christian emperors were perhaps more in two minds than clerical propaganda suggests; but it still seems odd . . .

The house was occupied until the Arab period. Norman William the Bad, *c*. 1160, seems to have objected to the place, and threw it down; a few cottages then occupied its ruin until a landslide obliterated them and preserved the ruins for us. They were first found in 1716, though excavations did not begin until 1881, and then only on a small scale; systematic work of uncovering the whole building began in 1950 and still proceeds – which makes each visit a fresh pleasure. The *mosaics* are now under a shelter which is shaped to give an idea of the form of the original building.

Although little now remains of the superstructure, the combination of the skilful sheltering and the ground-plan itself – rising upon several levels – provides the glorious floors with a wholly comprehensible setting. One bitterly regrets the loss of almost all the wall decorations, and of the vaulting.

The entrance (*Map* 1) was through a kind of triumphal arch leading to a court or *atrium* surrounded by a portico (*Map* 2). On the north is a large chamber which held a statue of Venus and may have been a shrine (*Map* 3). Through this, and a vestibule, the *bath* could be reached. On the west, the *large lavatory* (*Map* 4) can be entered, though originally the entrance was to its own western side. The marble seat has gone from this companionable convenience. Eastwards was the entrance to the *tablinium* (*Map* 5) giving on to the rectangular peristyle surrounded by four porticoes and with an elaborate fountain and pool in its centre. Opposite the tablinum door is an *aediculum* or shrine to the household gods (*Map* 6). Going left from the entrance, a doorway leads off, left, to a triangular courtyard giving access to the *small lavatory* (*Map* 7) – this initial emphasis on lavatories makes an odd introduction to a palace. It is a most comfortable and sumptuous office, however.

At the north-west corner is a vestibule (*Map* 8) where the mosaic shows a lady with a boy and girl and two slaves going to the bath. By their dress and the boy's squint, this has been thought to be a portrait group of the imperial family. The vestibule gives on to the bath, the *Salone del Circo* (*Map* 9) being the first chamber entered. The mosaic here shows a comprehensive illustration of late Roman circus-sports. The next chamber is the *frigidarium* or cold room (*Map* 10) – an octagon with radial apses, two being vestibules, the two larger ones plunge-baths, and the other four rest-chambers; the mosaics show the dressing which took place here and, in the centre, sea myths. In the small room beyond (*Map* 11), the scenes are of bathers being massaged, appropriately to the *aleipteron* it is. Beyond, again, are the long *tepidarium* (*Map* 12) – warm room – and the *caldaria* (*Map* 13) – hot rooms – where the loss of the pavements reveals the *hypocaust* below which heated the rooms.

Off the north side of the portico (*Map* 14) are sleeping rooms, some with fore-chambers like private sitting-rooms. Some of the geometric-patterned floors were damaged by Norman alterations. The fourth room off the portico (*Map* 15) shows seasons, the inner chamber amorini fishing from an interesting boat and, in the background, a representation of just such a villa as this was. The larger room (*Map* 16) is called the *Píccola Cáccia* after its detailed mosaic

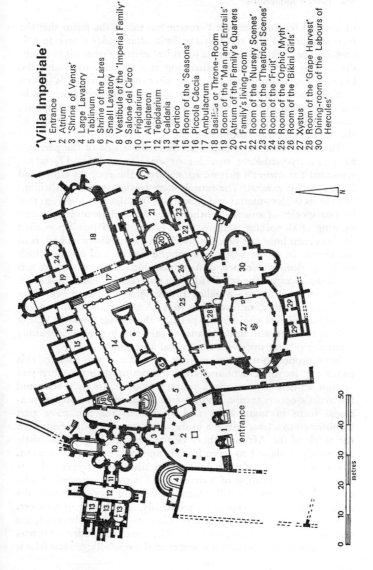

'Villa Imperiale'

1 Entrance
2 Atrium
3 'Shrine of Venus'
4 Large Lavatory
5 Tablinum
6 Shrine of the Lares
7 Small Lavatory
8 Vestibule of the 'Imperial Family'
9 Salone del Circo
10 Frigidarium
11 Aleipteron
12 Tepidarium
13 Caldaria
14 Portico
15 Room of the 'Seasons'
16 Piccola Cáccia
17 Ambulacrum
18 Basilica or Throne-Room
19 Room of the 'Man and Entrails'
20 Atrium of the Family's Quarters
21 Family's living-room
22 Room of the 'Nursery Scenes'
23 Room of the 'Theatrical Scenes'
24 Room of the 'Fruit'
25 Room of the 'Orphic Myth'
26 Room of the 'Bikini Girls'
27 Xystus
28 Room of the 'Grape Harvest'
29 ——
30 Dining-room of the Labours of Hercules'

entrance

N

metres
0 10 20 30 40 50

of hunting scenes. (Stewart Perowne has raised the point that the man standing to the right of the little altar under a tree in this mosaic appears to be wearing a liturgical garment over his hunting-dress. This man is clearly officiating at a sacrifice to Diana, the hunters' patroness, either before or after the hunt which is shown as if in concurrent progress. This suggestion has been taken up in the appropriate scholarly quarters and if it proves to be the case, this mosaic will constitute a very early substantiated instance of the use of liturgical vestments.)

Three flights of steps rise from the eastern side of the peristyle to a seventy-yard-long corridor or *ambulacrum* (*Map* 17) which separated the owner's private rooms from the rest. At either end is an apse (or *exedra*). The mosaic here is a masterpiece, thrilling both in its subject-matter and execution. Its subject is hunting: that by one species of animal of others sets the background for man's hunting of all species, and the great beasts' retaliation upon him; for here men hunt for fun, for food and for curiosity and sport in the circus. In either apse are symbolic figures and scenes which probably denote Africa and Armenia, and in the centre of this continuous design the sea divides the two continental land-masses, while on to – and off – a galley riding upon it, exotic beasts are loaded, and then disembarked in Italy. A stocky and commanding gentleman directs affairs; it is perhaps the owner himself. Young nobles, hunt servants and peasants all take part in this vivid masque upon our relationship with the animal kingdom.

No reproductions can give a just reminder of the effect of this pavement. Its movement and vivid conviction dwindle when you are not actually in movement yourself along it. Its bold style and the artist's concentration upon a free suggestion of three-dimensional form in man, beast and landscape – for the most part emphasized to a lesser degree in the other mosaics, but a feature of the work of the African school of the period – is impressionistic and surely designed to have its full impact when trodden upon. The russet and woodland colour throughout has a tempo and tone resonant as the beating of a drum. Looking at this together with the mosaics in the 'royal' rooms, gives you an opportunity for realizing what was happening, spiritually, in this late Roman era. Where the everyday scenes are so alive and closely observed, the animals snarling and neighing with life, there is a sudden weakness about the mythological scenes, and even the symbolic ones. Africa is no Lady of the Beasts as Artemis was: she is a perfunctory embodiment. The marine deities in the living-room, Polyphemus with Ulysses in one antechamber, and Eros and Pan in the other – even the tepidly erotic scene in the great man's bedroom – these are all archaistic and lack all conviction of faith. These mosaics are the direct ancestors of those Byzantine–Norman ones elsewhere in Sicily. The likeness is already here at your feet; and the circle is completed when you visit La Zisa (p. 137) and the Sala di Re Ruggero (p. 124), at Palermo, where the freedom of these mosaics – lost in the high formalism of Byzantium – is revived. A direct influence can be postulated since this was a royal Norman house and these mosaics were known until William I, presumably out of puritanical zeal, destroyed the palace.

The rooms off the southern side of the peristyle include the summer living-room with a damaged pavement representing the Orphic myth (*Map* 25) – Orpheus vapid among fine beasts – and a chamber in whose anteroom are the all too famous 'bikini girls' (*Map* 26). Lest you are now struck by their aesthetic insipidity after the others (or, conversely, have been surprised the others were so brilliant compared with well-known reproductions of these) let it be said at once that these are a later work of the fourth century overlying the original pavement. They have their appeal, these ten girls at their not very arduous exercise, and they show a charming naturalism; but the floor lacks the design and the quality of the earlier works.

At this point you have to retrace your steps and take the path running around the outside of the shelter as far as it will go to enter the *master's suite* of the private apartments, passing on your way the now open basilica or throne-room (*Map* 18) whose floor is lost. The master's suite consists of three chambers, one (*Map* 19) with a large mosaic of a man and entrails, another (*Map* 24) with an attractive fruit mosaic, together with the already mentioned mildly erotic mosaic marking the bedroom (to the left of 19).

Moving over to the entrance to the quarters of the rest of the family – these are centred on an *atrium* (*Map* 20) with a living-room behind (*Map* 21). The mosaics in the southern vestibule (*Map* 22) show touching nursery circus-scenes; while in the inner room (*Map* 23) are theatrical scenes with musical instruments and interesting Greek letters indicating musical modes.

Back on the outside one arrives at the *Xystus* (Map 27), an egg-shaped court with porticoes around three sides. Off this open rooms, one with a pavement of vintage scenes (*Map* **28**). At the east end is the large apsed dining-room (*Map* **30**) with the one really effective mythological subject on the floor, a magnificently turbulent 'Labours of Hercules' to which the artists could translate their knowledge of wrestling and the circus fights between men and beasts. In the apses are Hercules glorified by the conquered giants, and Lycurgus and Ambrosia. This splendid banqueting-room must sound almost the last fanfare of that heroic and masculine valour upon which latter-day paganism relied for its impetus – virility without the Goddess; brute strength lacking any concomitant charity.

You must return to Piazza Armerina to rejoin the No. 117 bis.

[71 km.] **Caltagirone**, a surprisingly prosperous town for the inland region, built over three hills up and down which run narrow medieval streets of considerable charm. All views of the town are enhanced by the use of local coloured tiles and finials, etc.

This site was occupied from the second millennium B.C. A hellenized Siculan town with Sikel connections also, it presently became a Greek one during the Syracusan expansion. Its name derives from the Arab *kal'at* and *gerun* – or 'castle' and 'caves'. The Genovese conquered it in 1030, but their stay was a short one. The town was destroyed in the earthquake of 1693 and, as one can still see, it was badly bombed in July 1943, when more than 700 people were killed.

The fine façade of the *Corte Capitaniale* carries carving by Antonello and his son Gian Doménico Gagini, the latter most probably having been born here. This building survived the earthquake. It houses a *Museo Cívico* where a variety of prehistoric and later antiquities, and local ceramics, are on show.

In the *Palazzo degli Studi*, in the wall of the staircase, is mounted a very good relief of sphinxes and dancing satyrs from the early fourth century B.C. from Monte San Mauro.

The church of *San Giórgio* has an interior shrine with a beautiful painting of the *Trinity* attributed to Roger van der Weyden, while the church of *Santa Maria di Gesù* contains a most lovely Antonello Gagini of the *Madonna della Catena*.

Hotels
2nd Class   *Artu.*
4th Class   *Trinácria.*

[102 km.] **Vizzini** occupies an ancient site which may be that of *Bidis* which Cicero mentions. It claims to be the scene of Mascagni's *Cavalleria Rusticana* and Verga's *Mastro Don Gesualdo*.

In the church of *Santa Maria di Gesù* a moving *Madonna and Child* by Antonello Gagini stands on the high altar. Locally, it is known as the *Madonna Bianca*, and is dated 1527.

The literary claims made by Vizzini are disputed by **Francofonte**, a town ten miles down the Lentini road from here, where the Municipality occupies the pretty eighteenth-century Palagónia palace adjoining the older feudal castle.

[132 km.] **Palazzo Acréide** is the successor of ancient Akrai, first of the Syracusan colonies.

In the modern town, the *Church of the Cappuccini* contains a *Stigmata of St Francis* by Vincenzo da Pávia.

The *Palazzo Júdica* (No. 10 Corso Vittório Emanuele) contains an interesting private collection of antiquities from Akrai and neighbouring sites formed by Baron Judica. The vases, Siculan and Greek, are a fine group; the domestic utensils in bronze intriguing; and some of the sculpture and terra-cottas are good.

In the church of the *Convento dei Minori Osservanti* there is a beautiful *Madonna and Child* by Francesco Laurana. He never tired of this subject, and never failed with it.

The remains of *Akrai*, founded in 664 B.C., are fairly extensive and decidedly interesting (see p. 212 for its history).

Greek Theatre. This is of a fairly late date (probably towards the end of Hieron II's reign), small and holding only 600 seats, but well-preserved and beautifully sited. Somehow you get a very nice flavour from this simple, semicircular structure lying in the tilled fields, covering what was – you are sure of it – a most pleasant little town to live in. The *Bouleuterion* to the west of the theatre was a small council-chamber. The area of the *agora*, abutting on the above, has still to be uncovered completely.

Latomie – behind the Theatre. These quarries are pitted with niches belonging to the Hellenistic Hero cult (see p. 242) and Byzantine rock graves.

Templi Ferali, on the east of the hill. In a vertical cliff-face two great rectangular chambers have been cut, their walls honeycombed with small, votive niches. These appear from inscriptions, still legible in some of the niches, to have been shrines of the dead.

Santoni – below the Templi Ferali in the valley of the Santicello. These twelve rock-cut sculptures representing Cybele are thought to belong to the third century B.C. The reliefs also show this Great Goddess of the east attended by priests and other related figures of myth, the Dioscuri, Hermes and Marsyas, lions at her feet and other now unidentifiable deities. Though these are of rough workmanship they have an impressive emotional power of their own. They have an aura of great religious devotion – something that is perhaps lacking now in the calculated beauty of the skeletons of the Doric temples.

To see these you must ask the custodian of the theatre to conduct you and open the shelters put up for their protection – a necessary thing, though one which has diminished their old power, emerging from the rock face mysteriously.

[175 km.] Syracuse (p. 211).

ENNA TO CATÁNIA

Route 1 S.S.192. Fast but dull road. 92 km. No accommodation *en route*.
Route 2 S.S.121 via Adrano. 105 km. A beautiful though not always a good road.
Rail Direct connections.
Bus Direct connections, Route 1 ; none by Route 2.

ROUTE 2

Accommodation en route At Agira ; Adrano.

[18 km.] **Leonforte.** There is a fountain in the village, the *Granfonte*, with a score of jets. This extravagance was built in 1651.

[31 km.] **Agira.** Once a Siculan town that was colonized with Greeks by Timoleon in 339 B.C. Here Diodorus Siculus, the first-century B.C. historian, was born.

Agira was also the scene of the 'miracles' of a saint called Philip of Argira, an apocryphal figure whom it is thought may have been a christianized version of Herakles, the city's protecting deity in pre-Christian times.

The church of *Santa Margherita* is a big church in which is a painting of the Magdalene good enough to have been attributed to Veronese, though this is now denied.

In the *treasury* of *San Salvatore* there is a late-thirteenth-century mitre of red silk, sewn with pearls, coral and enamelled silver discs, a most evocative medieval treasure. The Treasury also contains a fine Pisan abbatial staff, topped by a crucifix, of the fourteenth century.

Hotel
4th Class   *La Rinascente.*

[59 km.] A turning on the right to **Centúripe**, 8 km. off. The town rides a ridge 2,400 feet up, facing Etna, and has several times found this an uncomfortably strategic spot to be in. As *Centorbi* it was a Siculan town and the birthplace of the great doctor Celsus who wrote under the early Empire. Frederick II destroyed the town to punish a rebellion, and Charles of Anjou repeated the exercise. In 1943, the Hermann Goering Division defended the town for two days against the 38th Irish Brigade, which eventually stormed it.

The little *Antiquarium* in the Município houses a collection of local Hellenistic and Roman finds among which some of the small terra-cotta figures are delightful. Centúripe anciently manufactured pottery of an individual type which is represented here also.

[69 km.] You come to Adrano.

Adrano

Hotel
4th Class   *Messina.*

As *Adranon*, this was a foundation of Dionysius I of Syracuse, probably replacing the older, Sikel settlement at Mendolito, where such a great hoard of bronzes (to be seen in the museum at Syracuse) was found. Dionysius named the town for a local indigenous god. Some of its Greek wall can be seen near the *castle*, which was first built by Count Roger, though remade to some extent and given its curtain of towered wall in the fourteenth century.

The *Chiesa Madre (dell'Assunta)* is of Norman origin. The nave is divided into aisles by sixteen basalt columns which are antique, and probably come from a Greek temple. In the transepts are paintings by Zoppo di Ganci. The polyptych over the entrance to the Chapel of the Holy Sacrament belongs to the local fifteenth-century school of Messina.

Museo Archeológico

In the castle – which allows you to see its chapel with a fine Norman doorway and some early frescoes.

Open Weekdays 09.00–13.00 and 14.00–16.00; Sundays and holidays, mornings only; entrance free.

This excellent museum houses an important collection of prehistoric wares and other finds, among which the whole Casteluccian culture is particularly well represented. Also displayed is material both from the site of Mendolito and Adrano itself.

[85 km.] **Paternò**. Frederick II of Aragon died here, *en route* for Enna.

The fine *castle* is fourteenth-century; restored in 1900. It has a grand hall and a chapel with frescoes worth seeing – the keys are to be had on application at the Município.

[105 km.] Catánia (p. 257).

ENNA TO TAORMINA

Route S.S.121 from the Quadrívio di Misericórdia, joining the S.S.117 to Nicosia after 20 km., then turning on to the S.S.120 and again on to the S.S.114 for the last lap – not an easy road, nor a particularly good one, though a wonderfully beautiful one to travel; 168 km. to the Taormina corner.
Rail No direct connections, change at Catánia.
Bus No direct connections, change at Catánia.
Accommodation en route At Nicosia, Troína, Randazzo.

[44 km.] **Nicosia**, a very picturesque town that was important in the Middle Ages. The local dialect is said to 'betray the Lombard and Piedmontese origins of its early colonists'. A landslide in 1757 damaged a part of the town.

The *Cathedral of San Nicola* has a fourteenth-century *doorway* which is really good; a fine *campanile*; and an arched *portico* on the north. Inside, it has a *Martyrdom of St Sebastian* by Salvatore Rosa and a *St Bartholomew* attributed to Ribera. Its *choir-stalls* of 1622, or thereabouts, are attention-worthy also.

The church of *Santa Maria Maggiore* contains a huge and felicitous marble polyptych made by Antonello Gagini between 1499 and 1516. It shows the *Nativity of Mary, Annunciation, Nativity of Christ* and the *Assumption*. There is also a throne said to have been used by the Emperor Charles V on his visit here in 1535.

The *Castle* ruins are Norman.

Hotels
4th Class   *Centrale;*
              Pátria.

[77 km.] **Troina,** the highest town in Sicily, with a population of some 14,000.

An old site and anciently holy, traces of its walls from the Greek era survive at the pinnacle of the town. It was one of Count Roger's early conquests – in 1062 – and here in 1064 he was besieged for four months in the company of his remarkable wife, Eremberger, and 300 knights; one of the few really bad moments in his conquest of Sicily. To commemorate it he founded the convent of St Basil (now a ruin near the Capuchin convent), and raised a castle at the top of the hill. In 1082 he created Troína the first see of Sicily, but soon the seat of the bishopric was moved elsewhere.

Instead of the castle, the *Chiesa Matrice* crowns the town today. It rises beside an open *belvedere* where the view is indeed a beautiful one. Originally built in the twelfth century, current stripping of overlays of later decoration and alterations seems likely to reveal more Norman fabric than had been expected, though the proportions of the nave have a genuine twelfth-century splendour. Parts of the original pavement have already been uncovered. It contains two late Byzantine *icons* of the Madonna. In the *treasury* are a fine pastoral staff of the fifteenth century and a square ruby ring said to have been presented to the church by Roger. The *crypt* is original.

The *Church of San Silvestro,* where that saint's body lies, is also very old, but it belongs to a confraternity and the key takes up to a day to obtain.

Hotel
4th Class   *Ancipa.*

[106 km.] A turning on the right leads in 8·5 km. to **Bronte,** a town of oddly battlemented *campanili* and mostly interesting as the dukedom bestowed upon Nelson in 1799 by Ferdinand IV. The family still owns it, together with an enormous estate hereabouts.

[113 km.] Turning on the left to *Santa Maria di Maniace* or *'Castello Maniace'*: originally a convent founded by Queen Margaret of Navarre, the mother of William III, to commemorate the victory in 1040 of Georges Maniakes, who, with Norman help, defeated the Arabs here during his short campaign, 1040, to regain the island for Constantinople.

Maniakes is said to have built a small castle here, certainly a church or chapel since he gave it an icon painted by St Luke. Margaret endowed the place as a Byzantine monastery in 1174. The famous Peter of Blois's brother, William, was its first abbot. The small church is the most interesting among the exciting remains of the monastery. It still houses the precious icon. The apses fell in the earthquake of 1693, but most of the rest survived, notably the wooden *ceiling* and the gorgeous *doorway*. The female *statue* by the altar may be of Margaret herself. This is a memorable monument from the past.

Ferdinand IV gave this estate to Lord Nelson as part of the dukedom of Bronte (thereby depriving Palermo hospital of a valuable endowment, and at no cost to the King), when it was converted into a house. It still belongs to his heirs. To visit, apply at the Administrator's office.

William Sharp, the Scottish poet who wrote under the pseudonym of Fiona Macleod, died here in 1905 and is buried in the hillside *English Cemetery* beneath an Iona cross, strange-looking in this countryside.

[126 km.] **Randazzo** has never been destroyed by volcanic or seismic action and has preserved its medieval appearance despite the damage it suffered in 1943 when, the Germans having made it a strongpoint, the Allies bombed it. The *Palazzo Finocchiaro* dates from 1509 and the *Museo Vagliasindi* contains some excellent Greek vessels from a necropolis in the neighbourhood. (Admission is by consent of the owner.)

Hotel
3rd Class   *Motel Agip* (5 km. west along the S.S.120).

[168 km.] Taormina (p. 275).

SELECTED ENGLISH BIBLIOGRAPHY

GENERAL

Cronin, Vincent, *The Golden Honeycomb* (Rupert Hart-Davis, London, 1954): primarily an essay upon the religious art of Sicily.

Guercio, Francis, *Sicily. The Garden of the Mediterranean* (Faber and Faber, London, 1968): by an Anglo-Sicilian.

Maxwell, Gavin, *God Protect me from my Friends* (Pan Books, London, 1958): about the bandit Giuliano.

Maxwell, Gavin, *The Ten Pains of Death* (Longmans, London, 1959): about the tunny fishers.

O'Faolain, Sean, *South to Sicily* (Collins, London, 1953): delightful, though not very informative.

Peyrefitte, Roger, *South from Naples*, trans. J. H. F. McEwen (Thames and Hudson, London, 1954): down to earth, personal; the author in Catholic mood.

Quennell, Peter, *Spring in Sicily* (Weidenfeld and Nicolson, London, 1952): an aesthete's account.

Schwarz, Heinrich, *Sicily* (Thames and Hudson, London, 1956): excellent introduction to Sicilian architecture.

HISTORICAL

Finley, M. I., *Ancient Sicily: To the Arab Conquest* (Chatto and Windus, London, 1968).

Smith, Denis Mack, *Medieval Sicily (800–1713)* (Chatto and Windus, London, 1968) and *Modern Sicily: After 1713* (Chatto and Windus, London, 1968).

These three companion volumes brilliantly survey the whole of Sicily's history, from the Stone Age onwards. They can be consulted in reference to the subdivisions, below, but are best read for the rhythm of the island's extraordinary history and for the way they place this in that of the rest of the Mediterranean and European or African worlds which so much affected it.

Guido, Margaret, *Sicily: an archaeological guide* (Faber and Faber, London, 1967): a full and vivid guide to the ancient sites, excavations and collections of Sicily. Published in 1967, it is more up to date than Woodhead (below) in some details and is itself to be brought up to date shortly.

PREHISTORY

Bernabò Brea, Luigi, *Sicily Before the Greeks*, trans. C. M. Preston and L. Guido (Thames and Hudson, London, 1957): indispensable for the period.

GREEKS

Ayrton, Elisabeth, *The Doric Temple* (Thames and Hudson, London, 1961): a beautiful and useful introduction to Doric architecture.

Dunbabin, T. J., *The Western Greeks* (Clarendon Press, Oxford, 1948): most comprehensive, but partly outdated.

Green, Peter, *Armada from Athens* (*The Failure of the Sicilian Expedition, 415–413 B.C.*) (Hodder and Stoughton, London, 1971): a very full account of the Expedition.

Woodhead, A. G., *The Greeks in the West* (Thames and Hudson, London, 1962): lucid and scholarly account and evaluation.

NORMANS, ETC.

Masson, Georgina, *Frederick II of Hohenstaufen* (Secker and Warburg, London, 1957): a vivid and sympathetic biography.

Norwich, John Julius, *The Normans in the South: 1016–1130* (Longmans, London, 1967) and *The Kingdom in the Sun: 1130–1194* (Longmans, London, 1970): these two volumes recount the whole story of the Normans' southern adventure, their achievement and its decline in vivid detail, with deep sympathy and understanding. There is, too, an appreciation of all the surviving buildings of the period in Sicily. This immense labour seems to have sprung from admiration of those buildings and works, and to have been undertaken to satisfy the author's curiosity about their makers; we are infinitely the richer for it, whether we read because we are already interested or as a bait to whet the enthusiasm.

Runciman, Steven, *The Sicilian Vespers* (Cambridge University Press, Cambridge, 1958; also Penguin, Harmondsworth, 1960): a rousing and scholarly study of the period, its origins and its aftermath.

These four books could be read in conjunction: Norwich, Masson, Runciman, in that order.

EIGHTEENTH AND NINETEENTH CENTURIES

Acton, Harold, *The Bourbons of Naples, 1734–1825* (Methuen London, 1957) and *The Last Bourbons of Naples, 1825–1861* (Methuen, London, 1961): brilliant, if partial, studies of this extraordinary family and its epoch.

Brydone, Patrick, *A Tour through Sicily and Malta* (W. Strahan and T. Cadell, London, 1776): a delightful contemporary account.

Goethe, *Italian Journey*, trans. W. H. Auden and Elizabeth Mayer (Collins, London, 1962): includes a section on Sicily.

Hobsbawm, E. J. E., *Primitive Rebels* (Manchester University Press, Manchester, 1959): includes an excellent essay on the Mafia.

There are many books about the Risorgimento; a lively first-hand account is:

Abba, Giuseppe Césare, *The Diary of one of Garibaldi's Thousand*, trans. E. R. Vincent (Oxford University Press, London, 1962).

G. M. Trevelyan's three-volume life of Garibaldi – *Garibaldi's Defence of the Roman Republic*; *Garibaldi and the Thousand*; *Garibaldi and the Making of Italy* (Longmans, London, 1907) – remains the standard biography although it is heavily biased in its subject's favour.

SICILY IN FICTION

The following are works of fiction by Sicilians describing the life of their fellow islanders:

Giovanni Verga's stories tell of the lot of the peasantry with savagery. D. H. Lawrence's translations, gathered into one volume, are now a rarity. The following titles are available:

Cavalleria Rusticana, and other stories, trans. D. H. Lawrence (Jonathan Cape, London, 1928).

The House by the Medlar Tree, trans. Eric Mosbacher (Weidenfeld and Nicolson, London, 1950).
The She Wolf and other stories, trans. Giovanni Cecchetti (University of California Press, Berkeley, 1958).

Roberto, Frederico de, *The Viceroys*, trans. Archibald Colquhoun (MacGibbon and Kee, London, 1962): tells bitterly of the Catanian nobility's adjustment to the unification of Italy.
Lampedusa, Giuseppe di, *The Leopard*, trans. Archibald Colquhoun (Collins and Harvill Press, London, 1960; also in Fontana): tells of the same melancholy adjustment made by a Palermitan nobleman of genius.
Lampedusa, Giuseppe di, *Two Stories and a Memory*, trans. Archibald Colquhoun (Collins and Harvill Press, London, 1962): the Memory is exquisite and evocative; the fragment of a novel is savagely descriptive of 'Edwardian' Sicilian society.

PRACTICAL

Carta automobilistica (motoring maps) Nos. 25, 26 and 27 (1 : 200,000), Touring Club Italiano: 1969 edition.
Travellers' Italian (Jonathan Cape, London, 1965).

Frederick II of Hohenstaufen wrote a treatise on *Falconry* which is still (apart from medical advances) the standard work on the subject.

GLOSSARY OF ARCHITECTURAL AND ARCHAEOLOGICAL TERMS

abacus	upper, square section of a Doric capital (Gk.)
adytum	an inner shrine (Gk.)
antefix	an ornament on the eaves of a roof hiding the juncture of two rows of tiles (Lat.)
atrium	either an entrance hall or an open central courtyard (Lat.)
bothroi	small pits for votive offerings to chthonic gods (Gk.)
bucchero ware	native pottery, black or red
cella	enclosed interior of a temple (Lat.)
conch	concave doming of a vault
crepidoma	steps surrounding and mounting the stylobate of a temple (Gk.)
curia	administrative building (Lat.)
cyclopean	type of wall-building using big irregular stones with smaller ones filling the interstices
dipylon	twin-towered (Gk.)
dromos	street (Gk.)
echinus	the convex section of a capital (Gk.)
entablature	the whole ornamented band across the top of the columns of a temple below the roof
entasis	a slight curving of the lines and a gradation of spacing of components of a building to give an illusion of lightness to its mass
guttae	drainage spouts, often shaped like lion-heads on Doric temples (Lat.)
heroön	sacred place or enclosure (Gk.)
hexastyle	having six columns across its end
hypogeum	underground part of a building or artificial cave
kouros	figure of a youthful athlete or god (Gk.)
krater	bowl for mixing wine and water (Gk.)
metope	section of frieze above a temple's architrave: either plain or carved in relief, and alternating with triglyphs bearing three upright grooves (Gk.)

naos	as cella; though usually the eastern or principal chamber within a cella (Gk.)
narthex	a western porch outside, or a vestibule just within an early church
oinochoe	a jug (Gk.)
opisthodomos	western vestibule of a temple, sometimes blind (Gk.)
ostensory	a monstrance
pediment	triangular part over temple's ends, disguising the pitch of the roof
peripteral	surrounded by columns
peristasis	total ensemble of a building (Gk.)
peristyle	system of colonnading
pronaos	eastern vestibule of a temple leading into the naos (Gk.)
prostyle	an open portico, with columns, in front of a building
sekos	sacred enclosure (Gk.)
sima	cresting (of the cornice) (Gk.)
stoa	a covered portico colonnaded on one side (Gk.)
stylobate	platform on which a temple is built
temenos	sacred enclosure surrounding a temple (Gk.)
tholoi	(tombs) skep or bee-hive shaped (Gk.)
trabeation	entablature
transenna	open-work grille at entrance to a Byzantine chapel
triforium	a wall passage opening to the nave, above the side aisles and built in the thickness of the wall (Lat.)
triglyph	tablet decorated with three vertical grooves which divides one metope from the next (Gk.)

INDEX

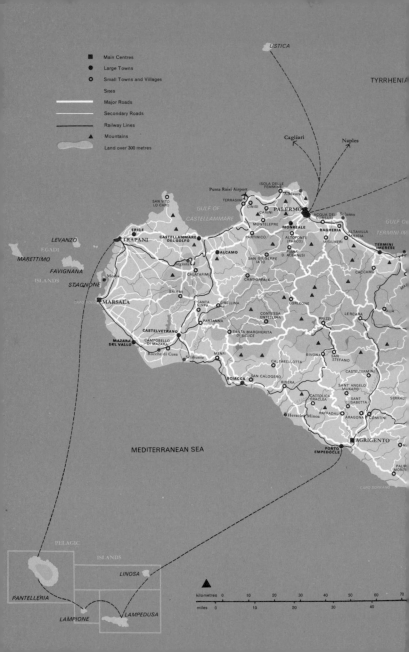